On the Wings of Mercury

'*From the cool forest tracks of Putaruru to the heat of the Olympic Stadium, Lorraine Moller's autobiography is a powerful and remarkable story.*' **Kathrine Switzer, pioneer of women's running, and author of** *Marathon Woman*

'*The best autobiography and possibly the best book I have read, full stop. Sports books are a dime a dozen but this book offers much much more. It's the story of Lorraine's journey, the journey of a great athlete, but above all else, a great person.*' **Chris Pilone, Olympic coach to Hamish Carter**

'*This is the most compelling autobiography I have ever read.*' **Peter Snell**

'*This book is one to enjoy time and time again. It is an inspirational life story told with great humour and honesty. I loved it.*' **Nina Rillstone, international marathon runner**

'*Lorraine inspires with her wit, wisdom and understanding of the universe and how we may harness her power to achieve great things. Her free and limitless spirit sparkles on every page. Lorraine Moller is so much more than an accomplished sportswoman. She is one of life's extraordinary people.*' **Allison Roe, MBE (shares the same star sign)**

Winning the 1987 Osaka International Ladies' Marathon.

Courtesy of Osaka International Ladies' Marathon and Sankei Sports

ON THE WINGS OF MERCURY
THE LORRAINE MOLLER STORY

Lorraine Mary Moller

To Taryn,
Many Thanks for
your support to
women runners.
New Zealand calls!
Lorraine Moller

Longacre Press

Events in this book were reconstructed from the reliable sources of diaries, letters, and scrapbooks, and less reliable recollections from me and others. Everything else was sourced from the reservoir of other dimensions accessed through the imagination, the accuracy of which is totally unverifiable.

I have attempted to describe events and people as I perceived them at the time, often from my own place of smallness. In the telling no offence is intended to any person mentioned.* Each encounter described has brought me to a new level of understanding on this marvellous journey of love, so while I have endeavoured to write candidly, it is also with the utmost gratitude to each character described, for you have all been my teachers.

———————————————————

*In a few instances I have not used the person's real name.

ISBN 978 1 877361 99 9

A catalogue record for this book is available from the National Library of New Zealand.

First published by Longacre Press, 2007
30 Moray Place, Dunedin, New Zealand.
Reprinted 2007

Book design by Christine Buess
Front cover design by Nick Wright
Cover photograph: Commonwealth Games, Christchurch, 1974.
Courtesy of the *Waikato Times*
Printed by Astra Print, Wellington

www.longacre.co.nz

CONTENTS

Foreword 7
Prologue   Dragon-slayer 9

PART ONE – MERCURY'S CHILD

Chapter 1   A Running Start 15
Chapter 2   Piddler 21
Chapter 3   The Window 30
Chapter 4   Olympic Heroes 38
Chapter 5   Incentives 42
Chapter 6   Breasts and Big Muscles 48

PART TWO — RUNNER

Chapter 7   Role Models and Rivals 55
Chapter 8   Winning Isn't Everything 61
Chapter 9   Great Temptations 66
Chapter 10   Cosmic Consciousness 74
Chapter 11   Tit for Tat 83
Chapter 12   Running Out 89
Chapter 13   Phoney Baloney 95
Chapter 14   Erroneous Zones 101

PART THREE — MARATHONER

Chapter 15   Mr Ron 113
Chapter 16   Snow-bound 117
Chapter 17   Checking In 122
Chapter 18   The Crash-mobile 129
Chapter 19   Queen 136
Chapter 20   Breaking Times and Tissues 149
Chapter 21   Wedding Presents 160
Chapter 22   Rough Crossings 164
Chapter 23   Roller Coaster 172
Chapter 24   Beyond Repair 176

Chapter 25   Vivaxis 185
Chapter 26   Breathing Space 189
Chapter 27   Scrabble Squabble 195

PART FOUR — OLYMPIAN

Chapter 28   The Messenger 205
Chapter 29   The Anointed One 211
Chapter 30   Squares into Wheels 220
Chapter 31   New Channels 225
Chapter 32   A Classy Affair 233
Chapter 33   Love Beams 242
Chapter 34   Killer Instinct 248
Chapter 35   Crackpots and Creampuffs 256
Chapter 36   Flaming Dove 263
Chapter 37   Chop Chop 270
Chapter 38   Gang-bushed 277

PART FIVE — MEDALLIST

Chapter 39   Percolations 287
Chapter 40   Cleared for Take-off 293
Chapter 41   Broadsided 301
Chapter 42   Into the Fire 304
Chapter 43   All that Matters 311
Chapter 44   Three Weddings and a Funeral 317
Chapter 45   Last Call 323
Chapter 46   Meeting Zeus 329
Chapter 47   Rock Bottom 335
Chapter 48   Gold 341
Chapter 49   Death 345
Chapter 50   Making Magic 349

Epilogue   Dreamer 355
Career Highlights 357
Acknowledgements 359

On the basis of consistent, world-class performances, Lorraine Moller has proven to be New Zealand's greatest female distance runner. Her credentials include three victories in the Avon International Women's Marathon, a win in the 1984 Boston Marathon and three times a winner of the prestigious Osaka International Ladies' Marathon. In a feat still unmatched today, Lorraine completed four consecutive Olympic Games, commencing with the first marathon for women in the 1984 Los Angeles Olympic Games. The climax of her career was an Olympic bronze medal in the marathon at the 1992 Barcelona Olympic Games.

On the Wings of Mercury is the most compelling autobiography I have ever read. Rather than a sports book filled with events and statistics, it is a book written by a sportswoman. Lorraine takes the reader on a fascinating odyssey: moving from her early childhood experiences, which helped shape her as a runner and person, through to the mature, articulate woman she is today — who at her best could beat anyone in the world.

Lorraine is a storyteller of considerable skill and she writes with an outstanding command of language and use of metaphor. Throughout this powerful story she holds the reader's attention and respect. It is unusual for an athlete to write their own story without journalistic assistance, but perhaps this is what has enabled Lorraine to better explore her innermost thoughts, her own motivations and spirituality. This is a candid, superbly written autobiography, providing the reader with a rare insight into the high and low experiences of an elite athlete.

Peter Snell
Dallas, September 2007

At the Barcelona Olympic Games, 1992.

Dragon-slayer

If a man wishes to become a hero, then the serpent must first become a dragon: otherwise he lacks his proper enemy.
— Friedrich Nietzsche

1 AUGUST 1992, BARCELONA, SPAIN

Legend tells of fire-breathing dragons that lurk in the bowels of the earth beneath Catalonia. What I sense this summer afternoon of 1992 in Barcelona as I survey the race course is that the road stretching between me and my dream is a steamy tar-pit of reptilian breath, threatening to suck the water out of my skin and desiccate my precious hope for gold.

I have prepared well. Handling such strength-sapping conditions has taken as much a flip of the mind as a bodily acclimatisation. Ever since I was a child the summer force of Helios has been my nemesis. But over the past year I have deliberately sought the heat and worked with it by degrees: at first tolerating it as a necessary evil, then respecting it as a condition that could be worked with, and finally coming to relish it as a force to be harnessed for victory. For the last three weeks I have been comfortably working out in the midday oven of the Mediterranean.

This, my third Olympics, is probably my last chance for gold. Others think that at thirty-seven I am past my prime, but I don't care. They do not know that a fire of my own smoulders deep in my belly, re-vitalising my cells and fuelling my ambition. I want to be an Olympic Champion more than anything I have ever wanted and today, I have vowed to myself, I am willing to run fearlessly into the furnace to achieve my goal.

As I stroll out into the sun's unyielding glare to the start line I feel a conviction that I am going to do well. This balmy air that will quickly send rivulets tumbling down the insides of my arms actually feels pleasant on my cool skin. While my rivals were edging each other out for refuge in the shifting shadow of the lone official porta-potty, I left the athletes' holding area for a nap on the wooden floor of a nearby surf shop, and topped it off with a luxurious cold shower. Now as my rivals nervously dash back and forth around me with their last minute sprints, I laugh to myself. Some have been warming up for thirty minutes or more. The mercury has shot up to 96 degrees and the heat rising off the tar-seal of the road is 118, hot enough to fry an egg — or a runner.

I catch the eye of Australian Lisa Ondieki, the reigning silver medalist and today's favourite. The stylish Lisa, with the porcelain face and ballet hairstyle, is sleek in her shiny green and yellow abbreviated outfit that is stretched tightly from crotch to shoulder.

Those lycra unitards are hot little cookers even with the mesh insert around the middle, I think to myself. I catch her eye and give her the Osaka Marathon look: *This is my race, I'm going to win.* I smile. I like her and I do not want her to think I am wishing her ill, merely transmitting the way it is. She turns away and nervously tugs down on the back of her suit.

We are called to line up in two rows according to alphabetical order. I am in the front row. Lisa takes her place next to me, which she rightfully claimed when her last name was Martin. But she has taken her new husband's name and her slip down the alphabet means she is ushered to the back line. In the affairs of ordinary men and women it would be a trivial matter easily shrugged off. But this is the Olympics where mortals, in seeking immortality, become pain-fully aware of any leadenness and read every nuance, hoping for a sign of celestial favour. The first contender has just been asked to take a back seat, a bad omen. I sense Lisa's vulnerability and I know already that on this day she will not be challenging.

I do a last minute check. The bare necessities: shoes, socks, shorts, singlet, watch. *Watch! What do I need a watch for?* The watch that measures my progress to the 100th of a second: my judge and jury, the final arbiter. If I trip and land on the road with my hands and knees skinned and bleeding, it is the stop button on my watch that my hand instinctively reaches for first. I have worn one while running for the past twenty years. Now, suddenly this runner's holy of holies is redundant. Extra baggage. It doesn't matter how fast I am running, the competition is my only measure. I just want to win. I toss it to one of our coaches on the sideline.

I release a hefty sigh, the last molecules of stale air. My watch is gone. The public expect nothing from me. Anne is retired. Mizuno has dumped me. Ron is dead. I am ready. Nothing stands between me and gold.

Nothing but myself.

Lorraine Moller

I dedicate this book to my mother, Maisie Moller, and to my father, Gordon Moller, the depth of whose love I could not fully appreciate until I had a child of my own.

PART ONE

Mercury's Child

Aspiring brownie, 1961.

Putaruru ballerina, 1962.

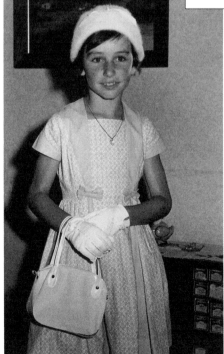

Wedding guest, 1963.

CHAPTER 1

A Running Start

Life is either a daring adventure or nothing.
—Helen Keller

JUNE 1955, PUTARURU, NEW ZEALAND

On the night of my arrival I started out slowly and finished fast, the same way I came to run marathons. In his rush to make my delivery, the doctor's flash new 1955 Studebaker, resplendent with the chrome grill that distinguished him as a man of consequence, broke down. He had to run to the only hospital in my hometown of Putaruru, all of a mile, making it just in time to wrap some forceps around my head and wrench me from my mother's sedated body.

Like my sister and brother before me, I was given a resounding slap on the bottom to make me cry, then handed to a nurse for processing. This procedure included a full scrubbing, whereupon I was catalogued and ticketed, straight-jacketed in large white cotton squares and then dispatched to the holding cell for newborns.

My father was allowed to visit afternoons between two and three p.m. when a nurse would hold me up to the viewing window for his proud perusal. Contact with my mother was forbidden for twenty-four hours as she was recovering from the surgical damage my arrival had inflicted upon her. After that I was brought to her for feeding at precisely seven and eleven a.m., three, seven and ten p.m. Being hospital property, I was loaned out only under the stopwatch of the good Catholic matron. She allotted thirty seconds for the nurse to scurry me to my engorged mother whereupon I was given nine minutes to suckle: five minutes on the holy right nipple and four minutes on the unholy left; and allowing another thirty seconds for the return journey, I was deposited back in my place of assignment at exactly ten minutes after the hour.

Such regulation had absolutely no beneficial effect on my promptness in later life. I can only conclude that such treatment served not to teach but to punish. And for what? Certainly nothing I had done, for up to that date I had committed no acts worthy of condemnation.

Somewhere along the line I adopted the assumption that God was punishing me for some original sin that goes with being human; perhaps for the incorporation of spirit into flesh that comes when one is being birthed into the earthly realm, or for the emergence from an orifice that caused the downfall of all of mankind, metonymically speaking. Regardless of these later adult cerebrations, certain core beliefs had been seeded, and I grew up knowing three things to be true: 1) I was fundamentally flawed; 2) if I were good enough (at what I did not yet know) I might at best be loved and at least be accepted, and 3) the only one I could ever count on was me.

The dash to my birth was tough on the doctor, my mother tells me, and I was the last baby he ever delivered, for shortly thereafter he had a heart attack, forcing him into an early retirement. She now proudly connects this with my running beginning, seeing it as a harbinger of how I would make others run, and break them in the process.

My mother had fortitude in her blood and molded us accordingly: ignoring our whining and rarely indulging us with mollycoddling. Being a third generation immigrant, my mother would have taken any modern day 'Super-Mum' to task, for she was the hub of the wheel in our household, raising six children, keeping the house and working the family dairy, all without daycare, divorce or Prozac. Her 'just make things work' modus operandi was shaped by both environment and heredity. The year she was born also marked the start of the Great Depression. Such harsh conditions served only to strengthen one descended from the Scottish House of Gunn: a hardy crew whose clan motto was, 'Feared by all, loved by none, the Gunn'. My mother's claim to fame is that her grandmother's cousin (on the English side) was the great opera singer, Dame Nellie Melba, whose talents neither my mother nor I inherited.

Mum says I was different. Not beautiful, not cuddly, not cute, just … different. I had taken that to mean that she too could see that I was tarnished and that was the kindest description she could come up with. One thing was certain: I was not your generic pudgy-faced baby. When I became more accomplished my mother upgraded me to 'special' and I suspected that she had reconsidered and wanted to be kind to my feelings. It was not until I became a mother myself I understood that she truly did regard each one of her children as special, as a mother is hormonally bound to do.

My Dad was not so diplomatic. He said I reminded him of a fledgling and he would suck in his cheeks, purse his lips and make a turkey-pecking gesture. Indeed, early pictures of me (of which there are few) show a skinny, bird-like baby, with a widow's peak hairline and a distinctive frown between my eyebrows.

My father was also descended from pioneering folk. Some time in the mid 1800s his grandfather, Wilhelm Wiggo Moller, bid his mother and father goodbye and embarked on the long ocean voyage from Denmark to this distant country, never to return. Settling in the farming community near New Plymouth, this strapping young man married my great-grandmother, also a Danish emigrant, and became a goods carrier with a fine team of draught-horses. On the side he was something of an inventor and reputed to have designed the first manure distributor. My father, I am convinced, inherited from him not only the hankering for new horizons and the single-minded focus of the self-made man, but also the shit-flinging gene.

He was a restless type but each new offspring was another link in the chain that connected my Dad to our town, Putaruru.

Putaruru was, and still is, a pleasant rural town of about 4,000 people. Back in those days it was the heart of the pine forestry with three or four sawmills on its perimeter. Being on the main highway

north and south, Putaruru had a reputation as being a 'thru' place
— somewhere you went to get to somewhere else. But as a place to
stay, for many it went nowhere: a dead end for trees and people alike.
Putaruru means 'the place of the owl' in Maori. The plaintive hoot of
the morepork owl could be heard at night around our town, 'Moore
pooork, moore pooork', hence its name.

My father must have convinced himself and his new bride that Putaruru was just a stopover. It was as good a place as any to begin their
ascent up the ladder of worldly things. He bought a corner section,
built a dairy adjoining a house to live in, and served up milkshakes
and ice-cream sundaes to locals and travellers. Over the years as his
family expanded, he grew into the little town until it was a habit he
called home. But his wanderlust was not fulfilled and inwardly his
longing resonated with the nightly cry of the morepork.

Apart from being born with two legs there was nothing written in my
genes to suggest that I would be a runner. My mother and father, and
brother and sister before me, had no particular interest in ambulatory
pastimes. Indeed for the first nine years of my life the only runner
mentioned was The Gingerbread Man, and I had no admiration for
where his talents got him.

I was, however, born under the sign of Gemini, ruled by the planet
Mercury, who in his godly semblance is the winged-footed runner
dashing across the heavens delivering celestial messages to mortal folk.
My mother says I came out running and never stopped. Mercury was
surely up on high, watching my legs going up, down, up, down, and
nodding in approval. I was his from the beginning.

In those days a baby's welfare was monitored by weekly visits to
the Plunket nurse whose chief job was to weigh the baby and plot
its growth in a little book. The steady movement of my legs made
me regularly regurgitate my milk. When I failed to put on weight
the nurse urged that I be taken off the breast and put on the bottle,
in the hope it would settle me. It made no difference and I continued to kick and sick. When I went on to solids I had peculiar tastes,
and enjoyed eating earth and eggshell, and had a predilection for the

fireplace where I would chew on the charcoal from last night's fire. Later on, I came to know the name of that condition: pica, or cravings caused by mineral deficiency. In particular I needed iron: the building block for red blood cells and a distance runner's currency for oxygen.

My other distinguishing feature was my big nose. Like a newborn foal whose legs are as long as they will ever be, I had an adult-sized nose with which I never quite caught up. When the Plunket nurse commented on the size of my honker my poor mother was so insulted she never took me back, even though the service was free. My mother now denies this but in my mind it has become legend.

When I was about three the nightmares began, and recurred now and then in those early years. The wardrobe that faced my bed, holding little girls' frocks with delicate smocking, and Fair Isle jumpers, was not so benign. I could detect sinister faces in the sweeping grain of the walnut doors, just waiting to do mischief with me when I nodded off. The moment I felt my feet rising I knew I was done for.

It was always the same: my bed tips up and is set on fire, my flesh melts off like cheese under the grill, my screams make no sound. A ghastly thin figure in hessian robes taunts me with a glass of water. I open my parched mouth but the hand holds the glass high and empties it on my head and I can feel steam evaporating off my skull. Ghoulish figures shriek in delight. I am Prometheus, nightly strung upside down, having not my liver picked out, but my skin scorched off, yet again. I am trapped until they are done playing and then I am discarded like a rag doll to this side of reality.

I ran crying to my parents' bed to seek refuge between them, and yet I knew that they could comfort but not protect me.

Eventually the wardrobe was moved into my brothers' room and my nightmares ceased.

As I grew older, my perpetual leg motion became purposeful. I possessed the pioneering spirit of my ancestors. With it I poked and ransacked every hiding place in our sprawling bungalow so that I knew where Santa hid the Christmas presents and where my mother stashed her comfort sweets. No space was too small to squeeze into but some were too small to get out of. I am grateful that I didn't end up living out my days in a laundry hamper. Also I had a persistent inner calling to put my fingers in electric sockets, and to jump into deep water before I knew how to swim. The dolphin lady Grace, from Kataia, says that I come from Sirius like herself and that such occurances are timely for little Sirians as they activate the DNA from our celestial ancestors. Whether or not that is true, I am grateful that my earthly father swam to my rescue.

My mother, exasperated at losing me almost every outing, resorted to putting me on a leash even though she found it repugnant. My second favourite pastime besides getting into things was getting out of them. I delighted in worming my way Houdini-like out of my harness and giving my mother the slip while she was shopping.

One day my mother took us on the annual Christmas shopping pilgrimage to Hamilton, the sprawling metropolis of eighty thousand people that provided all the surrounding farming communities with more sophisticated wares. She loved nothing better than to go to the department store; not just any department store, but Milne and Choyce, the choicest department store for 70 miles around. This day her shopping was interrupted when she suddenly felt the loss of tension on the tether. Dashing up and down the floors, she searched for me in vain. Afraid I had absconded onto the busy street, my mother ran out the front doors and noticed the crowd gathered at the Christmas display window, the sensation of the festive season. Then she caught a glimpse in the window. To her chagrin I was busily shedding my bloomers for the grand finale of a striptease amongst the three wise men. I curtseyed and the crowd clapped. I proceeded to piddle in the manger, as only a two-year-old can do with impunity, before my mother grabbed my hand and whisked me out of sight.

CHAPTER 2

Piddler

1958—1960

Piddling became my trademark. Especially in shop windows. The local fabric store came to have a distinctive odour on several bolts of material. Must have been imported from an exotic country, they sniffed. I could not help it. I was ill.

I was just a tot when I stepped on glass in my bare feet. I have a faint memory of my sister piggy-backing me into our house as blood poured from my foot. My wounds soon healed but a lump remained under my big toe. The doctor decided I needed surgery to investigate and I was confined to hospital. For three days the surgery was deferred and I was kept unfed and alone. My parents were refused visitation.

When my father came to collect me after the surgery, he says I was desolate and blank. Recalling the moment when he expected me to reach out desperately for him and instead seeing me stare into space as if he did not exist, he would shake his head at the injustice of it all. I do not remember this; the whole experience lies bound and gagged in the hinter regions of my mind, but I could always feel its black shadow lurking in the backdrop of my experience.

The doctors did not find anything in my toe. To my parents it seemed like a fruitless exercise that had needlessly distressed their child. Whatsmore when I was returned to their care I had a bladder infection that I had not had previously. They were told it was psychological and that I would outgrow it. Today they have a name for it: iatrogenic — something nasty that you bring out of hospital that you didn't have when you went in.

I did not outgrow it. In the following years anaerobic organisms blossomed on the unhappy cells like ragwort in a fallow paddock, until they had seeded and parasitized my nascent physiology.

In the first of his attempted escapes from the confines of small-town life, my Dad packed up our few belongings and with our reluctant mother and four kids in tow, he headed towards Surfer's Paradise on the Gold Coast of Australia. We travelled around in a Holden car, three in the front and three in the back. I always got a window seat otherwise I threw up. At night we took turns sleeping on the car seats or outside on a blow-up lilo with Dad. No-one wanted to top and tail with me because I always wet the bed so I usually got my own space. We stopped near Brisbane for a few months at a rental house while my mother took care of her fifth arrival, my baby brother, Bruce. The house was on stilts and had an outside dunny with a long-drop and a nesting chicken that laid claim to the toilet seat. There were two deliveries daily that you could set your clock by: the milk truck with the daily pints for healthy bones and teeth, and the ice truck, bringing huge blocks of ice for the icebox, to keep the milk from curdling.

While there I developed blisters in a neat semi-circle around my middle. The doctors said I was the youngest known case in Australasia of shingles, a title I accepted with pride. I was three years old and had set my first record.

When we returned home a year later I attended kindergarten and shortly thereafter, school.

By then it was established that I had a 'medical condition'. My mother accompanied me into the office on my first day, intending to explain this to the junior headmistress, Miss Hedgerow, who schooled the new entrants for their first year. My older sister and brother were both terrified of her; so much so that my mother or father had to literally drag them crying to school each day. It was by sibling osmosis that I feared her also. During swimming lessons this fearsome spinster had ordered two older children to hold my sister's reluctant head beneath the surface forcing her to be a starfish in order to build her water confidence.

I quivered behind my mother's back as I was introduced. Miss Hedgerow loomed over me, her body wide, her dark straight hair cut in a square frame to her square head. She spoke softly and smiled tightly, nodding as my mother explained my incontinence. I did not trust her. She was a giant slug licking her chops at the thought of consuming me limb by limb. I wanted to run but I was melded like a limpet to my mother's leg.

Miss Hedgerow thrust a Dick and Jane book in front of my nose. I nervously stuttered through a page. My mother had already taught me to read and write so it was assumed that I had attended school during the last year our family had spent in Australia. I was immediately dispatched to the second year entrants with the young sweet Miss Norman, thus escaping the full-throttled punishments Miss Hedgerow regularly meted out to her charges.

Some months later my father gave Miss Norman a ride home and, as the conversation turned to how well I was doing at school, my father could not resist touting my brightness by revealing that I had not attended school previously. The next day I was demoted to Miss Hedgerow's class to see out the year. I cried pitifully.

Whenever we had swimming lessons I bobbed underwater willingly. Determined not to suffer the fate of my sister, I held my breath for so long that on more than one occasion Miss Hedgerow signalled for me to surface by hitting me on the head with her shepherd's crook so the lesson could continue. This tool was not only used to wave threats and whack children, but also to hook the neck or leg of drowning children to haul them to safety if necessary, without Miss Hedgerow ever having to get wet.

By this time my parents were frequently carting me off to the doctor for my bladder infection. The doctor referred them to specialists in the cities. Repeatedly my body was invaded with needles and tubes, dyes, drugs and anaesthetics that pushed my consciousness out of my body as they did heaven knows what to me. And they never said anything, just hmmm-ed and wrote things down in secret files, as if my bodily processes belonged to them and were none of my or my parents' business. Even at that tender age, I knew it was not right and out of my tears grew an outrage and a deep mistrust of medical institutions and their agents in white coats.

The infection flared up so virulently that my urine burned the skin on my inner thighs I was sent to Auckland Hospital, three hours' drive away. Delivering me was a family outing, but my brothers and sisters were not allowed into the hospital so my mother went in to see me settled while my Dad waited with them outside.

When my mother stood to leave I begged with her to take me. Sitting on my hospital bed, I pleaded, 'Mummy, don't leave.' She turned and walked away. My cries became louder and louder until they were bottomless wrenching sobs of desperation: 'Mummy! Mummy! Don't leave me!!' Her footsteps echoed down the hardwood corridor, each resounding clack a little fainter than the last until the swish of the large doors at the end muffled them. She didn't stop. She didn't even look back. She walked away and left me. As the swing of the doors stilled I knew that she was not returning. My scream became silent, swallowed whole in one last bleak gulp and now petrified in my throat. Desolation overwhelmed me.

As I lay in the dark friendless ward I recalled an incident just a few weeks earlier. Mum had introduced me to some strangers, 'This is my daughter, Lorraine.' Seeing their blank uninterest in me, my mother sought to boost her credentials. 'I also have a very pretty older daughter at home,' she added. Now in hospital I knew with certainty the nature of my sin. My mother had left me here because I was ugly.

From then on I asked for my Dad to visit but never my mother. Not because I didn't want to see her — I desperately did — but to ask for her and be rejected was more than I could bear. I knew that with just one re-run of sensible shoes clacking away on a wooden floor, one more swish of the swing doors, one more gulp of silent emptiness, the feed-line to my heart would snap like a matchstick in a drunkard's fingers and my life would drain out of the fracture into the quicksand of oblivion.

Dad came to visit almost every weekend, pleased to be the preferred parent and referring to me from then on as 'Daddy's Girl', a claim that I both highly resented and grasped onto. I wanted to be Mummy's Girl and Mummy's Girl only, but failing that I would take Dad.

Years later he told me that when he arrived at the hospital one afternoon he found me on my bed weeping.

"Why are you crying?" he inquired.

"Because this is my sad time," I announced between sobs. "Leave me alone. I'll be finished in a few minutes."

I knew how to cope. I had also figured out the truth about life — that you mustn't ask for too much. I was better off settling for something less than to ask for my heart's desire and be crushed by disappointment. My Dad often told us, "You cannot have your cake and eat it too." This truism was the padded bumper bar intended to absorb the inevitable collisions with life's disillusionments. Previously I had not understood what it meant; now it registered as fact. I could not hope for it all. We both needed Mum and she was overextended. Dad and I had become bonded in disappointment: the left-out ones who had each other as a consolation prize.

"Hold still." The nurse scurried out of nuclear range. I was constantly being propped up on a monstrous X-ray machine that bombarded gamma-rays into little children like me with no shielding of the re-productive organs.

"But I need to go to the toilet," I called after her.

"Hold on. We'll be done in a minute."

I had been plied with water for the last few hours so that I would have a full bladder for the X-ray. She should have known better than to have asked a five-year-old with a bladder infection to hold on. I let go. I had almost come to like the feeling of the first warm rush of liquid on my legs.

When the nurse sauntered back to tend to me, that state-of-the-art radiation machine had urine running through its delicate inner workings and shortly thereafter died. Whenever my mother told the story she couldn't help sniggering over the height of pissing impertinence. I had destroyed a forty thousand-pound hospital asset, an amount that could have bought three decent houses in our hometown.

One morning a few days later I was brought my clothes and told to dress. My mother was coming to get me. After three weeks I was finally going home. I sat on my bed in the same green paisley pinafore and red cardigan I had arrived in, my heart thumping with anticipation. I wanted to run out into the corridor to find her, before she had a chance to change her mind, but I could not bring myself to move. I knew from the look of anguish on the X-ray nurse's face several days ago that I was already in disfavour. They might keep me captive if I made another wrong move, especially one so forbidden as to cross the door's threshold.

For hours I dutifully sat, poised for exit. Every time the door swished my stomach lurched into my throat. The medicine trolley came and went, then the morning tea trolley with orange cordial and an arrowroot biscuit, and later the lunch trolley. The nurses scooted in and out and the doctors made their rounds and occasionally someone got wheeled off.

When my mother finally appeared I started to cry. She always dressed smartly for the city: a belted colourful dress with a starched petticoat, and red lipstick. I thought she looked beautiful, but now she seemed distant and mysterious, a Madonna in the mist. I no longer trusted her. She cheerily kissed me on the cheek. "You're going home today."

As we walked through the swing doors at the end of the corridor I felt a twinge of triumph. The big doors to the outside were only a short passage away. I had the urge to run, dragging her with me, but she had stopped at the check-out window where a nurse flicked through files. I stood clinging to her side, clutching my little cane suitcase that had once held a picnic set and now contained my dressing gown and slippers. We were directed to an office just ten tantalising steps closer to freedom.

Inside a looming and somber man stood from behind a daunting wooden desk. He was a fearsome god. I forced a smile, knowing my fate lay in his hands. Ignoring me, he addressed my mother, his voice droning like an idling car engine. Using a diagram and a pointer, he explained to my mother that I had reflux causing an 'unarrested infection in my ureters' that was spreading. "When it reaches her kidneys," (which he pointed to on either side of the chart) "then," he shook his head solemnly, "there is nothing we can do."

My ears were pricked, absorbing his every word, as they did when Mum and Dad were having a hushed argument. Either he assumed I was too young to understand what he was saying or he just didn't care, for he spoke as if he were a repairman and my mother had a broken toaster under her arm.

The term 'unarrested infection in the ureters' became branded into my brain. These babbling big words meant what I had always suspected to be true: God had abandoned me and I was on my own. *This being the case, I'll cut off the path of the infection before the point of no return*, I said to myself as I focused in on his roadmap of my body and mentally established a blockade at mid-ureters. When I eyed him again he had deflated, no longer God but a rather stupid man who had missed the obvious of enlisting my participation in the matter. I knew I would not die. I was cut out for something special and carking it interfered with my ambition. I would be a famous film star like Shirley Temple or a ballerina like Margot Fonteyn.

At that time in my life I implicitly understood something that adults seem to have forgotten: that we do have control over our own bodies. I forgot that many times as an adult, too; but sometimes when I was in the flow, and running with complete confidence, I would remember that feeling and know that I could will my body to do my bidding. On those days I was unbeatable.

When I walked out into freedom that day, leading my mother, I felt euphoric. The world was mine for the taking.

During playtime we frolicked on the jungle gym in the middle of the playground. We liked to shimmy along the parallel bars on our armpits with our legs hanging. One day I sprinted to get there for first turn. Somehow the bars had been shifted. Instead of parallel they were converging. Even though it became increasingly tighter, I went on, pushing until I was completely wedged in the middle of the jungle gym and helpless to extricate myself. Kids continued to play around me until the bell rang when they all ran back into the classroom. I continued to dangle like a dress on a hanger, quite happy to do nothing, for nothing was all I could do.

I could see my classmates through the window at their little wooden desks. Then one boy pointed vigorously in my direction. Suddenly Mrs Peters came bounding across the playground, her womanly figure heaving in all directions. She did not seem to believe me that it was not painful, and desperately tried to unwedge me, to no avail. I was quite comfortably hanging out as I watched her scurry over to Miss Hedgerow's classroom for help. Now they both came, bosoms and bottoms pitching and falling with each step like medicine balls on a trampoline. Between them they could not budge me or the equipment so Mrs Peters reassured me while I watched Miss Hedgerow trundle urgently away to recruit help from the senior school.

To my secret delight the playground was soon abuzz with all the male teachers who launched a full-scale operation of collective manpower to dislodge me. Since all other school activities had now ceased, the children hung from their classroom windows which formed a neat little amphitheatre to this drama, witnessing the higher powers scurry and grunt and sweat for the benefit of one dangling waif.

I knew I was pushing it but I could not forgo the perfect opportunity to piddle. A little puddle splattered at the feet of Miss Hedgerow and Mrs Peters. "Never mind dear," Mrs Peters comforted while Miss Hedgerow nodded. "We'll have you fixed up in just a moment." The sense of power was intoxicating. Not only had I discovered that my shortcoming could be the source of command, I had also found my life's calling. I wanted to be on stage.

My years in primary school took a new turn and I rushed through my schoolwork and devoted my spare time to writing plays which I then produced, starred in and directed. My leading character was almost always a witch or a royal sorcerer, which I acted out with great verve.

While I fantisized about casting spells, I also aspired to become a ballerina; a famous one, of course, like Anna Pavlova or Margot Fonteyn, both of whose pictures I collected and pasted into scrapbooks. There was no ballet teacher in our town so I had to be content with socked feet crisscrossed with hair-ribbons, a tiara I had made out of cardboard and a borrowed ballet dress. I pranced around our house on my tippy-toes pretending I was the sugar-plum fairy or a dying swan.

"Look Mummy! There's a fairy!!" a little boy yelled. I had run up town forgetting that I was in costume. (On my first day at Brownies, the junior prelude to Girl Guides, I was assigned to the gnome clan instead of the fairy family. Afraid that I had been categorised by looks, I steadfastly refused to go back.) So now, being mistaken for a fairy was the single biggest compliment of my childhood, and knowing that I could probably never top that, my yearning to fly about on stage in a tutu was, for the most part, satisfied.

Years later when I was almost a teen my father took me on the three-hour drive to Auckland to watch the Royal Russian Ballet perform *Giselle*. Any lingering ballerina longings were finally squelched. The prima donna had a big nose and calves like grapefruit breathing behind her bony shins.

I moved on to a fantasy about becoming a film star. That dream was fed every Saturday morning at 10 a.m. The flicks (moving pictures), which cost sixpence each, began formally with 'God Save the Queen' played by a motherly lady on a piano in the corner of the old Civic Theatre (and later by gramophone when the new Plaza Theatre opened with all its modern conveniences and the price soared to ninepence). We all stood reverently to sing our allegiance to Her Majesty. Once an older boy was thrown out for remaining seated, a good lesson to us all. Then the cartoons came on as a prelude to a Shirley Temple, Hayley Mills or a Doris Day movie. I was captivated. The star was always beautiful and perky and she got everything she wanted by the end. This was the life for me.

CHAPTER 3

The Window

Forget not that the earth delights to feel your bare feet
and the winds long to play with your hair.
— Kahlil Gibran

1961

The infection once again grew out of control. I pissed acid all over the house like an abused puppy. Blood tests showed my white blood count to be dangerously high. I came home from school to find my little cane picnic case had once again been packed with my red flannel dressing gown and my slippers. Dread gripped my insides. This meant only one thing — I was being sent back to hospital. I felt guilty. I was being punished for my childish transgressions and this was how God sent naughty children to hell. I was just six years old.

My father owned a toy shop and he could now combine the trip to Auckland with a few business stops on the way. My compliance was secured with the bribe that I could choose any doll I wanted from the doll factory: a companion to take to hospital with me; a small consolation that I accepted because it was the best I was going to get out of my wretched prospects.

Inside the factory I zeroed in on the wall of walky-talky Princess Bride dolls, searching for one like my sister's, the one that my mother had unfairly given her because she was first-born, most loved, worthy and pretty. But my father quickly steered me to the smaller dolls, the cheaper dolls for the less lovable. As I dilly-dallied he grew impatient, grabbing one from the shelf.

"What's wrong with this one, she has a pretty ponytail like Auntie Brenda, don't you like pretty ponytails? Hurry up now, we have to get a move on." He was always in a hurry, impatient to get the job done, running to escape the betrayals of his heart. Hospitals, loneliness, parents, toys and life all added up to one thing — I could not have my cake and eat it too. I took it sullenly, the growing resentment towards my father poisoning my trust of him.

My dumb doll sat on my bed as I did, neglected and unloved.

Left in hospital I was lonelier than ever, the misery compounded by the misery of my previous visit. I longed for my mother and helplessly sobbed into my pillow for her every night. A mean nurse came by one evening and asked me why I was crying. I told her it was because I hadn't seen my mother for a long, long time.

"How long have you been here?" she asked abruptly.

"Months and months," I replied.

She came back later after looking at my chart and berated me for lying. I had been there just five days. "Don't be such a big baby," she scolded. "Other children have been here much longer than you."

From then on my suffering went underground, the flow of tears dammed inside, the whimper muffled.

After two weeks on powerful new antibiotics I was declared cured. On her last round before lights out the nice nurse told me I could go home on Friday of next week. The next day, I wrote to my parents, lead pencil on blue lined paper, telling them to come and get me next Friday.

When my mother arrived to escort me out I was downright jubilant. We sailed through the swing doors, paused at the glass window and went on to the doctor's office. This time, however, he barricaded the door.

"Wait outside," my mother instructed. "He wants to talk to Mummy."

As I stood at the door I could hear his muffled voice only. When my mother emerged I could tell from her grim face that I was doomed.

She put her arm around my shoulder.

"It was a mistake. You have to stay here a bit longer."

Fear gripped my insides, strangling the feeling out of them and leaving me with a strange deadening sensation throughout my body. I changed back into regulation pyjamas and returned to my bed. This time when my mother left I could not bring myself to look up.

I later learned that a specialist from America was due to visit in two weeks time and the doctor, keen to share the success of my case with him, had decided to keep me incarcerated. By the time the overseas expert arrived, however, my condition had deteriorated to its worst ever and I was no longer the success story my doctor had banked on.

My bed was in a children's ward with two rows of six. Although we were moved around fairly often, this time it was my good fortune to be placed for the rest of my stay at the far end of the room next to a large window.

Behind the headboard was a doorway to the next ward that had been sealed off. There was a little viewing window in the door that I could peek through if I stood up on my mattress. A girl, bigger and older than me, perhaps nine or ten, was curled under the covers, her face, fish-belly white, pulled into her chest. I knew she was deathly ill for two reasons: first, the brightness that I usually saw around living things was dwindling around her, and secondly, although the big window threw shafts of sunlight towards her, she had turned away from it.

One mid-morning the silent movie of my mind was interrupted by piercing screams of pain from behind my bed. I jumped up to spy through the glass. The white girl was hunched over on her knees, her back arched like a bow, while a nurse braced her shoulders and another wrestled her legs into lock-down. A doctor loomed over the bony spine with a fat syringe and was pushing it into her lower back. My breath froze. A nurse saw my little face at the window and snapped the curtain across. The girl screamed again and then caught her breath in a series of short, fraught gasps before her voice trailed into a pathetic snivel like that of an animal caught in a leg trap.

A few days later I noticed the curtain was aside. The girl was gone, her bed freshly made with sanitised white cotton sheets, tightly pulled and tucked with institutional precision. I asked the nurse where she had gone. "Away," she snapped. I knew then that she had died and while I wanted to cry with despair, the relief that I had not made friends with her helped me fight off the tears.

The next day there was another kid in the bed that had swallowed the girl up. I wondered how likely it was that I was sleeping in a bed in which a child had died. The more I thought about it the more convinced I became that the beds themselves harboured death; they were exit portals for children's souls and if I did not keep looking out the big window to connect with the outside world mine would swallow me up one night, too.

One day as I gazed out the window, a woman ran by. Her well-oiled limbs skimmed over the grass so effortlessly that she seemed to be floating. The whole world seemed to move beneath her, as if she gathered all of creation with the air she inspired, and released the trees, the sky and the very ground she ran over, through her pores. I had never seen such a creature before. I was awestruck. She looked up to where I was and stopped. She was looking right at me! She waved. *Did she know me?* I waved back. Her eyes met mine and she smiled. Then she ran on.

I tingled inside with a strange exhilaration. Something important had just happened. This otherworldly being had done more than look in my window, more than see me. She had given me a transmission from the future and I knew in that moment that sooner or later everything would not only be okay, it would be fantastic.

Back at home my parents received a letter from the hospital saying that they could offer 'nothing but prayers' and to come and get me. After five weeks in hospital, tests showed that virulent bacteria were having an orgy in my lower belly. I was worse than ever and not responding to their increasingly large doses of antibiotics.

When I arrived home I quickly resumed my place as middle child.

In a standard altercation with my brother that normally would have deteriorated to a fist fight he told me that he was not allowed to hit me, "Because ... because ... because ..."

"Why because?"

"I'm not allowed to tell you."

"Because why?"

"Because ... because ... Mum and Dad said you're going to die!"

My brother denies ever saying this and it is quite possible I said the words first; after all, I had heard them before in hospital. But I also knew for a fact that they were wrong and I argued so tenaciously with him that he couldn't resist. His punches always hurt like hell and resolved most arguments in his favour, but it was worth it. I had satisfied myself that he was lying and I would continue living.

I would never have admitted to anyone that Death stalked me at night. As I lay in the nether land between waking and sleeping, it would silently slip in through the scar of my big toe and creep up my left leg and then the other; a fist-headed serpent roaming for pockets of despair to grasp on to. Like a vacuum cleaner it sucked the life out of each cell, reaching upward. Quickly my legs were unknown to me, as if they were petrified tree trunks from the ice age. And still it stealthily moved up, rapidly and precisely vanquishing my torso, inch by inch. I would struggle to wake, to yell out, but I was paralysed and my voice was a frozen splotch of white somewhere on a hospital wall. It was not instinct or heart or voice but always a sharpened sword of willpower summoned from the centre of my brain that I grasped to ward off my intruder. The battleground for my life was at the top of my throat, the narrow isthmus leading to central command. *Stop!! I won't allow you to enter!* It always worked. Defeated, the Death Entity would spit and slither back from whence it had come.

I took to wiggling my foot as I went to sleep, as if a moving target were some insurance against this thief entering. "Stop scratching!" my sister would yell. "I'm not scratching, I'm wiggling," I would yell back.

Even though I was declared incurable, I continued to take massive doses of antibiotic pills. When I broke out in a rash all over my face, arms and legs, my mother marched me over to the doctor who diagnosed me as allergic to sulfur drugs and my medication was changed. It made no difference and once again my mother marched to his office, conveniently located directly across the street. The doctor, scrambling for answers, added two more drugs, one to speed me up and the other to slow me down. My mother, reflecting on the doctor's feeble explanation, was fast losing faith in allopathic medicine and quietly flushed them down the toilet.

The rash persisted. Every year from then on through high school it appeared with the first strong sun of summer. A few itchy red bumps bred more, and soon my limbs and face were a fierce mass of blistering irritation. Afterwards my skin peeled off in sheets: the annual shedding of the serpent that sought to feed on my life. I spent these days inside, missing school and our family's outdoor activities, with wet cloths soothing my burning limbs.

If it was not sulfur drugs that caused it, it was a grass perhaps, which bloomed in late spring, the doctor said. He recommended calamine lotion. My Dad was convinced my body was sloughing off the toxic residue from years of drugs. Gradually I outgrew it in my late teens. It occurred once more some twenty years later. My skin blistered as I watched a movie about a witch burning.

With no further solution offered by allopathic medicine, Mum went behind my father's back and took me to a colour therapist. Miss Whitcombe was an elderly spinster who had been a nurse in the tropics. My mother told me that she had been diagnosed with leukemia, a death sentence in those days, and had been cured by a colour therapist. From then on she had dedicated her life to the practice of radiesthesia: a form of vibrational healing. She returned to care for her aged mother in Wanganui, where my mother's parents also lived. On the pretext of visiting her folks, my mother drove us the five hours through the bleak Desert Road and over the hairpin turns of the Parapara Gorge seeking help for me.

Miss Whitcombe's house was a gloomy old bungalow with a straight concrete path up to a porch, and windows like mysterious inky eyes. A tall, grey-haired woman with the willowy figure of a schoolgirl opened the door. She greeted me kindly and took my hand which she held in hers while she talked. Her hand was smooth and cool, not wrinkly as I expected of an old woman's, and she spoke with a calm authority that instilled a confidence in me.

While my mother sat in the living room with lacy curtains and a musty smell, she led me into a stark spare bedroom with dark wooden furniture. I found the whole affair both spooky and fascinating.

One at a time she asked me to hold either vials containing specimens from her collection of elements, or coloured swatches of cotton thread. Then she consulted her instruments, switching back and forth between a pendulum which swung wildly in either direction, and a pencil-shaped glass pointer that, with her eyes closed, she rotated. I knew she was tuning in to determine which ones were right for me, so I kept very still so as not to disturb her concentration.

Back home, at bedtime, my mother placed a chair by my bed for the copper coil that transmitted the healing frequencies into my sleeping body from the coloured threads (orange or teal, according to Miss Whitcombe's instructions). I did not understand it then, any more than I understood X-rays and antibiotics. I only knew I trusted her, and that her treatment did not require I leave my mother.

Miss Whitcombe prescribed sulfur powder to cleanse my blood and fight the infection. My mother put this in the belly of dates, since these were one of my favourite foods. Pure sulfur has a rotten-egg taste and a crunchy texture that grated my nerves. To this day, similar crunching sounds put me on edge, such as the grinding of dry snow underfoot or wads of tissue paper being compressed. But I did as I was told, without complaint. The antibiotic drugs from the doctor were poisoning me Miss Whitcombe said. From eight a day which I had taken for months on end she put me on a series of cycles of four, three, two, and one, on consecutive days and then an equal number of days without to give my own immune system a chance to kick in.

Soon our cupboard was overflowing with unconsumed antibiotics and yet the doctor continued to write the prescriptions and my mother continued to pick them up from the chemist shop in our little town where everyone knew everyone's business. Even though the doctors had written me off, she knew that going against them was risky.

When my test results came back the doctor said, "Something funny is going on here." I was improving and he couldn't account for it. My mother had previously asked him what he thought of colour therapists and the like and he had said, "They should all be burned at the stake!" So now she bit her lip. I continued to recover.

CHAPTER 4

Olympic Heroes

Always to be the best and distinguished above the rest.
— Homer, from *The Illiad*

AUGUST 1964

The 1964 Olympics were being held in Tokyo and Peter Snell was a national hero. I was nine years old and finally had my first running role model. Every day at school the newspaper accounts of his and his teammates' medal-collecting runs were recounted to us. We pasted the reports onto cardboard placards and hung them on our classroom walls and wrote essays about what it takes to be a champion. The teacher told us of the dedication of our Olympic athletes; that they ran every day to get fit, and they won because they never ever gave up. Besides, she emphasised, they were from New Zealand which was the best country in the world because it had everything anyone could ever need to be strong and healthy, and that we were the luckiest people in existence. I believed her.

When I got home in the afternoon our parents continued to talk about our athletes who wore the black singlets of New Zealand with the insignia of the silver fern and how they had done "pretty well, by crikey!" I could hardly contain my excitement. In the distance running events Peter Snell won two gold medals, and John Davies won a bronze medal, as did Marise Chamberlain, just for us! I was so very thankful. The whole world now knew that New Zealand had the best runners in the world. I might have been doubly grateful had I not felt a sense of collective entitlement to their accomplishments. It had been made very clear to me that those medals belonged to the little country that had raised those athletes and because I was a Kiwi, that included me.

When Dad hoisted me onto his shoulders above the crowds a few months later I could see the entire track. It was night-time at Selwyn Park in Hamilton and floodlights lit the gliding forms of Peter Snell, all muscle, and John Davies, all bone, and others as they circled the dirt track. As much as I admired Peter Snell, I cheered for John Davies, because John was local, and besides, in New Zealand, you always cheer for the underdog. I learned that when it comes to finishing bursts, muscle beats bone: I watched Peter Snell forge ahead to the tape, kicking up clumps of dirt with his spikes and tossing them with his high back kick into the faces of his competitors as he went. I screamed along with everyone else as I clutched my father's head so I didn't fall off.

By the time I finished primary school I enjoyed the freedom of running around the field without wetting my rompers and of swimming without peeing in the pool. The Memorial Baths and the Putaruru Amateur Athletic and Harrier Club (PAAHC) were next door to each other at Glenshea Park. The pool was unheated and freezing. The day's temperature was posted at the entrance so you could check it out before you paid. I quickly learned that if it were below 63 degrees F, which was often, death was likely, and wheezing, which felt like death, was certain.

I turned my attention to athletics mainly because it did not involve lung-clamping cold water. Every Thursday evening on the grass track, kiddies' races were held over 50 and 100 yards. I was not the fastest, I tended to galumph rather than zoom along, but inevitably, three-quarters of the way through, I arrived at the feeling of my torso travelling like a royal carriage atop perfectly calibrated wheels. The next moment I was no longer running but flying on silk and for a second I would feel that I could beat anyone — and then the race would abruptly end. I was regularly beaten by another girl in my age group,

Lynnette Morse. She taught me my first lesson in humility. No matter how hard I ran, gritted my teeth, and willed myself to go faster, she trounced me, every time, hands down.

Everything changed when I went to high school in 1968. That was the year Mercury delivered me to the world of running, the year that marked the end of my bladder troubles, the year that I graduated to the senior division of the athletic club which met every Wednesday evening. For the first time in my life races longer than 100 yards were offered. In my first race of 440 yards, I conquered Lynnette, easily. By the end of that one lap of the track I was enraptured. In that extra 330 yards I had found my stage.

The boys' Phys Ed teacher at high school became my first coach. I was flattered to have his attention especially as he was one of the most popular teachers in the school. Mr Merito was commonly known as Happy Feet, a play on his name that you could use to his face without rebuke, even though my sense of propriety precluded me from ever doing so. Stocky and with a boyish face, he had that easy-going up-beat manner of his Maori ancestry, and on bus trips and school socials he was never far from bursting into song, guitar in hand. I always ad-mired those whose voices soared joyously out of them and lifted the spirits of others. I longed to be a songbird like my great-great cousin, Nellie Melba, or even a strummer sitting on a rock belting out 'Ten Guitars', as Mr Merito frequently did.

Looking back, his running advice was dubious but for his bestowal of interest I followed his counsel unquestioningly. Before the regional champs he told me that I must stretch my legs. Under his direction I folded my legs over and under each other, threw them backwards and forwards, and wrapped them around my torso with the vigour of a highland dancer. The next day my muscles were staging a sit-down protest. I could barely run. The solution, Mr Merito advised now, two days before the race, was to stretch more to further condition my muscles. So I did, throwing them around not quite as vigorously as I had the day before. Consequently my legs hurt even more. My father rubbed them with wintergreen liniment, digging into the sore spots with his thumbs, which made me wince and hammer the ground with my fist. Drawing on my fortitude, shaped by my former years in hospitals, I grimaced and won the race anyway. Pain, I discovered, was not a problem if it were not slowing me down, just a pleasure-sapping inconvenience.

Coming up were the Waikato Secondary School Champs. I was entered in the 880 yards, the half mile event. I'd only run two of them before but in my ignorant bliss I believed I could win.

CHAPTER 5

Incentives

No matter how good you are at something,
there's always a million people better than you.
— Homer Simpson

1969

My Auntie Christine had left an abusive marriage and come to our place for refuge. When the doorbell rang one day the whole family answered. Her estranged husband stood on our doorstep intent on repossessing her. When he became belligerent my Dad engaged in a quick kerfuffle and to our amazement tossed him over the railing of our veranda. He landed on his side in the grass, whipped out a comb to swish back his Elvis locks and scurried away muttering threats against my Dad.

Christine stayed. Though twelve years older than me she became my best friend. We spent hours sitting on her bed playing Chinese Checkers, pausing to sneak out to the burger bar for fish and chips to chow down while we obsessively jumped pegs. She told me all I needed to know about growing up.

Mini skirts were the rage and every few weeks Christine would enlist my help to take another inch off her skirts, measuring and pinning as she boldly took her hemline higher and higher. She worked in my Dad's shop and I marvelled at how she had perfected the bob for arranging things on shelves below waist level. In exchange for my help she showed me how to shave my legs and pluck my eyebrows.

She loved to read romance novels and one evening she clutched one to her chest and sighed, "When you're in love you long for the other person deep inside you. It's an ache that keeps you awake at night and makes you do crazy things."

I knew what growing pains were and an ache anywhere didn't sound too wonderful. And what crazy things you might do exactly, she didn't elaborate on. Her ex-husband, she said, had written to her to say he slept with her nightie under his pillow. A strange notion. I could not understand why she didn't have possession of her own nightie. Nor for the life of me could I ever imagine my Dad being entwined in my mother's nightie. Perhaps it was something to do with the type of nightie. These things I pondered for a long time.

For my upcoming race at the Waikato Secondary School Championships Christine offered me an extra incentive. The fashion rage was for cotton dresses knitted on oversized needles and she told me that if I won she would knit me one. I was desperate to be a pretty princess but I felt more like a warty witch with a big nose and white legs. The cotton dress, I decided, was my entrée to beauty and popularity. I had to have it.

Waiting for my race in bare feet and my school rompers I saw my competition and suddenly I didn't feel quite so confident. Girls several years older than me were warming up in spiked shoes and tracksuits, doing exercises. They looked very professional. When the gun blasted it was nervousness that catapulted me into the lead. I led all the way until 660 yards when one of the older guns in spiked shoes sprinted past according to her coach's carefully calculated instructions. Coming down the home straight, the fear of not getting my hand-knitted dress jolted me into overdrive and I discovered what a finishing sprint was, and that I had one. I won and got my dress.

After the race a man in an official Waikato Amateur Athletic Association (WAAA) blazer came up to me and told me I was a good runner and that I should run cross-country. I was so flattered that someone with WAAA written on his pocket would thought me worthy, I joined up for the winter season running junior girls' cross-country.

My first cross-country race was a mile long. Because I didn't have any concept of distance or pacing I ran it the hard way again — flat stick from the start. By halfway my legs wobbled and my lungs seared but I still won and that was reason enough for me to suffer again the next week.

My third such race was in my home town and as there was no junior women's race, I was entered in the senior women's event, over two miles long, twice the distance I had ever run, and against seasoned competitors over ten years my senior. Val Robinson was several times the unofficial runner-up in world cross-country events (the women's event had not been officially sanctioned by the world body) and clearly dominated all the local events. Pam Kenny, also a tough and talented all-round athlete, usually took second place to Val. But I didn't know that then. I just ran to win.

The race started and Val Robinson cleared out to the front. I careered along the sheep ruts in the paddock side by side with Pam Kenny.

"Are you okay?" she asked. We were halfway through the race and I could not answer; I needed to breathe. "Perhaps you should slow down," she cautioned.

No way. She's trying to trick me because she doesn't want me to beat her. I fastened myself to her side like a Siamese twin, sucking for air, white in the face. As the finish line came near, my legs were going numb and my view was reverse telescoping. With the last few available oxygen molecules in my brain I reasoned that if I could not feel, then I may as well run as hard as I could. So I sprinted. Up and down, up and down, my wobbly legs knew how to do that.

Twenty-eight years later I was giving a public talk in Putaruru and was recounting this story. At precisely this point in the narration, a woman leapt to her feet, waved her arms excitedly and yelled, "I beat you! I beat you!!" It was Pam, now on the fast track to senior citizenship but still looking as she had in the sixties. It stopped me short. I remembered beating her, I was pretty sure of it, and would have continued my story along those lines but her emphatic outburst made me doubt my memory so I left it there.

I do know that I collapsed into a jelly heap on the finish line and since my legs would no longer support me, my Dad carried me to the car and took me home. He left me with instructions to soak in a warm bath, his cure-all for any distress, while he returned to the awards. I sat in the bath for about two minutes then tossed on some dry clothes and my wet sneakers. Taking the short-cut across the railway tracks, I sprinted back to the clubhouse. When my Dad walked in I was in the process of accepting my trophy.

Dad decided that I must train, and he would do it with me. He could not have me flogging myself to death, especially in public, and he reasoned that, with a mind that outperformed the body, I must bring the body up to par with its master. He consulted with John Robinson, Val's husband, who wrote me my first training programme. Mr Merito had just been usurped but I did not give it a second thought.

Three times a week Dad and I frolicked around the park, up and down the hill in loops, racing and jostling, Dad throwing in sprints randomly, while I loped behind to catch and pass him when I could. I came to relish running with Dad, especially when it was raining. Barefooted and soaked to the skin we would skid through the puddles trying to knock each other over.

Dad had bush wisdom, theoretically illogical but totally practical. He believed we all have a phoo-phoo valve, which now and then becomes clogged with the lint of conventional living — which we must blow out or we will slowly suffocate. After a few runs Dad expounded to anyone within shouting range that a heart-thumping scamper in the fresh air was the best strategy for clearing the ol' phoo-phoo valve, and promoted himself as the poster boy for this fact.

When the locals got wind that Moller's daughter was a runner of promise and that the old man was taking her out running, they began to corner him around town. "Don't you think that you might be ruining her?" Dad's reply was always the same: "The day I kick the bucket doing too much running is the day she's over-training."

And that was probably the truth of it. We were very evenly matched in pace and fitness, though my rate of improvement outpaced his.

But for a few years we enjoyed not just the challenge but also the camaraderie. Best of all we got to know one another with the kind of unspoken intimacy that develops between running partners.

Mr and Mrs Drummond were the president and secretary of our club: an older couple who had no children of their own. Mr Drummond was an imposing and generous man in both stature and personality. Tall and plump-bellied with white thinning hair and shaded spectacles, like an executive Santa Claus, he always took charge, running the meetings with correct protocol and given to long congratulatory speeches at interclub meetings that culminated in thanking the ladies for the morning tea. He was a senior manager with one of the mills in town and had been President of the New Zealand Amateur Athletic Federation. Mrs Drummond was tall and slender with wavy greying hair and merry eyes that smiled at you through black-rimmed spectacles: Mr Drummond's right hand woman, always ready to take his orders and carry them out with a cheerfulness that brightened his serious undertakings. She had been the Ladies' Chaperone to the 1960 Olympics in Rome. Together they adopted me as a sort of running granddaughter and took me to meets all around our district in the only car in our town with electric windows.

At the Waikato Championships on the grass track as a 14-year-old I caused what the press called an upset by winning the senior 440 yards title, beating the invincible Val Robinson and veteran Pam Kenny. I presumed it was referred to as an upset because the women I beat were upset. Barefooted, I had not just broken the magic 60 seconds for one lap of the track, but had run under 59 seconds. I knew this was fast because Mr Drummond was quoted in the newspaper as saying I was destined for the Olympics. I was flattered and excited. If anyone could spot a champion it was Mr Drummond.

My season culminated in the National Championships over 880 yards. There was no event for junior women so once again I ran in the senior event. It was held at Mount Smart Stadium in Auckland, a cinder track not suitable for bare feet and so my father bought me my first pair of spiked shoes. There were four nails in each leather sole: long shiny steel prongs to grip the moist soil in cross-country running but too long for cinders. Dad took them to the workshop in a service station to have them ground down to regulation size. That meant that when the next cross-country season rolled around I would have to get a new pair.

I made the final easily and lined up against a field of New Zealand's best. They were all at least eight years older than me and I suspected they regarded me as a little punk who shouldn't really be there. There were two women, in turn, that I didn't take as seriously, Shirley Somerville and Heather Thomson. Shirley did not run, she pranced, like a Lipizzaner horse with a plume on its head. I had first seen her prance at a cross-country race in Auckland, with her hair in rollers covered with a sheer scarf to keep them in place. Along with the other pretty blonde, Heather, she sported a pencilled-in Marilyn Monroe mole on her face, a vanity in my mind that distinguished them both from this rugged group of scrappers. Heather wore hers high on her right cheekbone, Shirley, on her left upper lip. Heather claimed she had hers first and that Shirley copied her. Obviously they had their own competition going. Surely I would beat them both.

But, I discovered, never judge the tenacity of a woman by her make-up. Coming around the final bend in last place, I passed Heather. Shirley had already quickly pranced out of striking distance. I could see the thought wash across Heather's face as I passed, 'I'm not letting a kid beat me!' And she knitted her brow and crinkled that little black dot to sprint me off.

I finished eighth, taking a huge chunk off my 880 yard time with 2:13.7, a time that got my name in the prestigious American magazine, *Track & Field News*, as one of the fastest ever for a 14-year-old. I had never heard of *Track & Field News* but I knew it was important because Mr Drummond saved it for me.

CHAPTER 6

Breasts and Big Muscles

1970

Puberty was invented to humiliate humans. I could see no other reason for such a savage morphing of one's own tissues. As much as I wanted to shine I spent a good deal of my energy trying to conceal this hideous proceeding. Complicit with Mother Nature, my mother refused to allow me to wear stockings at my first school social. The shiny nylon veneers held by the fasteners of a suspender belt were a rite of passage she intended deferring until my legs were 'mature enough'. I spent the entire evening sitting on the long wooden bench with my skirt pulled over my knees and my legs tucked under me so that no-one would notice I was wearing long white socks.

Painfully self-conscious, I learned to keep my head down to hide my nose. In class I always chose the desk by the wall and sat with my chair sideways so that my profile would be turned away from the direct line of vision of the golden boy: the one who was handsome and brainy and flirted with pretty girls with small noses.

"Lorraine, don't you think it's time for a brassiere?" my mother asked one day as we drove up town. My whole body lurched forward in a big yes but I was embarrassed. The word 'brassiere' was an old biddy mocking my burgeoning tits. Why couldn't my mother be cool and just say 'bra'?

I was the second to last girl in my class to get a bra but couldn't bring myself to ask her for one. I simply rolled in my shoulders and crossed my arms to conceal the evidence.

When I changed for gym class I was teased by the class bully, not because I was underdeveloped, which I wasn't, but because I was braless and thus 'uncool'. On top of that, some of the 'in' girls started coming to school braless. They were considered outrageous. That should have been good news to me but being 'without' was only avant garde if you had been 'with'.

"Oh, I don't care." I shrugged at Mum and stared out my window.

But she had decided it was time and drove me to the lingerie shop where she bought me a 'teen brassiere': a series of criss-crossed straps not unlike the harness I wore as a two-year-old.

I heard tell that if I did too many sit-ups I would have trouble giving birth when the time came. There were whispers that if I ran too hard my uterus would fall out, the latter being a warning bandied about the world over, like the one about wearing clean underwear in case you got run over and taken to hospital.

At girls' school assembly where feminine issues were addressed, our headmistress warned us of the consequences of entering the annual school cross-country race.

"If you have seen the Russian shot-putters on television with their bulging muscles, this is what you risk if you run," she barked at us in her stern Scottish brogue.

I had, and Russian ballerinas to boot. For boys the cross-country event was compulsory but optional for the girls so she was kindly attempting to save as many girls as she could from the dire fate of masculinity through muscularity. I was seriously concerned. I wanted to run but not at the risk of muscle-bound legs, random feminine parts falling out and, worst of all, growing a moustache.

I decided to monitor this very closely by conducting my own study of one on the masculinising effects of running on adolescent females. I measured my calf size and logged it daily. When and if they reached a critical mass, not yet decided upon, I would stop running. This lasted about ten days and then I became bored with it. My muscles had not changed one iota.

The following season my long-awaited period finally arrived. I was mortified. I ran home from school, skipping class, and told my mother who gave me a pillow-sized sanitary pad to wear between my legs. As I struggled with the buckles of the elastic belt that held it in place I despaired whether my life was worth continuing. *How can I go through life with this every month? Why couldn't I have been a boy? It's not fair!*

The only vindication was that this event had somehow matured my legs and my mother let me wear stockings to the next school social.

I continued to train with my dad and to race most weekends, out-distancing everyone in my age group and carrying off the trophies: usually merchandise from a local store. Among my precious prizes were numerous salt and pepper shakers, his-and-hers towels, his-and-hers pillow-cases, a ceramic mouse, and a wire toast rack. I carefully arranged them all on my dresser.

Menstruation took its toll. As the months passed it became increasingly difficult for me to rouse myself in the morning. My mother took to bringing me breakfast in bed so that at least I ate before tearing off to school.

Soon my legs felt stuck to the ground when I ran. But I persisted, uprooting them from each step until my runs were done. I felt tired all the time, snapped at my brothers so they left me alone, and had trouble concentrating at school.

The biology teacher asked me to stay behind after class one day. Old Mrs Johnson reared race horses and knew her physiology. She pulled down my bottom eyelid with her bony finger. "Just as I thought," she said and sent me home with a recipe for cooking liver. My mother served it up but I found it disgusting and refused to eat it.

Mr Merito called me into his office for a little talk.

"When you first started running," he started in, "everyone said you were too young and that you would get burned out. But I didn't believe them. Now it's evident that they were right. You are burned out. Give up! It's over for you!!"

I could feel tears welling up and I fought to suppress them.

No!! I tried to yell, but my protest stuck in my throat below hearing range.

"You have to accept it," he said, looking at me in an earnest fatherly way. "You're finished." And he dismissed me.

I was miserable. The evidence was in his favour, but how could he declare me finished and wipe out my dreams just because he was bigger than me? I thought of the smarmy doctor announcing that I was going to die years ago and indignation rose up inside me. Mr Merito was wrong, I knew it. I was destined for the Olympics. Mr Drummond had said so.

Again the school cross-country champs were coming up and I entered just the same, defying my teachers. When the gun went off, I ran to the front. My legs had a sinking feeling, as if I were a water buffalo foundering in deep mud. It baffled me that my competitors let me run to the fore unchallenged, that their expectation had predetermined the outcome. When I crossed the finish line in first place my head was swimming and my legs were disappearing under me. A teacher caught me as I passed out and my parents were called to collect me. I was taken to the doctor who confirmed that with a hemoglobin count of 8.9 I was indeed very anaemic. "Any lower," he said "and we will have to put you in hospital." That threat was needed for me to follow instructions. I was put on a course of iron and banned from running for three months.

I wondered if Mr Merito was right, after all, and that at 15 I should announce my retirement. But somehow, underneath my despondency, I had an inkling that my destiny as a runner was just about to unfold.

Murupara School relay, 1972. Lorraine running the anchor leg. *Waikato Times*

PART TWO

Runner

A throne for Anne Audain, 1974 Commonwealth Games in Christchurch.
Dianne Rodger is on the right. *Waikato Times*

CHAPTER 7

Role Models and Rivals

1971

When I recovered, Mr Drummond took my career in hand and along with Mrs Drummond drove me to Tokoroa, a timber-producing town some 15 miles up Highway 1, and introduced me to a coach who could shape my talent: none other than John Davies, the man I had cheered for when he had raced Peter Snell some five years earlier.

Now, he was more than the pair of stick-insect legs that I had seen on the track. He was a real person observing me through large black-rimmed spectacles, a flesh and blood Olympian, and a bronze medalist. Immediately I took to his contained, intelligent manner and reassuring voice that was often punctuated with chuckles. Where this was leading I had no idea, but I knew that my potential had been recognised and that I was being delivered into the hands of a master.

Mr Davies took me for a run. He listened as I huffed and puffed beside him like the big bad wolf at a brick house. He knew exactly what I needed and wrote me an open-ended schedule telling me to build up my miles.

My dad took up the challenge and ran with me. He loved it, too, improving his own fitness and was convinced that the miles were processing all those childhood drugs out of my body. "Damn pills," I had heard him say to my mother, "not good for a kid." He had this theory that once they were sweated out the full power of my Viking heredity would be unleashed. My dad loved the idea of conquering Viking ancestors although he had no evidence of such. My mother did too. Despite my father's failings my mother admired his strength of body and mind. "Those Danes have dominant genes," she reminded me often. She had no idea back then that research would one day show that one's athletic ability is largely determined by the mother's genes, not the father's.

A few weeks later I met with Mr Davies and proudly showed him my training diary with a big 40 circled in red at the top of the page: 40 miles in one week. My fitness was improving rapidly.

Mr Davies soon moved to Auckland but continued to send me regular schedules. He had been a protégé of the legendary coach Arthur Lydiard, the man behind the slew of Olympic medals that the New Zealand runners had collected in the past few years. Mr Davies trained me according to the Lydiard principle: first building a base of endurance running to maximise my body's oxygen-carrying capacity so that it could handle, and recover from, increasing workloads. I did not question the schedules but dutifully carried them out to the letter. After all, John Davies was an Olympic medalist and not to be second-guessed. The difference in my fitness was profound. Over the next few months, along with Dad, I progressed to longer and longer runs in the Pinedale Forest, going three miles, then five miles and eventually churning out ten mile runs together.

We always sprinted to the finish, Dad would play to the pine trees as if they were an audience in a crowded stadium. He had confided in me during a ten mile bush run that he liked being alone out there so he could talk to his tall-limbed friends. As we ran he greeted various trees that lined our way with a nod and introduced me as his 'daughter Lorraine, the runner'.

As we bit into the last mile he put his hand to his ear. "Hear them cheering for us!" he instructed. I wondered if my dad was a bit nuts but doing as he said, I listened carefully. I swear I could hear a roar of encouragement building under the silence. Dad suddenly bolted for the finish and I took chase. Adrenaline surged through my muscles like electricity. He was John Davies, and I was Peter Snell at the Olympic Games, powering away from the flailing competition to win gold.

Most often I was faster in a dash so Dad used his bag of tricks to get a head-start on me: often he would quietly watch until I was lost in thought, and then dart ahead; sometimes he would ask me to stop and wait while he pretended to tie his shoelace and then he would sprint away; and other times he resorted to grabbing the back of my singlet and pulling me back as he launched himself in front. But when he was feeling frisky and felt he had a fair chance against me, he would playfully raise his hand to his ear and cock his head towards the trees. It was his signal to me that it was time to treat our tree audience to a good show of competition, and we would accelerate stride for stride until we were full-pelt racing.

"Don't tell anyone I talk to the trees," he warned me at the end of one such run. "They might put me in the loony bin and then you'd have no one to take you running."

Mr Davies wrote that I was ready to begin hill work-outs, a four-week phase of training specific to the Lydiard system. He explained that the hill work-out consisted of running up a long steep hill with exaggerated motion, running down quickly and then doing a series of strides along the bottom. This sequence was to be repeated three times in a session. Mr Davies had written across the page, 'Pump your arms!' But in his handwriting it looked like, 'Pump your anus!' I balked to read it out to my eager Dad. Ever impatient, Dad grabbed it from my hands. "Pump your … ahem…" he read, stopping short, and putting down the page. "Let's just go." I suspected that this was an advanced technique in training that when I was older I would come to understand, along with the secrets of the nightie. After I had lived in Boulder for ten years, my running partner told me that the secret to relaxed distance running was to breathe through your anus. I then knew this suspicion to be correct — it was some Zen art that I could never figure out how to do.

Now and then overseas runners arrived in town as part of a loosely arranged tour by Arthur Lydiard. When Mr Drummond asked us if we could take in an American cross-country runner and her husband for a few days we were very excited. She was a petite woman with doe-like eyes who had run on American teams. I was deeply honoured and Dad and I were excited to take them to the Pinedale Forest on our best run. The four of us made our way along the wide dirt logging road that had recently been filled with rocks for the traction of the heavy trucks. She wore a smart tracksuit and real running shoes. I was in my canvas tennis shoes that I always wore for roads. As Dad and I loped along we quickly realised that our guests were lagging. "It smoothes out soon," Dad reassured them and we slowed for them to catch us. I ran beside her, trying to think of something to say, when she suddenly pulled to halt and sat down on the moist forest ground, burying her head between her knees. Her husband hastened to her aid. "I can't run on this shit!" she wailed up at him. He picked her up and carried her back to the car. They left the next morning.

I felt bad. We had messed up. Perhaps we were doing this running thing all wrong.

Dad appeared at my door and plonked himself down on the end of my bed. "Don't worry. It's not our fault. I didn't realise that Americans can't handle rough surfaces. They train on golf courses all the time. It makes their feet soft."

That made perfect sense.

In the next season I ran high school champs, then regional champs, winning them all and setting records by chunks. When the Waikato Secondary School Champs came around, once again I was the favourite. This time I wore spiked shoes and warmed up like an old racing pro. The regulation uniform was black rompers (designed to disguise pillow-sized sanitary pads) and a heavy black cotton singlet, which I had sewn myself. But the regulations said nothing about socks. I had two pairs which I had found in a bargain bin, one fluorescent pink and the other neon green. They became my lucky racing socks. When I put them on I stood out. That day, wearing pink,

I won my races, setting Waikato records.

It so happened that the Royal family was touring Hamilton that day and the regal procession came by the school track meet, whereupon the top runners of the day were lined up to be introduced to her Majesty the Queen, Prince Philip, Princess Anne and Prince Charles. We were given a quick briefing. Curtsy when introduced. If talking to the Queen address her as 'Your Majesty'.

Rompers are not exactly curtseying attire, but I managed to bob and mind my P's and Q's. Prince Charles lingered for a while with me.

"Why do you run?" His clipped words seemed to be pushed out of his front teeth.

"To get there faster," I replied.

He smiled and glanced down. "And why do you wear pink socks?"

"To keep my feet warm." Then I added "Your Royal Highness" so he wouldn't think I was cheeky.

A few weeks later *she* moved into *my* territory, the territory I thought I had all to myself: that of running-girl prodigy. I was pipped. Her name was Anne Garrett and we first met at the North Island Inter Secondary School Championships, the first time a school event of this scope had been organised. She was 14, I 15, she the newcomer, I the established champion. Her coach was Gordon Pirie, the eccentric and flamboyant Englishman and long distance Olympian, and mine, the reserved and pragmatic John Davies. Anne and I postured at each other across the stadium, eyeing each other up and whispering catty remarks to our teammates.

I was warming up for my race in the fields outside of Hamilton's Porrit Stadium, when a voice called out, "You're wasting your time". I couldn't tell where it came from and assumed it was meant for someone else, but as I came by, again the voice yelled, "You're wasting your time".

I looked up. He was lanky, tan, athletic, 40-ish. I pointed at myself.

"Yes, you. What are you doing?"

"Warming up."

"Waste of time, ever seen a lion warm up?"

"No." I had only ever seen a lion in a zoo, where there was hardly room for the poor beast to turn around.

"Waste of time, no animal ever warms up except man. It's unnatural."

I did not want to contradict such certitude but my coach had sent me out to warm up. I ran on beyond his scope, cutting my loop short so as not to run by him again.

I told Mr Davies. "Sounds like Gordon Pirie,' he said. "Ignore him. He does that to everyone."

The race was 440 yards, one lap of the track. Anne and I ran neck and neck up the final straight, battling for the win. Our attrition rate was perfectly synchronised. Neither of us could get a micro-inch ahead of the other. We crossed the finish in a dead heat. In the days before photo finishes it was up to the judges who stood on a tiered platform at the finish line to make the call. They disagreed. It went to jury and a meeting ensued. The verdict came out. Anne Garrett was given the nod. My nose had let me down. I was crushed, she was jubilant.

Then an announcement was made. The referee had disqualified Anne Garrett for running inside her lane around the bend and covering less distance than me. I was declared the winner, and suddenly I was jubilant and she was crushed. The signature of our relationship was set and we became arch rivals for the next 20 years, taking turns at jubilation and despair, like partners on a seesaw.

From that day on, more than anyone else, I couldn't stand the thought of her beating me. Perhaps this was because we were so evenly matched and we were always vying for top Kiwi honours. She was often the grain of sand that irritated me so that I could find that bit extra in myself and I suspect I did the same for her, and thus Anne, I grudgingly admit, played a vital role in my success.

CHAPTER 8

Winning Isn't Everything

1971 — 1972

The half mile race on the track, the 880 yards — two laps — became my specialty event. During the summer track season there were meets almost every weekend, either in my region, the Waikato, or in Auckland at Mount Smart Stadium. Dad drove me to these meets, thrilled to watch me race and be around 'running' people. He always waited at the finish for me, ready to prop me up and walk me around until my shaky legs had worked off enough lactic acid to support me.

There was one woman who was supreme in the half mile event: Sue Haden, from Auckland. Sue was eighteen years my senior, a handsome woman, with a strong athletic build and a rather pretty face set with icy blue eyes and framed with a no-nonsense pixie haircut. She wore her determination for running like a knight's armour — there was no penetrating to the warm and fuzzy side of her, and if indeed she had one she never showed it to me. Dad said she just needed a few drinks and a good night on the town, and I suspect he fancied himself as a candidate.

For the first season of races I sat just behind her for the first 660 yards, then she would take off and I would finish the race behind her in escalating lactic acid debt, which felt like trying to sprint across a waterbed of ever-increasing density. Lactic acid is the by-product of anaerobic metabolism: the way the body copes with energy demands greater than the intake of oxygen can sustain. All runners come to know the burning feeling in the muscles of oxygen deprivation and lactic acid build-up when they push too hard, and learn that if they continue to run their muscles will very quickly become unresponsive.

However under Mr Davies' tutelage I came back the next year and instead of finishing 10 to 15 seconds behind Sue I was now only five seconds back and the 'waterbed' finish grew shorter. (NZAAA went metric at that time and the 880 yards became 800 metres, slightly shorter and about a second faster.)

Sue cornered me at an early season interclub match at Porritt Stadium as I was warming up. This surprised me no end since she usually said no more than a cursory hello. Her message was terse. She was sick of me sitting on her and wanted me to take the lead for once. I was puzzled. Didn't she know I sat on her because she was faster? But since she was so forthright, and fearsome to boot, I felt I had no choice. So I led.

Coming into the home straight, Sue sprinted past me for the win, a predictable move. As I watched her back, it suddenly occurred to me that I had been bullied into leading so that she could get a faster time for herself. A wave of indignation surged through me. I was being used! I discovered then that anger is a great antidote for wimpy mattress finishes. I sprinted and passed Sue with fifty metres to go, and won the race. She was stunned, so was I, and the press called it another upset. I had graduated to being her rival.

It had been a full day of racing on the Cambridge Memorial Field grass track and I had just swept the winnings in all the junior girls' distance events. As I was walking past the change rooms sucking on my orange ice block, I accidentally got an eyeful at the doorway to the men's shower. He was a grown man in his prime, athletic, well-built, and full-frontal naked. I quickly walked on and he did not see me. I should have been embarrassed, and I was, but the handsomeness of him had caused something strange to happen inside me. A ripple of warmth emanated from the pit of my belly like the unravelling of a sheer scarf in a strangely delightful and indefinable way. What I did know was that this running thing was laden with mysterious potential.

Sue and I competed against each other next on New Year's Eve at the seaside town of Tauranga, a festive meet on a grass track. Again Sue approached me before the race. This time I eyed her warily. She admonished me for clipping her heels in previous races. "Don't do it again!" she warned. I had a long stride and had to deliberately shorten it when running behind others. The moment I was unaware or they slowed the pace I was back to tapping their heels. Anyhow I had obviously upset Sue and now I had to be extra careful. Knowing now how motivating anger can be, I didn't want her mad at me.

When the gun shot off, Sue commandeered the front spot. After the last race she no longer wanted me to lead, preferring to go back to her old working formula. I settled into my familiar position, when, tap! I clipped her heel. I hoped she didn't notice. Then I did it again. "Sorry!" I yelled up ahead. When I did it a third time I knew I was in big trouble. We were not even halfway through the race yet. So I took the only option I saw open to me, and got out of her way by taking the lead. I sprinted in front of her, an unusual manoeuvre for me and a dicey one, but less dangerous than clipping her heels one more time. I ran the last lap in front. Coming down the home stretch I fully expected Sue to come whizzing by me, so I sprinted just the same... and won. Another upset. The prize was a full set of cutlery, a very grownup award which I saved for the time I would leave home.

Sue did not approach me again after that.

Walking back across the field at the end of the meet with my folks, we crossed paths with a young man, whom I had secretly had a crush on for a few years. Now that I was 16 I was hoping to be able to escape the clutches of my family and go out partying with him and his friends for New Year's Eve.

He yelled out, "Gonna come and sink some piss with the boys tonight, Lorraine?" I cringed.

My father looked at my mother. "Did you hear that? The cheeky young larrikin." Then he turned to me, "And what have you been up to young lady, that this joker thinks he can talk to you like that?!"

I knew I was done for. As much as I denied any mischief, I knew my father sensed that I was guilty of stirrings. There would be no going out this year. I would have to stay at home content with admiring my cutlery.

On the basis of my 800 metre runs against Sue I was selected to run for New Zealand. The team members, all under 23 years of age, would travel to Australia to run in meets against young Aussies. I was very excited finally to have the honour of wearing the silver fern of my country.

The first meet took place in the cool evening on an all-weather track in Sydney. I won the 800 metres comfortably. At the second meet in Canberra a few days later I felt sluggish. Although I won the 800 metres again, I was disappointed with my time of 2:12 since I had been running in the 2:08 range. I wanted it all so badly that I did not take into account that I was running on a grass track in very humid conditions in the middle of the day. All I could see was that out of two races I had made a backward progression and that by my final race of the week I would be humiliatingly slow.

On the way to the stadium for my final race I complained of my last-race lethargy to a team-mate hammer thrower.

"If you're feeling tired then take a couple of these." He flipped out some No-Doz caffeine pills.

I was suspicious. All pills to me were suspicious. "Are they legal?" I asked.

"These tiny things? Sure they are, just like drinking a few cups of coffee." He waved them under my nose, "I take them all the time. You won't feel tired for your race, I guarantee you."

I didn't believe his assertions about their innocence. This was a dodgy proposition, probably criminal. Across the Tasman I could sense my Dad's presence looming over my shoulder, shaking his head. *Don't do it! No, no, no!!*

I downed them and went out to warmup. By the time I stood on the start line, my whole being was atwitter with a drive for action the likes of which I had never felt before. I zoomed around the track, easily winning my Under-23 division of the match. I ran a personal best time of 2:05.1. Afterwards I ran another zesty four miles to cool down and would have kept going had the meet not finished and the bus been leaving. That night sleep did not come easily.

Cheat. What an ugly word. Whenever my brilliant run was mentioned I hung my head in shame. John Davies was thrilled. His eyes shone when he told me that 'Sue's face was as long as Queen Street' when he told her of my fabulous time. His delight made me feel worse. I could not admit to him that my performance belonged to a little white pill.

My Dad knew. He gave me The Look and I knew in that instant that he had read my guilt. I said nothing and neither did he. Inside I desperately wanted to see pride in his eyes, to prove my worthiness, to fill this hole inside of me. I knew there was only one way to dig my way out and that was on my own merit.

From that day on I decided I would always play it straight.

CHAPTER 9

Great Temptations

One must go forward, that is step by step
Further into decadence.
— Friedrich Nietzsche

1972 — 1973, DUNEDIN, NEW ZEALAND

With the end of high school approaching I had to consider what to do with my life. While I was considered academically bright it was running that I excelled in, but in those days sports as a career for a woman was not a viable option. The closest thing was to be a Phys Ed teacher. That sounded fun enough to me. I didn't really care as long as my higher education didn't interfere with my running. Mostly what I wanted was to get away from the restraints of home, and the Phys Ed School was in Dunedin at the south end of the South Island, as far away from home as I could possibly go.

My brother was already a student of Phys Ed and I was enthralled by his tales of student pranks and mischief-making. There was one character renowned for his party rendition of 'The Dance of the Flaming Assholes'. His performance entailed inserting a rolled funnel of newspaper between his butt cheeks and lighting it. As the paper burned down he would dance faster and faster. Even my father couldn't help smirking at that tale. I couldn't wait to get down there and come home with my own outrageous stories. (I never did get to see the Flaming Dancer. Apparently he was forced into early retirement after charring a vital orifice.)

My parents were not as gung-ho about my freedom as I was. While they did not often formally lecture me on the dangers of the world, they alluded to them. By the time I headed out the door on my grand adventure I was well aware of the three great temptations that if succumbed to would bring great shame upon my family.

The first was pregnancy. Mum would whisper to me on occasion about someone's daughter in town who had to 'take a long holiday in the South Island'. To have such a daughter would be mortifying to her, and we both knew that Dad would shoot the bloke responsible.

The second was partaking in drugs. There were none in high school that I ever came into contact with but in universities the temptation was apparently lurking in wait for innocents like me and with it came certain addiction. My parents had watched a documentary on television and they were worried for us. "Don't let anybody give you a drink if you don't see where it came from. Someone could easily slip something in it. And keep away from ma-ri-ju-wana." My mother would emphasise the "ju", as if to say, "I am familiar with the word so I know what is going on" and my father would nod in agreement.

The third danger was the Moonies. Do not talk to them in airports. Do not go to their meetings and never give them money.

My hostel accommodated both genders and when I arrived at the dining room for my first meal, I could not see any Moonies but there were handsome young guys everywhere. I was just seventeen years old and despite my parents' warnings I was chomping at the bit to experience forbidden delights.

I had been there just a few days when a weedy guy with Jesus hair and beard befriended me outside the hostel. He asked to come up to my room as he wanted to show me something. Not used to saying no to anyone, and being curious for experience, I led him up. He sat cross-legged on my bed and rolled a joint as he extolled its mood-enhancing benefits. I had never seen one before, let alone smoked one, so he demonstrated how to draw on it and hold it in deep before exhaling. I did my best but as soon as my lungs got a bite of it they rejected the intrusion so violently I thought I might expel my backbone. For the heck of me I could not understand anyone smoking, no matter what it was. I watched dumbly as he got suitably stoned and then, thankfully, he left. Amazingly I was not addicted. My room stank. I realised that if anyone investigated I would be thrown out in disgrace. When the Jesus Hippie called for me again I pretended I wasn't home.

I was standing on the steps of the Phys Ed school in my running gear, wondering which direction to run in when a group of men came trotting by. "Hey Chick," one yelled out, "come for a run!" That was how guys talked to girls back then. I was flattered. I sprang down the steps and joined in their pack. They were a group of about ten lunchtime runners, guys who worked in downtown Dunedin. They set a pretty mean pace and I was running hard to keep with them, especially up the hills. "Want a hand?" someone yelled as I panted away and suddenly there were three or four hands on my backside giving me a push.

Before long, every weekday at noon, I was on the steps of the Phys Ed School in my shorts, waiting for the lunchtime guys, and every week I became a little fitter. The parameters of what I thought was reasonable training were stretched until I no longer thought of myself as a limited girl, but as one of the boys, capable of running as fast and as far as my fellow athletes.

A Sunday run with the lunchtime guys was not the tame ten to 12 miles that I was used to but a rugged 20 miler over the Waitati hills in fog, rain, drizzle or, very occasionally, a smattering of snow. Soon I was clocking 90 miles per week, something that was unheard of at the time for a woman, except, it was rumored, by those mysterious East German steroid queens. For me it was pure fun. My running buddies readily accepted me into their fold, being both solicitous of my well-being and proud of my progress.

As I continued to get stronger my times improved. I was winning all the races, breaking records and getting my name in the news regularly. The lunchtime runners were in love with me. I loved them back. They were my running family. Their wives, who raised their kids and cooked their meals and washed their smelly socks, were jealous of me.

Every Monday morning when my photo appeared in the newspaper with the weekend's running results, the offended wife delivered it to the breakfast table with a moustache doctored onto my face. And if I set a new record, a husband or two would have to sleep that night in the woodshed, which, they assured me, they happily endured to be associated with 'Running Chick'.

Occasionally Dick Taylor showed up. He was soon to become the Commonwealth Games gold medalist for the 10,000 metres. Smooth-faced with a ready impish smile and a stocky lean body honed for competition, he was always ready with quips, which he dropped to the trailing runners who caught and passed them around like kids at a lolly scramble. We struggled to keep up with him and not daring to speak, if indeed we could, in case we missed the next hilarity. Eventually he would break the pack by bringing the constituents to their knees one by one, with laughter.

Dick had no compunction about running over the tops of cars that were in his way. One of the guys thought that was going a bit far and told him. I thought so too, but he was irrepressible and I held my breath as a car came to a stop sign right in Dick's path. Without so much as missing a stride, he opened the passenger door, ran through the interior and out the other side with a cheery "excuse me, just passing through" to the astonished front-seat occupants.

Alistair McMurran coached Dick Taylor and many others in the area. He was known simply as Ali. His smooth, elemental face reminded me of one of the garden gnomes which the lunchtime runners felt compelled to relocate from one front yard to another on their runs. Everyone liked Ali, if they noticed he was there for he usually stood on the periphery, a shy but astute observer. He had a gentle and unassuming nature which made people feel safe enough to reveal their secrets, a useful talent for a sports reporter with the *Otago Daily Times*.

When Ali asked if he might interview me I consented to a Friday evening appointment. He picked me up in his trusty old Ford Anglia and drove me over the remote shores of the peninsula, all the while asking me penetrating questions as I talked into his microphone. I began to realise that I had committed myself not to a 30-minute press interview, but to hours of soul-searching that would supplant my Friday night partying. As we headed into the mists rolling in from sea that stretched all the way to the polar ice cap I started to wonder if he were a serial killer. I scanned for something with which I could defend myself. The only thing was a ballpoint pen in my pocket so I kept running my fingers over its tip just in case.

There was no need. Ali wanted only to connect with someone he saw as kindred. In a way he was my first spiritual mentor, throwing out insights on the nature of life and competition, just enough for me to grasp and no more, but I had an inkling that beneath each grain of wisdom conferred there were layers of truth I was not yet ready for.

When I went home during the university break, Ali sent me long typewritten epistles which impressed me deeply. 'An athlete who crosses out the little "i" and allows the big "I" to shine through and be dominant must achieve good things for themselves and others,' he wrote. 'Any person who achieves fame in any sphere should use it for the good of others — so that the lot of humanity can be improved and the general consciousness of the world uplifted.' Such lofty aspirations were couched in glowing praises for my talent as a runner. He was convinced that I would be the greatest female distance runner New Zealand had seen and that one day I would win a gold medal for my country. Ali's words made sense to me. They confirmed what Mr Drummond had already told me. I was destined to be a champion. Now I could easily envision a greater reason for such a destiny: one day, gold medal in hand, and my halo shining brightly, I would shower humankind with my deeds of philanthropy.

But my faith in the genuineness of Ali's prognostications soon took a tumble. In the New Zealand Cross-country Championship a few months later I failed to live up to his (and my own) expectations. I had committed the first sin of racing — never do anything new — and downed a cutting-edge powdered milk drink called Sustagen on the start line. I had had no breakfast so followed that with two cream-filled doughnuts I had bought on the way to the race. I might normally have survived a start that was too fast, and perhaps could have given chase when Anne Garrett's team-mate, Allison Deed, passed me on a long uphill. But the stomach cramps were belly-bending and my pride mortally punctured, so I lay down on the hill in the middle of the race for an embarrassingly long time, until I finally got up and walked to the finish line.

The New Zealand Road Championships always followed the Cross-country Championships by several months. In his race preview, Ali wrote of me for his sports column, something to the effect 'while she is a good runner she has yet to prove she is a good racer'. His words were a sly blade that sliced into me when I read them. Suddenly the dazzling tributes from a mentor seemed to be no more than schmoozing from a reporter who would mock me publicly. When I saw Ali at the start of the women's four kilometre road race I would not speak to him. I was wearing my suede Puma road shoes. Each shoe weighed over a pound and they were as stiff as clogs, but they were brand new and as red as my anger, and I loved them. I trounced my competitors soundly, including Anne Garrett and Gordon Pirie's newest teenage protégés, Allison Deed and Barbara Moore.

Afterwards Ali wrote to me explaining, 'My article was meant to make you mad … and to engender within you the determination to win.' When he added that my win was evidence of his good judgment, I remained offended. I might have forgiven him if he had admitted that my victory was testimony to my fine racing ability, but he didn't. He didn't know that to interfere with my running was to wrestle with my dragon. We barely spoke again for the rest of my time in Dunedin.

My brother introduced me to Jake. A second-year student, he strutted the raw exuberance of Tarzan out to conquer the jungle: lank hair over dark eyes that glinted with the youthful confidence of testosterone, a wide-boned jaw ready to rip flesh with his bare teeth, shoeless feet with dusty soles that splayed out and blended with the ground, and a muscled caveman body designed to both dodge dinosaurs and perpetuate the species.

My Dad would have had him sussed in two minutes: would have

called him a randy dog lurking for an opportunity, a gorilla in mating season; and he would have filled him with the fear-of-Gordon and given him the heave-ho with a well placed punch if necessary. But, by my own design, Dad was not 'within cooee' to keep me from the pitfalls of lust and ignorance.

We floated around in nighttime student gangs: well-brought up kids looking to the herd for direction in navigating our emerging sexualities. We all applauded as Jake dazzled us by doing flic-flacs on the pavement, scaling mission-impossible walls, and somersaulting off lampposts.

Very soon he took to unsolicited nighttime visitations by climbing up the wall of the hostel and leaping in my third floor bedroom window. He made no bones about his intentions: he wanted to make a woman of me. My mother had warned me not to go the whole hog with a boy because 'once they get it something chemical happens in their brains and they have to keep getting it'. I certainly did not want to get landed with some albatross of a guy with a sexual addiction to me. That fear had kept my curiosity at bay until now, but now I was beginning to see my virginity as an affliction of childhood for which I needed a fast cure. Jake hardly seemed the type to wait panting for his next favour of the home-comfort variety, but for the sake of decency and out of deference to my mother, I held out for about two weeks.

One evening we were fooling around on my bed. He knew my curiosity was weakening my resolve and went for the final push. During the act, as I lay wondering if I should be feeling something special other than friction, he developed a strange low guttural voice. "Look at me!" he snarled. He had a Charlie Manson psycho-killer-look in his eyes. "You're fucking the devil!" I froze at the 'f' word, then I tried to wriggle free but he had me pinned. I looked up and his eyes burned into mine for a moment of eternity. They had become the flashing eyes of the dragon, gloating in conquest, and I felt a cold surge of fear up my spine. Satisfied he had made his point he leapt out the window and took flight into the night like Dracula.

His next visit through the window a few days later was purely to boast. He was a witch, he explained, who belonged to a coven of twelve others. In his bid for power he was seducing as many virgins as he could. He told me he had a contest going with his buddy, also a witch, as to who would be the first to reach ten. I was his tenth. Perhaps he was appealing to my competitive spirit for he genuinely seemed to think congratulations were in order.

We met infrequently after that — he spooked me too much and I was also deeply offended. I saw him because underneath my fear I was fascinated by the whole idea of sorcery.

So when he offered to read my tarot cards one evening I readily agreed. I had never seen tarot cards before. I drew The Tower, the symbol of having your old structures blown apart with a crisis, he told me. He then gave me his deck to keep. I figured he was trying to make amends so I took them. I kept the cards in a wooden box for the next 17 years, even though I could not bring myself to open the lid and touch them.

"We can watch you wherever you are," Jake told me one evening. "You belong to us now."

"But I'm going to Canada soon."

"Makes no difference. We can even help you win your races."

"NO!!" The strength in my voice surprised me and even he, my conqueror, was taken aback.

"I can win races without your help. Keep out of it!"

He had my virginity but as far as I was concerned it was a one-off deal. My running on the other hand was sacrosanct. I took to locking my window.

CHAPTER 10

Cosmic Consciousness

JULY 1973, CANADA

The 1973 Pan Pacific Conference Games was a five-nation track and field festival between New Zealand and Australia, USA, Canada and Japan, held every two years. This year it was being hosted in Toronto, Canada. I was selected to run the 800 metres. I had just turned 18 and felt very grown up.

The team gathered in Auckland at Mount Smart Stadium the day before we took off. We were issued uniforms, given itineraries and introduced to team management. The legendary Peter Snell addressed us briefly with tips for the touring athlete. I was so awed that I remembered nothing of what he advised, except not to eat too much fruit before the race. When the formalities were done with, I stepped on the track to do my last fast training, a 400 metre time trial. I whizzed around the cinder track in my best time to date, 56.4 seconds flat. I was especially pleased because John said Sue was standing on the sidelines with her coach who had his hand in his pocket on his stopwatch, secretly timing me.

On the flight going over the team spirit was evident. One of the sprinters had an infectious outgoing personality and when he swung his guitar onto his knee and burst into song everyone would join in for a good old sing-along, even those on the plane who were not with our contingent. A few of the guys voted me as the chick with the best 'gams'. I was flattered, even though I wasn't sure what 'gams' were and was afraid to ask in case they were something other than legs.

In those days management included a women's chaperone, whose job we all understood was to protect our virtue in this men's domain of sports. I was a little afraid of Miss Burkhard. She was the first woman I ever saw wearing a man's shirt and dress pants with fly, and who wore her hair in a short back and sides as if she could never be bothered with anything sensitive or frivolous save a smattering of bright red lipstick announcing her loud mouth. She was a muffin with too much baking powder in the mix, mushrooming out of her personal space and into yours. What's more, she smoked, wherever she felt inclined, and I resented having to sit in a car with her while she fagged away my vital oxygen and subjected my runner's lungs to her exhaust.

On our first morning in Toronto at seven a.m. she entered the room I was sharing with another runner without knocking, pulled back the curtains and yelled, "Get out of bed!" just because she had decided it was time to. There was no recovering from jet-lag or allowance for individual preferences. I started looking for ways to duck her authority. The obvious was to slip under her radar. Since I was the youngest she felt I needed extra chaperoning — the audacity of it. Didn't she know I was a university student, not just a bonafide adult, but one of the crème de la crème, New Zealand's future, and that it was my duty to experience all of life's fruits, and her national duty to facilitate that? She didn't see it that way. She was a bulldozer on 'Mission Control' and I knew that in a confrontation I would be flattened. So I hid quietly in the middle of the team and watched her moves so that I could evade attention.

On the day of the Games I ran first the heats and then the final of my race. I was very nervous but felt heartened when I saw a pigtailed, gangly 14-year-old line up. She was wearing USA colours. *Now here's someone I can beat*, I thought.

I could barely feel my body. As I lined up for the final my hands were tingly and the doubts in my head were noise competing with my heartbeat. The race whirred by: a blender of legs and elbows chopping me into little pieces. When it spit me out at the finish I was fifth: the safe place in the middle, out of the limelight and yet considered acceptable enough. The gangly girl won easily. Her name was Mary Decker.

After I had warmed down I joined my teammates in the stands. In good Kiwi style they were downing the beers and yahooing. "Have a brewski!" someone yelled at me and, keen to join in the fun, I downed an oversized champagne glass full of beer. I had not eaten for some hours and was dehydrated from the run so pretty soon I was feeling woozy. The buses were departing for the athletes' hostels and I lined up in the shadows until Miss Burkhard had gone. Then I jumped on board with the noisiest, drunkest New Zealand crew around, which had attracted the noisiest, drunkest Australian crew. I knew for sure this would be the fun bus.

It was an orgy. They were shaking beer cans and spraying everyone on board, chanting *nah-nah, nah-nah, nah-nah, nah-nah, hey, hey, hey, get your gears off*, and coercing some drunken idiot to down-trou. (I could never look. It was all too horrible.) For the grand finale, someone had taken on board a rubbish bin full of food scraps which they were joyfully distributing around the interior. I was covered head to toe in beer and potato peelings. The driver screeched the bus to a halt and refused to drive any further if things did not settle down. It did, until we were safely underway again and the antics resumed.

When we arrived my head was buzzing from the alcohol and all the screaming and laughing. One of the male runners offered to help me up the stairs to my room. Keeping a careful lookout for Miss Burkhard, we made it to the dorm corridor, whereupon he proceeded to smooch with me in the shadows outside my room. He was a handsome, charismatic guy with running superstar status, somewhat older than me. I was in no state to protest, nor did I want to.

I cannot recall the transition, and perhaps this was the hallmark of an extremely smooth operator, but it seemed one moment I was fully clothed in the corridor and next I was minus clothes on the bed in his room. He was going for the whole kit and caboodle, as my mother would say. This was way more than I was up for. I knew I needed to act fast, so I started to cry. It was an instant show-stopper.

"What's wrong?" he asked.

"Please don't," I sobbed, "I'm a virgin." I failed to add 'once-removed' as it would not bolster my case.

My seducer, I discovered, was an honourable human being. As he sought to comfort me I could see the silhouette of his manhood as a sinking shadow puppet on the wall. He moved to turn on the light but I stopped him, preferring to crawl around on the floor to find my clothes, than have him see me naked. I made it to my room in a rather dishevelled state and gave my roommate a look that said, 'What are you looking at, I always walk around with my clothes on inside out and back to front, especially when they are beer-soaked and covered in food'.

The next morning at seven a.m. when Miss Burkhard ripped our curtains apart, the light was a rude assault on my eyes. We were off to Niagara Falls for a team sight-seeing bus tour.

The ride was hell. Rolling along the highway at 70 miles an hour, I could feel a nausea welling up in me. I made my way to the front of the bus.

"I am going to be sick," I tried to whisper discreetly.

"What?"

"I feel sick."

"Speak up!"

"Stop the bus!" A group behind me yelled. "She's going to chuck!"

The bus screeched to a stop. I quietly threw up on the concrete shoulder while everyone looked down on me. When I re-alighted I knew the word had got out that I was a wild one and everyone knew I was hung-over after a wild night of sex and booze.

When our team went separate ways for post-Games meets, I was in the group that did not include Miss Burkhard. I relaxed, slept till noon and raced in the evenings, which I did creditably. Whatsmore, I got to hang out late with the guys. Run hard and play hard; this was the Kiwi male way, and I could see no reason why the Kiwi female should not adopt it also. But I never ever in my life drank beer again.

In Victoria, on our last stop of the tour, Dick Quax pulled me aside.

Dick was already approaching superstar status. He and the other Kiwis, Rod Dixon and John Walker, would soon become known as the Big Three, world-beaters who would herald a new golden era of distance running after Snell, Halberg, and Davies. Dick, John and Rod were all on this team. As a trio they were in some ways a complementary set, like the Three Musketeers: fine-looking and vibrant, with a hint of rascal in each; all quite different in expression but belonging together as superior athletes. Others were jealous. They grumbled when the Big Three returned from the Adidas factory laden with the latest gear: crisp white tracksuits with stripes and hoods, and kangaroo suede shoes. I took note. Too much success had its drawbacks — people resented you for it.

I was envious of the Big Three, too, but not in a hateful way. I looked up to them as the epitome of excellence. They were paving a road for me. One day, I hoped to strut around the stadium sporting all the latest gear from a foreign factory, like they did.

I always thought of John Walker as a lion. He was king in his event, often winning with his barrelled chest beating for the tape and his long blonde mane alight with animal power. In his lion-ness he seemed to be a magnet to victory and would later become one of the most celebrated milers the world has ever known.

If John was earthy, Rod seemed to be ruled by his feelings. Tall and gangly with an affable personality and twinkling eyes he made me think of an afghan hound, eager for attention, willing to perform superbly for it, and possessing an extroverted and fun-loving nature that Kiwis either loved or hated. As a relative youngster he had already won a bronze medal in the 1972 Olympics in Munich.

And then there was Dick, the eldest of the three. I identified with Dick the most. He was the thinker, his features handsomely craggy, his eyes narrowed into constant surveillance. Above them his eyebrows arched like barriers guarding his private assessments. He was definitely an eagle. Also coached by John Davies, Dick had undertaken to keep an eye on me, as eagles do. This was a responsibility which, like most things in his life, he took seriously. He was concerned that I was developing a bad reputation and wanted to tell me in a big brotherly way to cool it. Since that night in Toronto the guys were hitting on me at every opportunity: brushing up against me or inviting me to their room for a party for two. Dick listened as I tried to convince him that I was much more innocent than it appeared. I could not find the words to explain that I was naïve; a Putaruru girl just left home; a country kid who was taught to be nice to everyone. I had not yet been to the sharp-knee-in-the-groin finishing school of etiquette for young ladies on sports teams.

A part of me also felt it wasn't fair. As a female I was being judged by a different yardstick. If I had been a guy my perceived sexual expression would have been gauged as wanting, as a girl it was wanton. I was beginning to see a parallel in the athletic arena. Guys had more licence to be sexual, physical, aggressive, ambitious, self-serving, extroverted, competitive and successful, than girls had.

"My dad always said you can't put an old head on young shoulders," Dick sighed.

"Yeah, well, everyone probably thinks I am having an affair with you too."

Dick looked around. We had been talking closely for some time. "Probably."

"My point, exactly."

From then on we understood each other. Dick had my trust.

Back at university the gaze of the witches was no longer my concern and I slipped back into life with a new ease and confidence. I got myself a nice boyfriend; well, actually two — one on the third floor of the hostel and one on the eighth, which worked out very conveniently. Between my studies, my running and my social activities, life was very full.

I had a thirst for the esoteric and attended a few churches but it seemed to me that they all churned out the same old rhetoric and offered nothing mystical at all. Their answers to my questions were inadequate: steeped in dogma which served only to turn me off. But when I went to an introductory talk on transcendental meditation I was intrigued. The instructor, a fresh young man named Ian Crooks, described being enraptured watching the American sprinter, Jim Hines, win the 1968 Olympic Gold in the 100 metres.

Ian's eyes flashed with awe, "The guy was in cosmic consciousness!"

I nodded in agreement. I had taken little notice of the sprints but I took his word for it. Ian sent me home with a little booklet that had graphs of reductions in heart rate, blood pressure and the like after meditating, and I sent these on to John Davies to get his opinion. (Now that I was in university I had graduated to calling him by his first name.) John wrote back saying, 'If you do this, you won't even need to train!' He was being facetious but I took his comments as an endorsement. I couldn't have cared about the scientific studies, I wanted to run in cosmic consciousness, which I imagined to be a blissful oneness with the universe that delighted those who watched, like Ian. So I paid my money, and with my white handkerchief and flowers as offerings, I was given instruction in TM with my personal mantra.

Faithfully I sat repeating *aing, aing, aing* in my head, 20 minutes twice daily. I expected something profound to happen but after three months I was still sitting for 20 minutes repeating *aing, aing, aing* and it felt much the same as when I started. Besides, I could see no remarkable gains in my running. I had hoped for something more, perhaps a hallucination with messages from angels followed by a world record run or two. I might have been disappointed but for the realisation that the divine direct-line, which I was seeking through TM, I had already subscribed to through my running. It was at that point that my runs took on a new dimension besides conditioning for races: they became my meditation. From then on, a solitary 12-mile run enveloped in the mists of Mt Cargill never failed to take my mind down tributaries of deep and original thoughts that enticed my brain and re-vitalised my body, until one day I reached the conclusion that somewhere, some time, on a run like this, I might find cosmic consciousness.

A girlfriend of mine at university categorised everyone by nature as either cats or dogs. Cats have attitude, sensuality, style, and possess diamond shaped faces and almond eyes. Dogs are loyal, honest, unassuming, uncultured, with long faces and round eyes. She looked at a person and knew immediately if they were a cat or a dog. It seemed to explain the world for her and enabled her to make sense of human behaviour.

I asked her once as we lounged in the hard wooden chairs of our bleak concrete block common room if God were a dog or a cat, but she could not find a definitive answer. "Dog is God spelled backwards so perhaps God is a dog, but then again, cats think they are God," she pondered. She cast her green eyes heavenward and a bridal veil of wild brown hair spread over her shoulders.

"I don't see cats and dogs in people," I told her. "I see lines and circles." I had been pondering this theory on my runs for weeks now. "Lines are narrow, contracted, and two dimensional. Lines are our unfinished business from other lives, our potentials yet to be lived."

I was into past lives back then. I thought it an outrageous concept so I loved to throw it on the table whenever possible.

"Circles, on the other hand, are lines that have had both ends stretched and stretched until finally they join," I continued, making a taut circle of my arms.

"Being complete, they are the sources of our strength. People with a majority of lines are Line People and those with a majority of circles are Circle People. Line People, being more in contraction than expansion, like security and structure and are comfortable with their limitations and conventional living. Circle people are seekers. They yearn for adventure, freedom, truth and autonomy."

I had first heard the word *autonomy* in class a few weeks before when we had studied Maslow's *Hierarchy of Needs*, and had been saving it for an occasion like this.

"You and I are Circles," I declared confidently. It was obvious to me that most students were Circle People.

She nodded. She had a radical streak and was definitively Circle. "And what is God," she asked, "a Line or a Circle?"

Touché. We were now in the full swing of our intellectual sparring, the milk filming over in our forgotten mugs of instant coffee.

"Neither," I found myself explaining for the first time, "God is a Sphere."

I found it strange hearing my own words because I was not sure then if I believed in God as a sentient being, although I was prepared to accept the concept of an Eternal Everything.

"In the beginning," I continued, "we are all made of lines which are actually pieces broken from the axes of the Sphere of the Eternal Everything. Call it God if you like. So we all start out as Line People and as we go through lives we gradually hook up our lines and become Circle People." I was on a roll now.

"And then what?"

"We enlarge the circles by living in them."

"And then what?"

"We flesh them out."

"Like, more ... dimensional?"

"Yeah, yeah. Exactly! We expand energetically!!"

Unfazed by my enthusiasm she forged on relentlessly. "And then what?"

"I don't know... perhaps they all merge together to form a sphere."

"You mean like God?" She gasped at the sacrilegious implications.

"Maybe," I shrugged.

"Hmmm. Interesting ... but there's just one thing."

"What is that?"

"How can something that is infinite have a shape?"

She had me there. I was only 20 and thought I was smart but I really didn't know too much at all.

And all this stuff about lines and circles? I had made it up to top the cats and dogs theory. But once uttered, it stuck, and for the first time I considered that encircling my lines could be a way through to cosmic consciousness. How actually to do that, I had not the slightest idea.

CHAPTER 11

Tit for Tat

JANUARY 1974, CHRISTCHURCH, NEW ZEALAND

The trials for the Commonwealth Games were in Christchurch at the end 1973. University had finished and I made my way up to the South Island city where one of my boyfriends lived, a fine-looking guy with the physique of a Greek god. I was captive to his handsomeness. It made me feel pretty. What's more, he was captain of one of the football teams and training to be a doctor. He genuinely wanted to save people from suffering and his idealism on top of his good looks and fine prospects made him the perfect catch. My mother had always fancied that one of us might be a doctor or, failing that, marry one.

The day of my race, he came to watch me for the first time and I was anxious to impress him in turn with my running brilliance. Too intent on appearing in control *and* nonchalant I forgot to focus on the task at hand, the 1500 metres, and failed to make one of the required top three places.

The coach of our Olympic running champions, Arthur Lydiard, showed up on the warm-up track as I was getting ready for the 800 metres, my last chance to make the team. While I was not coached directly by Arthur, he was The Godfather to runners and anyone coached by his system, no matter how many generations removed, he saw as family. A short stocky guy, he talked fast and directly, standing square on and fixing his eyes on yours. There was no getting around

83

him, nor would you want to, for his one on one attention was a great compliment and when the master spoke you were compelled to listen.

"What are you doing, mucking about on the track? You're not paying attention. I saw you waving to your boyfriend in the stands! You should have won that race! Now get out there and do what you've trained for and make that team!!"

"Yes, sir," I mumbled weakly, and I went out and qualified for the 800 metres for the Commonwealth Games, because I had been commanded by Arthur to do so. My boyfriend was duly impressed.

The Games were held in Christchurch in January, perhaps the biggest sporting event New Zealand had hosted to date. Held every four years, the Commonwealth Games are like a mini-Olympics to the participants. I was entranced with the whole affair: team meetings, being issued with uniforms, staying in the athletes' village, mixing with the other athletes, and of course racing against runners from all over the British Commonwealth.

The athletes' village was surrounded by a high wire security fence and we were issued with identity passes to enter. The women were housed in a compound within the compound, so all females had to go through a second checkpoint to our quarters from which the men were barricaded. I couldn't figure out exactly what they were protecting us from with this strange arrangement. Obviously the people in power, all men themselves, considered that the fairer sex needed protecting from the fearsome libido of the athletic male. But I, for one, did not want protecting. So I spent a good deal of time outside our compound in the men's domain, not only because it did not smack of a convent, but also because I was entranced with a particular high jumper.

I took to meeting Claude down at the high jump pit on the practice track at dusk. He was tall and long-limbed and moved with a luxurious swagger, as if his skin were a silk robe. He jumped that way too.

"Stand, Lorraine, right here, *ici*." He pointed to the ground in front of the landing pads where the bar would have been. There was no bar.

I was the bar. He loped towards me then flew like a bird clean over my head. I didn't duck. I wanted to show him I was a good sport.

"Lorraine, Lorraine," he chuckled and patted the pit, inviting me to join him in the soft landing pads. I loved to hear my name with the rolled *r*'s of his native tongue as he pulled me towards him.

"*Voulez vous faire l'amour avec moi ce soir?*"

I had a pretty good idea what he was asking, but I played coquettishly dumb.

"*Je ne comprend pas*," I replied — the one French phrase I'd mastered in school that had never failed me in class, and now helped to defend my virtue. My teacher would have been proud of me.

"Just say, '*Je vous désire,*'" he tutored and I repeated the phrase after him and laughed, playfully slapping his roaming hands as we wrestled around on the big foam blocks. It was youthful horse-play; all hot breaths and giggles. We never asked about his girlfriends or my boy-friends — indeed we knew little about each other. We did know that in two weeks' time we would be back in our regular lives, so today we would revel in romance. Soon we would simply be trinkets tucked away in each other's memory box.

In the evening, back in the women's dormitory, I confided the secrets of my evening tryst to my roommate. She delighted in every detail. I lamented to her that the next evening I could not meet Claude as usual, since I was meeting my boyfriend.

Next evening as I waited at the village gates to be picked up, I spied Claude in the distance sashaying like a Siamese tomcat towards the practice track. On his arm was my roommate.

When I arrived back at our quarters that night she was not there. The lights were off, our two mature married roommates asleep in their single beds. I carried out my revenge in stealth. I short-sheeted her bed and I arranged the wastepaper bins in front of the door. Then the table that served as our dresser I saw it glinting in the moonlight: the foil wrapper with the four rows of seven. She had confided that she had gone on the pill to regulate her period for competition. *Sure,* I thought, pushing it under a pile of magazines. Then I brushed my teeth, climbed into my bunk-bed and lay waiting.

Crash! Bang! Clatter! In the wee hours of the morning the opening door skittled the metal bins across the wooden floor. "What the hell!" one of the older women yelled before she snored off again. I lay silently on high alert, pretending to be asleep. My roommate put on her pyjamas and now was fumbling at the dresser in the dark. "Shit," she finally muttered. I sniggered to myself. She climbed into bed. "Shit," she muttered again. "For crying out loud, shut up and go to sleep!" the older woman yelled. I was feeling slightly satisfied. In the dark I saw her shadow heading towards me and she climbed up onto the bunk above mine. That night I became a violent sleeper, tossing and turning so that the bunk lurched like a dinghy on the Strait of Magellan. I kept at it until daylight.

"Oh man, I hardly slept at all." She was bleary-eyed as I leapt out of bed bright and refreshed and keen for the day's training.

"Boy, someone made a lot noise last night."

The older women were glaring at us.

I shrugged and looked in the direction of the offender. "I was asleep by ten."

"I'm sorry for waking everyone," she offered meekly.

"Yeah, what ungodly hour was that anyway?" I chimed in, perhaps a little too emphatic with the word "ungodly".

"That bunk needs screwing into the wall," she muttered to no-one in particular.

We shared no more secrets but I did hear her say that she got her period the day before her event.

Through heats and semi-finals I qualified easily for the final along with my teammates, Shirley Sommerville and Sue Haden. When I lined up on the start line a few days later against names I had read in *Track & Field News* I was aflutter with awe and sick with anticipation, my knees were weak and my hands tingled with pins and needles. When I looked up to see row upon row of tiered faces staring back at me, I suddenly wished I was invisible, away from their judging glare. *What if I can't keep up?* I didn't want to finish last and embarrass my family who were up there somewhere. As I toed the start line I remembered the three C's my Dad had drummed into me: keep Cool, Calm and Collected. It was good advice that was totally useless.

Bang! The blast of the gun was always welcome. Suddenly the dam of adrenaline was released from the viscera into moving muscles. I found myself in a flurry of limbs jostling for position on the bend. I remembered my coach John Davies' advice. *Stay on your feet, give yourself enough room to stay out of trouble, keep up with the leaders as best you can.*

'Keeping up.' I didn't realise back then what a limiting expectation this phrase set. It implied that whomever you were keeping up with was superior. If Arthur had been my coach he might well have told me to forget about the others and to go out and win in no uncertain terms. John did not understand how much my confidence wavered, and that I was constantly gauging my ability from his words. He neither overpowered you with his high expectations, Arthur-style, nor showered you with visions of fulfilled potential as Ali had done. Rather he approached opportunity rationally and conservatively.

Now here I was, 'keeping up' as best I could, cautiously tagging the leaders through the 400 metres and the 600 metres, and then as the others claimed the medals I sprinted home with what I had left. I was stunned. It had all flashed by so quickly and I had missed it. I wanted to shout, 'But wait, I wasn't quite ready. Couldn't we start over?!' But the cheers for the winners saturated the stadium and there was no-one remotely interested in hearing my excuses.

The race was won by Australian Charlene Rendina, a chunky, seasoned power-pack with a withering finishing burst, essential for an 800 metre specialist. Sue Haden was second. I had finished fifth. Fifth. Fifth again. Just plain old fifth. Disappointing fifth. Nothing fifth. I was missing that something extra and I had no idea where it was. As I walked along the track, recovering my breath and pondering my place, I spied Mrs Drummond, who was officiating at the high jump, excitedly waving to me. "Look." She motioned at the giant scoreboard and there was my name down the list of results: 5. Lorraine Moller

NZL, 2:03.6. Although disappointed I was pleased to have run a personal best. My fifth place, now qualified with a personal best time, had become 'commendable fifth'. When Anne Garrett failed to qualify for the final in the 1500 metres, my fifth became 'better than Anne fifth', the sweetest lemonade I could squeeze out of that placing.

One night, back at university, I was engaged in good-natured banter with my boyfriend when he called me 'Big Nose'.

"Don't call me that," I cautioned.

"Big Nose! Big Nose! Big Nose!" he taunted.

"I'm warning you, don't say that again or I'll get you."

He rose to the challenge. "Big Nose!!' he teased again, intoxicated with the power of the upper hand and smugly secure in his handsomeness.

"Little Dick!" I called back. I really did not have enough experience with male members to distinguish a small one from a big one, nor did I know enough about the male ego to understand the depth of the blow I was delivering. But the next time I saw him he had a new girlfriend.

CHAPTER 12

Running Out

MARCH 1975, MOROCCO

New Zealand had a very strong tradition in cross-country at the international level and so was sending full teams of ten men and five women, including me, on a five-week tour of Europe, culminating in the 1975 World Cross-country Championships in Morocco. Although I am not statistically inclined, I did recognise that this was a very favourable ratio.

The team first met at the home of the team manager, a pleasant guy who became affectionately known as Maxwell after Agent 86 of the 'Get Smart' series. He hosted a cocktail party so that we could all get acquainted. Maxwell's wife, we noticed, had weepy sores all over the left side of her face. She explained that Maxwell had received his smallpox vaccination for the trip and had rolled his 'poxy' arm across her while asleep one night. She had contracted smallpox in her face. This was not a good omen.

Maxwell was a volunteer who had served dutifully in the athletics federation for years and now, as was the custom, his good service and dedication to the sport was rewarded with an overseas trip, as manager. The trouble was that Maxwell had never been out of the South Island of New Zealand before, and travelling through Morocco would prove challenging. Whatsmore, the team of athletes he was chosen to lead were all savvy travellers in their own right and not exactly thrilled to let Maxwell call the shots.

When we gathered at the airport, Maxwell gave us instruction. He had read that in airports bags are often stolen right from your side, so he advised us to put our feet through the handles. When it came time to board, he was on the concourse anxiously ready to usher the team onto the plane, but he couldn't find us. We were hiding around the corner and, on cue, we rounded the bend lugging our hand luggage with our feet with exaggerated slowness. "No, no!!" Max shouted. "That was not what I meant!"

Within two weeks he had used up the allotted funds for the trip and was wiring back to the Federation for more. Not only did he have no experience with haggling but he had trouble converting sums in his head and was repeatedly taken advantage of by taxi drivers who added zeros to their fees and grabbed for the biggest notes he flashed in front of them as he struggled with the currency. We hit him up for everything we could, including sangria, which we drank by the pitcherful in the evenings as we partied amongst ourselves after hard days of training and travel through the south of Spain. One of the guys drank so much one night that, when he threw up, the regurgitated contents included the little umbrellas that decorated the drink.

By the time we got to Gibraltar, Maxwell had run out of money again and the Federation was not responding. When we most needed the luxury of our Western comforts, we were forced by budget to travel the cheapest way possible. We made a stomach-churning trip to Casablanca on a dubious ferry, where we took a train into the interior of North Africa. The long ride on the wooden benches played hell with an athlete's sinewy buttocks. The toilet was a hole in a cabinet that dumped onto the train tracks. There was no food service and we were ravenous, but we had no money to pay for food anyhow. We managed to score a bag of oranges off boisterous ragamuffin boys who raced onto the tracks from nowhere whenever the train stopped, then pulled down their pants and waved their bottoms at us as we pulled away. Finally, after what seemed like an interminable number of hours, we arrived in Rabat.

Rabat was teeming with activity — chaotic, passionate, and seedy. I was enthralled and a little nervous so, along with my teammates, I observed without question the three team rules: do not drink the tap water; do not go out without a male; and run in long pants. Many of the Arabic women, especially the older ones, were veiled, and a bare-legged woman running in the streets was a glaring anomaly. So we women wore long pants and ran with the men and we all drank nothing but Coca Cola, even brushing our teeth with it. During the day we moved as a group, negotiating the medina with its stalls, and bolstering each other in haggling for exotic wares. Before long we were garbed in kaftans and funny hats, wearing curlicue shoes and carrying leather bags that had been cured in goat's urine.

At the hotel, we were fed well the first night. But by the next day when we sat down to eat, hotel management had got wind that we needed to be on the budget programme. Each plate delivered to the table consisted of two tiny ribs, two tiny kidneys and a tiny liver, rat-sized I thought as I politely pushed them to the side of my plate and laid my silverware in the finished position.

Just two nights before the race Maxwell attended the managers' meeting as required by the International Amateur Athletic Federation. We were hungry and we blamed him for the budgetary constraints. We knew these boring meetings dragged on for hours, which provided a great opportunity for a team party — in his room. We ate and drank well and charged it all to room service. I felt a little guilty ordering from a menu that charged the equivalent of $12 for an orange juice and $5 for a few peanuts, but was bolstered by the guys chanting one of their team mottos, "If you don't eat, you don't shit and if you don't shit, you die!"

The World Cross-country Championships were held on a horse track. The surface was flat with a sandy base, and a few mounds of dirt had been bulldozed to form the hills required to define it as cross-country.

As we surveyed the course the day before the race I saw the long finishing straight and made up my mind how I was going to run. Sitting on the bus to go back to the hotel, I confided my plan to Euan Robertson, one of my teammates.

"You know how after you finish a race you always find that you have something to spare that you didn't know you had?"

"Yes …" he said, not sure what I was getting at.

"Well, I'm going to pretend that the race is going to finish 400 metres before it does. Then I will use that 'extra' so that at the end I am all used up and not wishing I had pushed harder."

"Sounds like a plan," he confirmed.

The next day we arrived at the race course in good time to warm-up. The preliminary events had already started — a series of horse races across the middle of the race course. Time after time the starting marshal on his steed brandished his rifle recklessly while he jabbered instructions to a thronging mass of testosterone on horseback. Bang! Off they galloped to the cheers of the crowd, the riders whooping and yahooing, arms flinging, legs kicking in a plume of dust that redistributed our race course. We runners might have been ants on a cricket pitch hoping not to get squished while we went about warming up, stretching and preparing for our big race.

I made my way to the bathroom. It was dark — just as well — and consisted of a concrete squat hole in the middle of the floor. Done, I pulled the chain whereupon a tide of water swept across the floor, washing my feet and soaking my racing shoes. I squished out to the start. Horse races over, most of the crowd had dispersed.

I started out quickly, as one must do in World Championships. It is a fine call: running fast enough for a good position without putting oneself into an oxygen deficit that is irrecoverable. As the race progressed I worked my way up to the front and by the time I turned onto the final four kilometre stretch I was in third place. The only trouble was that I was well and truly spent. I now knew why they called it a home stretch for it just kept stretching and stretching — and stretching. Soon my legs had a thick jelly-wobble feeling, as if there were molten lead seeping out of my shoes, and my vision was telescoping down to the ground just in front of my feet. What had possessed me to think that I always had something left when I finished races? Now that I came to rethink it, I could not recall ever having anything much left over at the end of a race and right then I came to appreciate that in previous races my energy had most often been impeccably distributed. This felt very familiar, but usually the finish line was sufficiently close enough when the gas ran out for momentum to complete the job. Today, this would not be the case. I had made a tactical blunder.

One person passed me, then another. I made a sprinting motion but my legs were sinking into the sand. The finish line was approaching in slow motion and fading into the ether at the same time. I staggered on then flopped across the line like a dying fish on a deck. Once again I was fifth.

Medical personnel ran to my aid, pushing my head onto my knees while I heaved for air and blood slowly pumped back into my brain. Someone pushed a foul-smelling liquid under my nose. "Drink, drink." In my stupour, one thing came to mind: not to drink anything except Coca Cola.

"Poison, poison," I stammered and pushed it away, just as our women's manager, Pam Kenny, came to help me to my feet. She had seen me run like this when, as a 14-year-old, I had raced against her in Putaruru. She was full of praise for my efforts, reporting to the press at home that: "I thought she was just fantastic. She ran herself to a standstill."

When I fully regained consciousness I worried that I had offended someone, but when I later walked past the medical tent, they pointed at me, chanting, "Poison, poison!" and laughed heartily.

I couldn't believe I was fifth again. That position kept recurring like a case of malaria. I could see the headline: *Lorraine Moller of New Zealand is suffering from a recurring case of fifthitis. There is no cause for concern; it is not contagious.* But I was comforted by the fact that I was the first New Zealand woman; and, along with my fifth placing, Heather Thomson's sixth, Anne Garrett's tenth, and Allison Deed's 29th, we scored second in the teams' competition to the USA. Best of all, I had finished ahead of Anne.

The race was won by Julie Brown, a talented young American woman whom I would meet head to head in the Osaka International Ladies Marathon 11 years later. Our men's team won the teams' competition, with John Walker taking fourth place. Euan Robertson finished fifth also, not having embraced the pretend-the-race-is-finishing-with-400-metres-to-go plan to the extent I did.

That evening, we arrived at the awards ceremony 30 minutes after its scheduled commencement. The food on the banquet table had all been eaten, every last morsel, save the picked-over carcass of a large snake.

Undaunted by our hunger, we waited for the prizes to be presented. A large table was adorned with gift-wrapped parcels. We couldn't wait to see what we got. When they finally got underway, the officials gave thank-you speeches and presented each other with the gifts. The pile dwindled and disappeared until there was nothing. We left empty-handed.

Hungry and crestfallen we headed to the Americans' quarters for a party of our own. Ushered into a hotel room, I found myself sitting on a bed next to an aloof, skinny, dark-haired guy with a moustache. Heather, of the beauty spot, was sitting on my other side, nudging me. "Frank Shorter. Gold medal," she mouthed waggling her forefinger in his direction. Suddenly I became self-conscious and sat in quiet awe, not daring to speak or even look in his direction. Julie Brown, our American hosts told us, was not the partying type and was already in bed. *So that was what it took*, I thought, *no fun at all*. I decided that I would emulate Frank instead; after all he was here having a good time and he had a gold medal.

The next day we left for home, giddy with excitement at the prospect of returning as champions and runners-up. This time we did not complain as we waited for Maxwell to dispute his room charges. When we reached Charles de Gaulle Airport we had a stopover of few hours for lunch.

With no money, Maxwell left us to fend for ourselves, pleased that he had led the winning team but keen to distance himself from our famished grumblings. We sat down in the cafeteria, turned out our pockets and ordered water and bread rolls to break in half and share. This perplexed our waiter no end and he kept asking until he understood that, although penniless, these were World Champions dining in his cafe. Suddenly our table was filled with a feast of French cuisine upon which we gratefully gorged.

CHAPTER 13

Phoney Baloney

1977 — 1978, KATIKATI, NEW ZEALAND

Trevor had a bush of untamed hair that made me think of the Wild Man from Borneo. I was in the headmaster's office at my old high school in Putaruru as a student teacher. After my graduation from Otago University I had attended Auckland Teachers' Training College and I was finishing my one-year stint with this assignment. Now that I was all grown up and to be a teacher myself, I felt quite unlike the gawky teenager I had been when I was last there, and I expected an upgraded status.

"Lorraine, I would like you to meet Trevor." The headmaster gestured towards the tanned, stocky man, a teacher at the school and just a few years older than me. The face inside the wild hair turned to look at me, locked in a gravity that caused premature frown lines between the eyes.

"Hello," he grunted and turned back to the headmaster. I had interrupted something.

Now there's a guy with a dark cloud over his head, I thought to myself as I slunk off. It was not a figure of speech. When I looked at him I had literally seen a cloud lingering around his temples, like a halo gone inclement. I knew that look well: as a child I often saw it around my Dad when he was out of sorts. Back then it was purely a keep-out-of-trouble instinct, so I knew when to approach my Dad and when to keep away.

Trevor became my boyfriend. Against my better judgment I responded to his overtures, mostly because he was an escape from my parents' domain into a social crowd my own age. He had a car, a little blue Mini Minor he affectionately referred to as 'Bluey'. He was prepared to take me places, and later on loaned me Bluey on occasion.

I had been named in the New Zealand team for the 1977 World Cross-country Championships in Germany the following March so I was filling in time until I left. I had no intention of embarking on a long-term relationship with Trevor and absolutely none of becoming a teacher. As usual, such a certainty about what I didn't want got me exactly that.

My plans went awry. Still in Putaruru, just before Christmas, I came down with toxoplasmosis after rescuing an injured bird in our backyard. My red blood count plummeted once again and I resorted to a series of iron injections. I could no longer run.

When I resumed racing a few months later I found myself coming up short. My health was not fully restored but all team members were required to pass a fitness trial prior to leaving, so I pushed myself. In race after race I was having trouble breathing and the time of 9:40 for the 3,000 metres was eluding me.

Tests revealed that I had exercise-induced asthma. When I ran hard it sounded like I had a whistle stuck in my throat and the doctor recommended that I have a scope down my airway in case I had accidentally inhaled a peanut or some such thing into my lung. Being a sentient consumer, I could have told him there were no unaccounted-for peanuts in my air system. But he did not ask and I thought he might find something else, like one of the stones I had stuck up my nose when I was four. I was desperate to run my time trial on the weekend and I needed a turnaround for this last attempt before the deadline. This man of title exuded such confidence that I expected something along the lines of a miracle.

Two days before my race the doctor 'scoped my lungs under general anaesthetic, in his office. When I came around, he told me that he'd found no foreign objects in my lungs, gave me an inhaler to suck on, and as he showed me to the door wished me well in my race. I walked to the bus station some ten minutes away for the hour-long ride back home.

On the day of my race I could not turn my head to either side. My throat was sore and the anaesthetic had left my legs leaden. I had no choice but to wave the team for Germany goodbye. I went home and defiantly tossed the inhalers in the bin.

John Davies had left his wife. For the past five years John had sent me regular letters with my training schedule attached, which I had religiously followed, but now I had not heard from him in months. Without the unshakeable reliability of his counsel I felt lost. I decided to follow the doctor's recommendation and have a painful bone spur removed from my heel. Once again I was under anaesthetic, and under the knife.

All went well, apparently, until I was coming out of anaesthesia. Semi-conscious I began crying out in delirium. A stern matron dressed me down. What was it about schoolmistresses and team managers and matrons? They seemed like one person, an archetype in different guises on call to wrestle my spirit into submission. Her scolding was barely discernable to me, just muffled background noise from some faraway world.

I woke up. She was standing at the side of my bed.

"I think I was asleep. Did you just say something to me or was I dreaming?"

"Of course I said something! You should have heard yourself carrying on! I can't believe such nonsense! You should know better, yelling out like that, trying to get attention. I won't have such behaviour in my ward. Got that?!"

I nodded. This time I got it.

My foot had been made into a nice little package, sealed and stamped as if ready for posting, and contained within a nifty little wire tent under my blankets. As the anaesthesia wore off pain took its grip as if steel wires were being winched across the top of my foot. The bandages were too tight. The matron checked them with a cursory glance and declared me fine. *What could she see without opening the parcel?* I wondered. The pain intensified. Another nurse came on duty. She gave me morphine and then more morphine. I begged her to take off the bandage but she said she was not permitted.

When Matron came back to the ward she scolded me for being a prima donna and told me to stop seeking attention. I took to counting minutes on the clock, watching each second click by and knowing that after a few hours I could plead for another shot of drugs which gave respite from the feeling that a rat was gnawing my foot off.

After 40 hours I could bear it no longer. With my heart beating savagely, I furtively loosened the bandages under the cover of my little tent until I felt some liberation from those rodent choppers. To my great relief, when Matron came in she did not notice that I had interfered with hospital property.

Two weeks after surgery, the surgeon unveiled my leg in his office. The surgical wound had healed but the top of my foot had a pressure sore the size of a fifty-cent piece, red-raw and oozing pus.

My outraged mother drove me to the hospital on our way home, requested the matron and made her look at my foot. Matron grunted a belligerent acknowledgement, but offered no apology. "It's the surgeon's responsibility," was her defence and without another word she turned about-face and clickity-clacked in her white heels off behind the swing doors.

I was called to come quickly. Mr Drummond was in the hospital dying of cancer.

Dad drove me over and we waited outside his room in a ward that no-one comes out of. Mr Drummond had just had a radiation treatment and was very nauseous. I could hear him throwing up with great gurgling mucus sounds. When the nurse ushered us in I was shocked. His once big aura was shrunken, and his robust body, ravaged by chemicals and radiation, was now grey and pathetic. I had seen that look before from my days in hospital; Death had him in his clutches.

Mr Drummond grabbed my hand in a desperate clamp and pulled me towards him. A sharp acidic smell hung around him and I found myself pulling back.

"I have been waiting to see you." He paused as another wave of nausea engulfed him and he fought to ward off more retching. "Promise me one thing."

"Yes, of course."

"Promise me that you will go to the Olympics."

I wanted to explain that it wasn't that easy, that I could not guarantee it, that I might not be fast enough — but there was little room here for explanations, contingencies or excuses. "Yes, I promise I'll try."

He squeezed my hand tighter. "No, promise me you *will* go."

I was cornered. More was at stake than a rash promise to an old guy having a sentimental moment. This was monumental, a deathbed pact not only between Mr Drummond and me but also with God. I knew I had to promise or be damned, and yet I had no way of knowing if I could deliver on that promise. In the past year I had lost the string to my Olympic balloon and now it seemed to be drifting away into the ether. But there was no time for prevarication; I would figure the details out later.

"Yes, I promise."

He pulled me to his chest and kissed me: a slovenly chemical kiss that made me flinch. He clung to me, to my youth, to my life, and then he finally let me go. Tears trickled down his cheeks. Within 48 hours he was dead.

I felt like a phoney. I could not even call myself a runner, and yet I had just promised I would be an Olympian. I wanted to hide away somewhere. My foot had left me with no racing prospects for a year and no imminent escape overseas for a grand adventure. I had no choice but to get a job. Not just any job: the requirement of my teaching bond was two years of country service.

Katikati was as good a hideaway as anywhere. On the east coast just over the Kaimai Range and only an hour from where I had grown up, it was not unlike my home town, just smaller and a little wealthier. The school was considered choice, and the headmaster said my running status would be good for the 'mana' of the school. So the job was mine.

I lived with two other teachers across the road from the school. I aspired to be an eagle flying the heavens, but here I felt more like a finch in a cage: hemmed in and cramped for freedom. Without the release of running I quickly fell into food-binge hell.

It began when I discovered a roommate's block of chocolate in the fridge with only the first two rows eaten. I marvelled at how she could be so disciplined as to leave it sitting there, and closed the door. Next thing I found myself back at the fridge peeling down the wrapper and polishing off the next row. *She will never notice*, I told myself and went back to marking my papers. After a few more trips to the refrigerator and several more rows, I realised that the second deadly sin of roommates — food theft (the first being the theft of a love interest) — would surely be noticed so I polished it off, limped down to the store and bought a new one, polished off the first two rows and replaced the original chocolate block with its replica.

This became a daily ritual. I put on weight, I got pimples, and I hated working. I loathed it so much that in the mornings I cried as I dragged my sorry feet off to school, as I had done the first few times when I was five years old.

Soon I graduated to full-blown food orgies, where I went to the store, bought all the sin food I desired and sat on the privacy of my own bed to eat myself to death. My feeble attempts at suicide by engorgement never worked. Glutted to the gills like a fois gras goose I inevitably fell asleep, only to wake up fatter, pimplier and even more miserable.

The great thing about life is that you get out of most things alive — unless you really screw up. If not for Trevor I might not have lived through it.

CHAPTER 14

Erroneous Zones

She was just a passing fiancée.
— Alfred McFote

1977 — 1978

Trevor was my lifeline. For almost two years we spent every weekend and all of the school holidays together. He was an adventurous type and under his guidance I learned to ski in the winter, to snorkel in the summer and to camp in the wilderness. During the August holidays of my second teaching year we became engaged. I was not in love but I felt beholden to him, not just for his company, but because in the previous year I had crashed his precious Bluey not once, but twice.

The first time, in a momentary lapse of concentration, I had gone off-road, through a barbed-wire fence and landed in a paddock. That was forgivable. With a little cosmetic reconstruction Bluey was as good as new. But when I rear-ended a truck that almost rear-ended the Katikati school bus my transgression was unforgivable. Bluey, the mini, had just been ridiculously minimised. When Trevor arrived that afternoon at my house he had tears in his eyes. I thought he might take me in his arms to comfort me, to caress my bruises better, and to soothe my shocked nerves that had also been jeered at by 30 school children hanging out the bus windows. But he didn't. He walked past me with his arms outstretched, "Oh Bluey, Bluey," he cried.

Marriage would prove that my protestations of remorse over Bluey were genuine. Everyone would see what a good person I truly was. But when I told my family I was engaged their crestfallen faces said otherwise. My father grunted. Gordy said Trevor reminded him of the mock turtle in *Alice in Wonderland*, who was always crying at the prospect of being made into turtle soup. My mother took me into the bedroom and asked me if I was in the family way.

The first day back at school I carried the sapphire and diamond ring on my elegantly cocked finger with a Mona Lisa smile on my face, demure and understated as one recently spoken for should be. The word quickly spread throughout the school. "Miss Moller is engaged!"

The first class of the day was cricket. The kids quickly scattered to their posts and I stood at the pitch, giving batting and bowling instruction. In the outfield, I spied 12-year-old Kelvin, out of my circle of influence, facing away from the game and making menacing gestures towards the next kid. I marched over and stood hands on hips, in my looming, authoritative schoolteacher pose. As I started in with my "What do you think you are doing young man?" routine — *smack!!* — the batter hit a sixer. The ball flew across the field hitting my finger at full-force and crushing my precious ring into a distorted joke.

The message from above had been delivered.

I was tossed into a dilemma.

True, I was having doubts, but undoing my pending matrimony was more trouble than I could face. Everyone around me was busy pairing up for better or worse starting the natural sequence of events for Line People in rural New Zealand: marry a bloke with a steady job, settle down in a country town with a weatherboard ranch you can call your own, and rear three or four snotty-nosed kids. There were people like that all around me in Katikati: men whose highlight was Friday booze night in the Private Bar of the local pub, and women who were on the public hospital's waiting list for their 'hyster' as if it were a rite of passage to some sort of freedom. Trevor was a reliable guy for that kind of life. When I thought about it I wanted to flee but I had nowhere to run. So I did nothing.

College friends of mine were getting married in New Plymouth about five hours' drive away. I borrowed Gary's little blue Vauxhall Viva and set off with Trevor and my teen brothers, Bruce and Gordy, in tow for a wedding-cum-skiing weekend adventure. Somehow we missed the wedding. Trevor wanted to ski on Mount Taranaki and since he was the alpha male in the group we were captive to his vote. We made it off the slopes in time for the reception, where I proceeded to gorge myself on festive goodies. That night I fell ill with abdominal pains which grew progressively worse. By morning I was in agony.

Our plan had been to take the few hours' drive to Mount Ruapehu for more skiing and, despite my condition, Trevor was not up for changing his plans. I piled in the back seat, unable to sit up, groaning all the way to the parking lot of this remote snowy mountain. Trevor and my brothers piled out to ski, leaving me writhing in the backseat. Gordy soon arrived back. He had searched out a paramedic who told him that I may have appendicitis and urged him to get me down to a hospital as fast as possible. Gordy now had to find Trevor who was happily whizzing down the slopes with Bruce. An hour later they showed up. Trevor, a little surly at cutting his recreation short, sped home, seemingly indifferent to the fact that every bump and twist in the road amplified my pain.

As soon as we arrived back Ravi, our local doctor and family friend, came over, examined me, and sent me off to hospital for what should have been a simple appendectomy.

Perhaps it was the sanitary smell that hit me when I first walked into the hospital, or the polished floors of the corridors where efficient heels clipped along carrying stainless steel trays and cotton swabs, or the sight of the swing doors that concealed medical procedures, but as soon as I entered a feeling of doom descended upon me.

Flee now, my instinct implored.

Don't be so dramatic, this is only an appendix, my rational mind countered. My voice of reason wore a business suit and kept records and promoted the institutions of society. She was a stern parent who kept my wild, impulsive child of instinct in tow. So, along with my street clothes, I stuffed my free spirit into a bag, donned a hospital gown and crawled into bed and waited. After a few hours the pain in my tummy subsided. I thought I was getting better and could probably leave soon.

The surgeon strode into the ward. Strikingly tall, with a head of thick dark hair and a carefully trimmed moustache, he moved stiffly with his wide shoulders back and his chin arrogantly tilted. Definitely a sergeant major type. Brusquely he checked me over, palpating my abdomen while his white-coated entourage looked on. Ah, the white coat. I knew what that meant: the licence to peer at anyone's privates. I knew the routine: the vehicle was signed over at check-in, so don't ask any questions, just lie back and detach. Sergeant Major said he would check on me again in the morning.

Next morning he marched up with another train of white-coated peerers. Without addressing me, he proceeded to poke my tummy. "Does this hurt?" "Does this?" Actually I felt pretty good. He hummed and haa-ed as he jotted notes on his clipboard; then, it seemed to me, in a spontaneous decision, he made a great flourish with his hand and ordered, "Take it out!" *Well*, I thought indignantly, *he didn't ask me!*

When the nurse came over to prep me for surgery I was fishing for information but didn't know quite what to ask; but I felt sure that I, and not just my appendix, should be involved in this.

"How big a scar will I have?" This seemed a legitimate question for a young lady to be asking.

"I don't know," the nurse replied flippantly, "some doctors make big scars, some make little ones." The image sprang to mind of Dr Sergeant Major leering over my vacant body with a machete.

Then she shaved off my pubic hair. She didn't ask. She just did it. As the nurse beavered away I lay there, stunned. I recognised her. She had been a student at Putaruru High School when I was a student teacher. This was not right. Once again I was being rendered power-less by this mighty institution and soon, when anaesthesia would force my awareness off to another dimension, there would be no keeper for my temple.

All done, she sent me to take a bath in preparation for surgery.

I lay in the tub reading the latest book off the stands, *Your Erroneous Zones* by Wayne Dyer, about becoming an authentic person who is the driver of her own vehicle in life. Every now and then I cast a glimpse at my defoliated pudendum, which served only to deepen my offence. As I sought to understand it, a cold horror clutched me and a voice in my head boomed, *Run! Run for your life!!* I stepped out of the bath and stood in limbo staring first at the plastic bag containing the clothes I had arrived in, and then at the green hospital operating gown. Something about the two spaghetti ties that served to leave a gaping split down the back was so repugnant that I knew what I must do. When I was little I could not run. This was not just about my appendix, this was about something much bigger: I could reclaim authority over my own life. My hands shook as I put on my clothes and my heart was thumping loudly as I walked/ran in stutter-steps out into the corridor, through the front door and down the street towards freedom.

Once clear I began to gallop to get a head start on any pursuing ambulances with orderlies bearing strait-jackets. My belly still hurt and I had to scrunch myself in a low Groucho Marx scamper. I found a shop and dashed in to use the phone. I called home.

My brother Gordy answered.

"Come and get me," I cried, "I have run away from hospital!"

"You can't do that!"

"Well, I have. Come — quickly!"

"You have to go back."

"No way."

"Do they know you're gone?"

"Of course not. I've run away … escaped, absconded! Get it? Please, come and get me, now! Hurry!!"

"Yes, of course I will, but on one condition. You have to ring the hospital and tell them."

"Okay, I will. I will."

"Promise?"

"Yes I promise! Now hurry up!"

Much as I loathed the idea, my upbringing of civilian decency still reigned. At once I made a second quick call to the hospital. I knew that if I hesitated I might never find the courage. Reception answered.

"How can I direct your call?"

"This is Lorraine Moller. I am scheduled for surgery in ten minutes but I won't be able to make it." When I hung up the owner of the shop was glaring at me.

Gordy arrived. He was a little miffed over the ruckus I had caused. He had called the school where my mother was teaching. The headmaster had recognised it as an emergency and relieved my mother. She had run to call our local doctor Ravi, who had left his practice to call the hospital, and very soon word spread around the community that Lorraine Moller had run away from hospital. Nothing like this had ever happened before and no-one knew what to make of it.

Gordy drove me straight to the hospital to pick up the remainder of my belongings. He walked in with me. The nurse stared down as she delivered my gear. She could not, or would not, look me in the eye. I was directed to the office where a grim figure sat behind a looming desk, lips pursed, hands tightly clasped. I knew who it was. The face was different but it belonged to Matron — Matriarch of the Line People. She presented me with documents to say that I had voluntarily checked out, and demanded that I sign. Under her starched white linens she was seething shards of broken glass. I picked up the pen attempting nonchalance but my hand was still shaking and it looked nothing like my signature. I had no idea what the papers said. She took them and straightened the edges, then glared at me, not speaking until she had my eyes.

"Doctor (Sergeant Major) says that if you drop dead on the street he would not lift a finger to help you!"

So much for the Hippocratic Oath, I thought, *I'm glad I'm out of here.* But I turned my eyes to the ground for although I was electrified I was also ashamed. For the second time that morning, I left.

Things at the hospital were shaken up. I heard that a few weeks later Dr Sergeant Major resigned.

When I got back home a posse of concerned citizens was waiting for me. Ravi, the doctor, listened carefully to my concerns. I was afraid I had embarrassed him and that he would chastise me for my stupidity. But when I finished recounting my side of the story he simply said, "I admire your courage". Then he gently explained that I was in grave danger and urgently needed an appendectomy. Now that I had done in my chips with the public system he arranged for me to be admitted to a private hospital.

That evening I was in a new hospital where a surgeon, aptly named Dr Jolly, carefully removed my appendix, making sure that the incision was very small. I heard that my appendix was so swollen he could barely get it out of the incision but dared not cut it any larger. Indeed the scar is barely perceptible. My reputation had preceded me and I have never been treated so well in a hospital as I was there.

Gradually over the two years in Katikati I recovered from my heel surgery, grasping back my identity as a runner yard by yard, then mile by mile. After my appendectomy I quickly recovered my health and fitness, and for the first time in years my optimism and self-esteem were switched on high. I began waking up very early before work and running down to the water's edge where I sat while the sun rose. Like a solar panel I absorbed the life of the new day and, charged up, I would fly home and skip off to school, singing.

By the last school term I was racing a little and was fit enough to vie in the New Zealand Cross-country Champs for a place on the New Zealand team for the World Championships to be held in Limerick, Ireland, the following spring. I desperately wanted to go, to get out of Katikati and away from school teaching. I was still shy of peak fitness and not race-ready but I knew if I was smart I stood a chance. The week before I studied the 3,000 metre course in the neighbouring town of Tauranga, searching for a tactic that would give me an edge on my better-conditioned opponents.

As I warmed up on race day I had no idea if I could make a place in the top six and clinch a spot on the team. My only thought was to accelerate at those places where everyone wants to take a breather, such as at the top of a hill and in the first few strides after a hurdle.

From the start I followed the leaders out. At the crest of a large hill with ten others I accelerated off a hurdle and sprinted down the other side. Suddenly I was a clear fourth. Though my thighs were burning and my lungs lurched upward for oxygen, I chuckled inside. *If I can hang in there for another lap I will have my ticket to freedom.* I jumped again and again sprinted. Now I was third. As we approached the hurdle on the hill for the last time I relished the heat in my muscles for I knew I would make it. I finished second.

I was elated. In five months' time I would be out of here. Anything could happen.

A week later when I visited home, Dad wanted to have a 'little talk'. Just the words 'little talk' got my hackles up. It meant we had to go somewhere private where Dad would deliver a vote of no-confidence in one of my decisions and ask me to change my mind — his words bundled up in hand-me-down parental horse-shit. There was no way ever to win one of those talks with my Dad. His tenacity would always bully you into submission.

It turned out he wanted to discuss the arrangements for my pending wedding. The next day he was going up to Auckland to visit his brother, Bill, and to book the reception at the famous Moller's Barn on Bill's farm, a place renowned for its rip-roaring parties, the idea of which I was relishing. If I were having second thoughts this was the time to let him know, he said.

I wasn't about to step through this gingerly-presented exit. I could be as stubborn as he.

"If you think I'm going to call it off, no way," I snapped. Then softening, I added,

"*I am* getting married, so go ahead and book the farm."

Dad's eyes narrowed. He was unconvinced.

"Daddy, I really do love him."

Dad's lip twitched into a faint sneer. He wasn't buying it and I knew it.

"Are you sure?"

"Yep."

At this point I expected him to go for the jugular. But today he had a headlock on himself. He was not going to fight me and force me into a position against him. He turned to go. This was the point of no return. My future would be set for the next 30, 40 or even 50 years! I had a chilling vision of myself, old and wrinkled, sitting in a tree crying 'Mooore pooorrk' as the Mock Turtle wept below. I leapt to my feet.

"Dad?"

He turned on his heels, "Yes?"

"Wait ... I was just thinking that since I am going to Ireland maybe we should wait till after that. What do you think?"

"I think that would be very smart," my Dad said.

That night I rang Trevor and called off the wedding. Then I sat down with our guest list and wrote out un-invitations, cancelling the invitations I had sent out a few weeks earlier. Not long afterwards I told Trevor I was breaking up with him. He cried and begged with me to reconsider but I held firm.

Running through the Pinedale Forest with Dad, 1980. *Ron Daws*

PART THREE

Marathoner

Finally, the finishing line! 1980 London Marathon.

Courtesy Avon Running/Yellowdog Productions

CHAPTER 15

Mr Ron

OCTOBER 1978, AUCKLAND, NEW ZEALAND

Around the 15-mile mark of the Choysa Marathon I previewed my blind date for the evening. It was the weekend of my cancelled wedding and rather than spend a weekend alone in Katikati, I drove to Auckland to watch these crazy marathon men run up and down the waterfront. I had little interest in the marathon. Women did not run in them and they were too long and painful-looking to be exciting. But since I had agreed to escort one of the overseas invitees to the after-marathon banquet I felt obligated to attend. I had bought a new dress for the occasion, a pale green frilly thing with a floral print. The only snag was that my shoes didn't match (red!) and I had no others and no chance of getting any since back then the shops were closed on weekends.

In the few seconds it took him to pass by me I glimpsed a solid runner with a herky-jerky style as if he had a short leg, a glazed look in his eyes, and an upturned nose that made him look like a Sneetch who had just lost his belly star. Unless they are winning, seeing someone in the latter stages of a marathon does not allow for the best first impression. Ron Daws was not having a good day. The leaders were way ahead and this American looked as if he would rather be somewhere else.

"Are you sure that's him, are you sure?" I badgered my nodding friend, Heather of the beauty spot, who had set me up with him. I wanted to say, "I thought you said he was handsome", but held my tongue. I was beginning to regret that I had agreed to this whole confounded proposition.

Ron was standing with Arthur Lydiard at the entrance to the banquet. He was tall, dark-haired, blue-eyed and very handsome. There was something in his bearing that emanated intelligence, the composure of an accomplished person who knew the world and had mastered it. Suddenly I felt like the country bumpkin with the big nose and the silly dress. I hoped it was dark enough that he couldn't see my shoes were red.

We sat together at our table. When he looked at me, it was with a stare that penetrated right through. I was disconcerted and found myself wondering if he could see what a minion I was. Already I had resigned myself to the moment when he would excuse himself and flit over to another table for more sophisticated company. But he didn't. He chatted, asking me about myself and listening intently as I struggled to sound more interesting than a country school teacher with only two channels on her black and white TV, who still called her parents Mummy and Daddy to their face, and who not so long before had ironed her damp blouse while wearing it, causing a third degree burn. I was much more comfortable asking him questions which he answered (what I knew to be) modestly. I didn't know where Minneapolis was so he drew a map on a serviette. I was impressed. He knew geography and cartography. When he let slip that he had been to the Olympics, I felt tingly all over. Then when he mentioned he had written a book published by Runner's World, I was about to swoon. He was from the movies: John Wayne, Elvis Presley and James Bond all rolled into one.

I invited him over to my parents' table and introduced him. Dad was particularly mellow, having run the marathon himself that morning. My mother was fluttery with excitement and ran over to me later during the evening and whispered in my ear, "I always knew you would end up with someone like this!"

"But Mum," I protested, "I have only just met him."

"I know. But he's just right for you."

I took it to mean that here was a handsome, charismatic, accomplished, polite man who matched my mother's inflated opinion of me.

Ron stuck with me that evening as my date. I was used to blokes who dumped the girlfriend for most of the evening, drinking up at the bar with the other blokes while they sniffed around whatever else was available, returning for the odd dance just to keep the woman in tow. No wonder my mother came to the quick conclusion that Mr Ron was Mr Right.

After a few hours the evening was in full swing and I was enjoying my fourth set of dances with Ron. As we jived he looked at me with a big silly grin. I met his eyes: exuberant, unveiled, inviting me through the icy blue pools into the depths of his person. In that moment my feeling of inferiority disappeared and a sensation of great power surged through me as if I had just become Ruler of the Universe. I knew he was mine. He seemed small and vulnerable and I knew that if I chose to I could squash him underfoot like an insignificant bug.

Don't do it! a voice inside me cried.

Don't do what? Pursue him? Crush him? I was the country bumpkin and hardly the one calling the shots. I had to look away from Ron's gaze and regroup. He continued to dance, merrily unaware of the drama playing out in my head. At the end of the night we agreed to meet in a week, after he had completed his prearranged tour of the South Island of New Zealand. He kissed me goodbye. I was in heaven.

At the end of our relationship, when the ensuing power struggle finally turned in my favour and Ron was reduced to a self-confessed blithering idiot, I would understand my dance floor premonition and feel guilty because I hadn't listened.

While Ron was gone I pestered my brother until he sold me his Vauxhall Viva. A week later I zoomed up to Auckland again to meet Ron for his remaining two days in New Zealand. After that sweet kiss he had planted on me, I was stewed up with hope, consumed by desire, and ecstatic with fantasy.

I picked him up Sunday morning at Arthur Lydiard's place. It was a magical day that seemed to last forever. We ran, we ate, we went to a concert, went sight-seeing, visited my relatives, and talked and talked, telling each other about ourselves, about our love of running — beautiful, easy conversation, as if we were old friends catching up after lifetimes apart. That night we drove to the top of Mount Eden, a popular park-up spot, and made out in the car until we reluctantly decided that we had better take him back. When we arrived at Arthur's at about 10:30 p.m. the lights were all off and it seemed they had retired for the night. I lingered while Ron went to let himself in. Next thing he was back tapping on my window.

"I'm locked out," he whispered. "I've knocked but they're not answering."

"Well," I replied gleefully, "we can't have you sleeping on the doorstep. You'll have to come back with me."

We drove back to my friend Heather's place and, after a short negotiation about who would sleep on the floor, we both piled into a very squeaky single bed. By the next morning we had consummated our lust and were suffering the longing that is created when one lover must leave the other for a faraway land. We promised to write, and to figure out how to see each other again soon.

Ron wrote beautiful letters. He sent me gifts: earrings, clothing, poems, hand-made cards. I slept with his book under my pillow. He was my man, and I couldn't wait to see him again. My girlfriends were excited for me. Allison Deed (later Roe) enthusiastically declared, "You are so lucky to have an American boyfriend. Americans really pamper their women!" We launched into a discussion about how many cars and TVs he might have.

CHAPTER 16

Snow-bound

MARCH 1979, EUROPE

We awoke at the National Training Centre in Paris on our first morning to find it had snowed. I was on the New Zealand Cross-country team once again, travelling through France and Italy for competition and acclimatisation before heading on to Ireland for the World Championships. Our team of 12 men and six women was as spirited as the last.

Shrieking delightedly, we romped around throwing snowballs and shaking branches on each other until our hands and feet were frozen. Then we went training in long-sleeved T-shirts and socks on our hands, our pink legs churning rapidly to generate heat. I had never run in snow before. According to team lore, no-one ever missed a training run due to the weather or a meal unless you were sick; there was no whingeing about conditions; and one must reserve judgment and decline comment about the means of others to let off steam.

In this most bitter of European winters, we raced over cross-country twice in Paris and Seville in preparation for the World Champs.

After the race in Paris, we returned to our dorms chilled to the bone. The facilities were limited and rather than wait we discovered that six skinny women could squeeze into a French bathtub. It took an impromptu team meeting to decide that the strange little basin next to the toilet was tailor-made for washing our muddy socks and we marveled at French ingenuity.

After the race in Seville we could not afford to linger. We had to catch an evening train to Rome and a connecting flight to Ireland via England the next morning. It was a train to trouble.

I took a seat in the cabin with the 'fun' group. Team management was next door, with the 'serious' folks. Someone had acquired a flagon of wine by dubious means and with the carriage rumbling and swaying in hypnotic rhythm, eight men and women got drunker and sillier as the night got darker.

The conversation turned to Euan Robertson's beard and the consensus was that he would be a 'sexy looking bastard' without it and what better time to relieve him of it than now. It was a group effort. Someone produced a cup to hold a dribble of wine, someone else a can of shaving cream, and a third a seriously-used plastic Bic razor. We were in the barbering business.

Euan was shorn like a sheep by a townie at the Putaruru Agricultural and Pastoral show. In a few minutes his beard was half gone and the razor was too blunt to finish the job. His face looked as if it had been devoured by moths. I slid onto the floor, clutching my belly with laughter. My gaping lips were too tempting for Jack Foster, keeper of the shaving cream. He squirted it into my mouth, instantly extinguishing my merriment. I gagged and heaved, sputter-spattering cream across the walls. A wrestle ensued for possession of the aerosol weapon and very soon the interior of the cabin and its inhabitants were decorated in white foam.

The door opened. The conductor looked around and closed it abruptly. A few minutes later he returned with our manager. Terry Baker had served in the diplomatic service in Paris and was perfect for this job. Unruffled, he quietly stated that it was in our best interests to cool it and start cleaning up. He said the conductor was very upset with us and patrons of the train were complaining that we were making too much noise. When the door closed, someone wiped a T-shirt across the windows and seats and we resumed out antics. Thirty minutes later the train came to a stop. We didn't even notice. When the door opened again, it was Terry with several stern looking, uniformed men, who glared at us. They closed the door and stood outside and gabbled away in Italian. The door opened again. Terry put his head in.

"The gendarmes have agreed not to take this any farther but you must cease your activities and pay for the cleaning of the cabin." In my drunken stupor I did not realise the gendarmes were police, or I may have shown more respect. We rifled through our pockets, tossing every last lira out the door at the feet of the conductor. The train started up again and dumped us at midnight in Rome.

For the next three days my food tasted of shaving cream.

The World Cross-country Championships — Limerick, Ireland

En route to Ireland we discovered there was an Aer Lingus baggage handlers' strike on so we decided that the men would come by ferry with all the luggage and we women would travel by plane. By now I was feeling the aftermath of my breach of the competitive athletes' Code of Excellence: *Save the hard partying until after you have raced*, and was coming down with a cold. The championships were just four days away and I was fried.

When we arrived in Limerick we were met by the proud organisers of this event who piled us into their brand new, plush vehicles courtesy of their sponsor. Our hosts suddenly had a bright idea — we were such a good-looking team of women they would drive us to the Cliffs of Moher and photograph us atop the shiny bonnets of these cars with the sea vista in the background — a certain sponsor-pleaser. It took over an hour to get there and for another 30 minutes the cars were manoeuvred back and forth with painstaking accuracy, the drivers taking every care not to drive us over the cliff. Inside we were becoming disgruntled. "What the heck are they doing?" we asked. "Why are they taking so long?" Finally the three vehicles were perfectly lined up. "At last!" we sighed. There was just one small oversight. The cars were so tightly aligned that the middle vehicle could not open its doors to let out the passengers. The whole venture was immediately scrapped and they took us to the hotel. Given our sightseeing detour, the men arrived soon after us.

It was noon a few days before the championships and Heather and I were sitting on the bed whiling away the morning with our teammates Kevin Ryan and Jack Foster. I felt safe because there was no shaving cream in sight.

Jack was something of an anomaly, the senior of the team and very, very fast. Because of his age he had a following among runners, especially those in the over-40 bracket. He also possessed a wicked sense of humour.

The phone rang. Kevin answered. He held the receiver to his chest and spoke to Jack.

"It's a fan," he said, "wants to bring his son up to meet you."

"Tell him to come on up," Jack instructed.

Heather and I prepared to take our leave but Jack had mischief on his mind. He pulled off his T-shirt and jumped into bed, patting the spaces on either side. Heather and I jumped in and pulled our sleeves off our shoulders and the covers up under our arms. Jack draped an arm around each neck. The scene was set.

Knock! Knock!

"Come in." Kevin pulled the door open wide and swept in the visitors.

"I'm sorry," the older man looked slightly panicked. "I was looking for Jack Foster."

"I'm Jack Foster." Jack pulled his arm from my shoulder and extended it out, welcoming and magnanimous, as if nothing was amiss.

The balding, ruddy-faced man met his hero's handshake hesitatingly, not sure where to look.

"And this is my son, Sean."

Jack thrust his hand out again. The youth, just bordering on puberty, looked at his Dad who nodded. Sean averted his eyes and shuffled forward to give Jack a wimpy handshake. I caught him peeking at my slight cleavage and he blushed.

"So, you're a runner?"

Sean nodded.

"Great sport," Jack enthused. "Keep it up."

A light smirk rippled across the boy's mouth.

"Nice meeting you. Thank you for taking the time." The father was back in the doorway, making for a quick getaway.

"Really it was no trouble," Jack replied sincerely, "You are most welcome, any time! Keep up the running, son!"

They both waved.

"Goodbye!" We all yelled cheerily.

On the day of the World Cross-country Championships it snowed. Under-the-weather, underdressed and not used to such cold conditions, I stood shivering on the start line. All can be lost at the start of cross-country and I lost it. I quickly became trapped in a bottle-neck behind dozens of slower runners on a single track. Somewhere at about the half-mile mark I lost my shoe in a bog but I hobbled on as best I could, lop-sided. As far as I know it is still there, a petrified relic in a field. My finish was somewhere mid-field but I was unfazed. I had my suitcase with a few belongings and my life savings of $1,000 in traveller's cheques. I was off to America to see Ron.

CHAPTER 17

Checking In

1979 — 1980, MINNEAPOLIS USA

I had no idea how far it was to the US. I thought it was maybe a two-hour flight, so when the loquacious American sitting next to me on the plane engaged me in conversation I thought I was safe. He talked at me the entire flight even when I closed my eyes and pretended sleep. I was too polite to tell him to bug off. Ten hours later when we finally landed, he was still talking as chirpily as if he had just been freshly wound. I thanked him insincerely for his company and made my way to my gate to Minneapolis. As I sat quietly in solitude the loud American suddenly appeared beside me. His flight was delayed and he had sought me out because he enjoyed talking to me so much. Finally his flight was called.

I positioned myself in front of the gate and watched the clock. It was now four o'clock. My flight was scheduled to leave at five p.m. and I was anxious to get on the plane and be reunited at long last with my one true love, Ron.

I awoke with a start. I looked at the clock. It was five! I scanned the concourse. A red velvet rope blocked the walkway to the plane. I realized everyone had boarded and my flight was about to take off without me. Grabbing my bags, I sprinted for the gate, leapt the cloth-covered barrier chain and ran down the concourse. The plane was still there but the doors were closed. I knocked on the door of the hatch, timidly at first then, gaining courage, I began full-fisted pounding. It worked. The door swung open and a flight attendant looked at me with a start.

"Can I help you?" she asked.

"Yes," I replied anxiously, "I just have to get on this plane!"

"Calm down, Miss, you can get this plane, just go back and sit in the boarding area and we will let you on just as soon as we let all the other people off first."

When I finally arrived in Minneapolis in March of '79, Ron was waiting for me at the gate, looking as handsome as I remembered him. It had been almost five months since we first met. We made our way to his car, an old Toyota with rust spots all over it and what looked like bullet holes in the windows. Out the back window hung a mangey looking black and white mutt with wild eyes, one blue, and one brown. Ron affectionately referred to him as Snarf, and explained that the dog had X-ray vision.

His house matched his car in character. It was tiny, more like a cabin, a bachelor pad with the sparse furnishings thrown any old place. On his kitchen counter were car parts and slabs of limestone that he intended to find some use for. Meantime they looked like permanent residents. The fridge was almost empty, save for a big bag of loose grapes with rotten ends, bought for 50 cents, Ron proudly declared, and some cinnamon raisin bread that Ron called Used Bread because it came from the day-old store. So much for my rich American fantasy. But, I reasoned, he was the artistic, sensitive type, a non-materialist with his values in the right place. Just the guy for me. My mother was right. I knew for sure then that I would end up with Ron, that he was my destiny. Here I was in Minneapolis, ready to add a woman's touch to this bachelor's life. In return he would usher me into the big wide world of America, sophistication, movie actors, big races, even the Olympics. I couldn't believe my luck.

Early the next morning Ron ate his two pieces of cinnamon toast, boiled water in an old aluminum kettle for his coffee and took off for work. He was a statistician for the Department of Labour. It sounded official, though it held about as much interest for me as a week-long game of cricket. Ron said his job had its captivating moments, such as when he wrote in a report that the demand for refrigerators was cooling off or that the numbers of elevators were up and down.

As he left, Ron cautioned me that there had been a rapist in the area so I should be careful. I didn't put a foot outside. After all, this was America and I knew that the rapist would have a gun. Instead I waited until Ron arrived home for a run. His friend Phil came to join us, and I am sure, to look me over and report back to his buddy.

It was winter. I changed into my running gear: shorts, and a long-sleeved top because it was cold outside. They laughed when they saw me. "You need a hat, gloves and long pants, or you'll freeze to death!" Ron proceeded to fish through his gear for some extras. I felt silly wearing long pants. In New Zealand only pooftahs wore long pants to run in. Hats and gloves were unheard of. I thought Ron and Phil looked like pooftahs, but being the foreigner I was willing to make concessions.

Outside the snow reflected the plump moon and sparkling stars, and made the path around the perimeter of Lake Nokomis clearly visible. As we ran, Ron and Phil regaled me with a popular Minnesotan pastime — tales of how cold it got. "Why, it gets so cold, your eyelashes freeze together and you can't open your eyes till you get inside, if you can find your way ... ha ha ... The tyres of your car freeze flat to the road and when you get it started it goes kerthunk, kerthunk, until it warms up into a round shape (true) ... and ... Every spring when the snow thaws they find all the missing runners who tried to make their way across snowdrifts, frozen in mid-stride." I never, ever went cross-country in the snow after that one.

One evening Ron offered to take me to the movies at the bargain theatre on Hennepin Avenue. His eyes glinted as he outlined the schedule: three Marx Brothers movies end-on-end for only one dollar. It was still winter and some degrees below freezing. I had by now learned to dress warmly. So when Ron emerged wearing lederhosen like a little Swiss boy going for a walk up the Matterhorn, my eyebrows rose.

"You're not wearing those, are you?" Knobby knees protruded from the cuffs of the suede shorts, and a little bib held his shirt in check.

"Yep!" he replied reaching for the car keys.

I felt ridiculous being with him, but knew I was being tested, so I didn't mention it again. I just kept repeating to myself, 'He's the one who looks silly, not me, he's the one...' Once inside, Ron's juvenile get-up did not look so strange. The only others there looked like homeless folk wanting a warm place for the evening. Ron was unfazed. He giggled all the way through, for over four hours. I endured.

After my movie marathon, Ron decided that what I really needed was to experience the ultimate icon of American culture: the drive-in movies. I had never been to one before, which Ron found almost incomprehensible. "Oh Gawd, I can't believe it!" I was excited. From what I knew, drive-ins were romantic affairs where the guy slipped his hand across the back of your seat and pulled you close during the sexy scenes.

The night of the drive-in we arrived early so that Ron could park in the centre at the front of the screen. In a surge of generosity he splashed out for popcorn, "Can't have a movie without popcorn!" — a bucket of Texan proportions, the likes of which I had never seen before. I snuggled down into my seat, next to my man, immersed in my American experience.

When the previews started we couldn't hear anything. Ron marched around the cars to the ticket box. He came back fuming.

'That's it, we're leaving!' and he started up the car.

"But why?" I whined. "The movie hasn't even started."

"Because my radio doesn't work and we can't get sound. They want to charge me five bucks to rent a speaker. I can't believe it!"

"But Ron, I'll pay the five bucks. I want to see the movie."

"No way! When I come to a movie, I'm not accustomed to having to pay for the sound also. We're leaving." And he drove off.

He didn't drive out the exit but headed for the entrance and parked himself at the ticket counter nose-to-nose with the line of incoming cars, refusing to budge until he got his money back. The facing cars were beeping. Ron had gridlocked the entire operation. I sank down into my seat as the guy forked over a refund. I never did get to go to a drive-in movie.

Despite Ron's infuriating and uncompromising principles, I quietly admired him. We had a lot in common, I told myself, like running ... and I couldn't think of anything else. It didn't matter to me that he laughed himself silly over the Marx Brothers or the Pink Panther or Fatty Arbuckle, or that he listened to Herb Alpert and the Tijuana Brass. He was 18 years older than me and was entitled to his tastes, which, considering his age, were those of my parents' generation. I just stuck to him and did whatever he did.

Our weekends were spent at races, which made me very happy. I joined in racing alongside Ron, finishing usually one place behind him, as a dutiful student who respectfully knows her place in the pecking order. Within two months I had run my first ten kilometre road race, my first ten-miler, and my first 20-miler.

Twenty miles for a race. It seemed to me a silly distance, good only for a training run. When the annual Stoughton to Madison Syttende Mai 20-miler in Wisconsin came around, I went along for the ride with Ron and Phil who ran it every year. Ron had drummed up some deal with the race director for accommodation at a big-game hunters' lodge.

The place was creepy. There were animal heads on the walls. The waste bins were elephant feet. As I lay on my bed hoping for a peaceful pre-race sleep, the lion king glared back at me, his jaws petrified in a silent roar. When I reached out to turn off my bedside lamp, my hand turned jittery as I realised I had grabbed onto an antelope leg with a shade. I didn't sleep well. But I have never found that sleep the night before a race is necessary to race and I have never been so tired as to fall asleep during one. This one was no exception. It was fun to race farther than I ever had before, and the long, rolling hills reminded me of my Dunedin days loping over the hills. When I won the race easily in a world-best time, I dismissed it as a training run and of not much use except as a build-up for some serious track racing at a later date. After all, the only people who ran these long races did so because they were too slow for the shorter stuff. The truth was, I was running to please Ron, and I could see that my win amplified his interest in me.

The next weekend I was off on my own to New York for the L'eggs Mini Marathon, a ten kilometre run just for women, organised by Fred Lebow, the race director of the New York City Marathon, whom I had met in Limerick. I was excited to be travelling to races as an invited runner, just like Walker, Quax and Dixon did in Europe, and a tad nervous to be flying across the USA all by myself.

At the airport check-in I was told the flight was a non-stop to New York, so when the plane landed I got off. I walked outside to the transport area and asked a taxi to take me to the Mayflower Hotel where the invited runners were staying. He hadn't heard of it. He called over another taxi driver and soon there were four cabbies having a conference. To help I pulled out my letter from the New York Road Runners Club with all my race information. He took a look at it, pointed at the address and sniggered with his buddies.

"This hotel is in New York. This here is Chicago!"

Thinking it might be a Twin Cities type situation I asked, "So can you take me to New York?"

"Lady," he said as if he was talking to a five-year-old, "New York is hundreds of miles away!"

I made my way back to the airline counter, crushed and lost. "I got off the plane too soon," I blurted to the clerk, on the verge of tears. They put me on another plane to New York and the cute story of the geographically-challenged foreigner became *New York Times* material.

Three weeks later there was an exodus of runners from the Twin Cities, all driving north for the Grandma's Marathon weekend in Duluth. I didn't have any intention of running a marathon and I can't remember if it was reluctance to go or disorganisation that caused

Ron and me to arrive in Duluth about ten p.m. the night before the race. We drove to the house of race official Dorothy Spencer, who came out in her nightgown to reluctantly hand me an official number so that I could run. Ron must have talked me up. But as far as I was concerned I had come along just for the ride — and a 20-mile training run.

When I arrived at the 20-mile mark of Grandma's Marathon the next day I was winning easily. My ride was waiting to pick me up but heck, a win is a win, and I was feeling good, so I waved them goodbye and ran on. I won comfortably in 2:37:36.5 which ranked me eighth in the world.

Ha! Marathons are nothing! I thought, *The cup event for runners too slow for the track.* So I pooh-poohed the whole affair, as I knew everyone at home would, even though here they were making a big fuss of me. But that was Americans, slightly off in their discernment of quality: just a bit rah-rah over everything.

Moller family, 1969: from left Gary, Vivienne, Gordon, Maisie (Mum), Gordon (Dad), Delwyn, Bruce, and Lorraine.

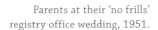

Parents at their 'no frills' registry office wedding, 1951.

Rotorua sprint, second to last, 1964.

Victory over Sue Haden in the 800 metre race at Porritt Stadium, Hamilton, 1973. *Waikato Times*

Meeting the Queen in Hamilton, 1970. *Waikato Times*

Opening ceremony, Commonwealth Games, Christchurch, 1974. (Placed fifth in line, looking up.) *Waikato Tim*

Running with Allison Roe at Takapuna Beach, Auckland, 1981.

Ron Daws with Snarf, car and canoe, taken in Minneapolis, 1979.

With Ron, 1980.

Wedding photo: from left Dick Quax, Sue Jowett, the bride and groom, 1981.

Running through the Pinedale Forest with Dad. *Ron Daws*

Portrait of author, 1980. *Ron Daws*

Running through the streets of London, Avon International Women's Marathon, 1980. *Peter Tempest*

First breakthrough in international marathon racing. Winning the Avon International Women's Marathon, London, 1980. *Courtesy Avon Running/Yellowdog Productions*

Giving an impromptu speech at the Avon London Marathon awards, 1980.

Courtesy Avon Running/Yellowdog Productions

On the podium at the Maratona Atlantica Boavista, in Rio de Janeiro, 1979, with American 'superstar' marathon runner, Bill Rodgers (centre).

CHAPTER 18

The Crash-mobile

Strife, only a slight thing when she first rears her head, but
her head soon hits the sky as she strides across the earth.
— Homer, from *The Illiad*

1980, MINNEAPOLIS

After a few weeks at Ron's home, I soon realised that someone was jealous of me — Snarf. This beast never failed to burrow his way into the middle of the sofa, forcing a gap between our two bodies. "Oh Snarf, that's my guy!" and Ron would kiss him profusely. I would have given him a doggie drop-kick out the door if I had been sure I was above this canine competitor in the pecking order of Ron's affections. So I feigned affection for it. Later, sensing my disdain for his best friend and loyal companion, Ron took any opportunity to hold me down on the floor with my arms pinned and let Snarf slobber my face with its washrag of a tongue, despite my protestations of disgust. Ron would yell delightedly, "Doggie kisses! Doggie kisses! See Snarf loves Lorrainey-Babes too!"

Home alone while Ron was at work, I got to taking the bus and going to the shopping mall, entranced by the plethora of bargains America had to offer. Filled with happiness this one day, I bought Ron a 'you're wonderful' Hallmark card and signed it 'From a Fan — XXX.' Then I put it in the mailbox. I had been in Minneapolis for over a month and was thrilled with my new circumstances.

"Any mail?" It was Ron's usual greeting when he walked in the door in the evening.

"I haven't checked," I lied.

Off he went to the mailbox and sat down to sort through it. He opened my card, then tucked it under some bills and, without a word, spirited it away. That evening he never mentioned it. It was then I knew that the disappearing card was a case of mistaken authorship. Snarf was not only one who was competing with me for Ron's affections.

The next day while Ron was at work, the search was on. Rifling through all his personal effects, I found my card on top of a stack of love letters, hidden under a book in a drawer. Her name was Tessa. She was stewing over my presence, couldn't believe he had got them into this mess. 'When is she leaving???' her letters implored.

I was devastated, outraged, and, I have to admit, my competitive spirit was piqued. I returned the stash of letters as I found it, deciding to keep my indignation to myself. This would be guerilla combat, and I needed to strategise. I figured I had the pillow advantage. I was also a vastly superior athlete to her. In Ron's eyes, this was not to be underestimated. Now I had the added bonus of the inside track on her, which she provided once or twice a week with her letters. If I hung in there I might drive her desperate enough to put Ron off her. As the months went by it became apparent from her frantic pleadings that I was gaining a sizeable lead. I felt both smug and guilty. I had become a snoop.

I was running by myself in the web of trails of Fort Snelling on the banks of the Mississippi. One moment I was bowling along on a threshold run (the fastest comfortable effort one can sustain without having to slow up at the end of the run) and the next I was seized with the feeling that someone had put a plastic bag over my head. I was on my knees fighting for a breath. For a moment I thought I would die and that no-one would find me for weeks, when I'd be all rotted and eaten by animals. Gradually I came around and gingerly set off on the solitary five-mile trek back home. This gave me time to think things out. *I don't want to be puffing on drugs. I don't even want to call it by its name in case it gets familiar and sticks to me. I have to get this under control, right now!*

Mentally I retraced my thoughts. They had gone where they often did these days — to Tessa's latest letters and her protestations of love for Ron. "You only care about her because she is a faster runner than me," she wrote. *Damn right I am!* I thought at the time. However as I had loped along, such bravado had dissipated and underneath much more tender sensitivities reigned. *How could he do this to me? Doesn't he care about me enough to tell her to take a hike? Why do I put up with this?* I had felt the rising heat of anger from my chest damped down with uncried tears, and a compact little clump formed in my throat. It was the same tightening that came when I had had to carry my little suitcase to the car and sit stoically next to my dad as we headed for hospital. And like then, I had swallowed it down and kept on course. This time, however, as I forged on, my airway had completely shuttered.

The solution was obvious. *I can't control Tessa or Ron, only myself.* I made a pact then and there: *I'll slow down at the first sign of tightening in my throat, even if I have to throw the workout or the race.* Following this plan, I did not have another full-blown asthma attack for the next 13 years.

If nothing else, Ron was getting comfortable with me. In my mind this gave me licence to work on him, for his own good of course. To date he had prided himself on four things, — that he had never owned a suit, that he had never spent more than $1 for a gallon of gas, that he had never spent more than $10 for a pair of jeans and never spent more than $50 on a car. But with much urging on my part he forked out $500 for a light blue VW fastback in good condition. I felt victorious. My influence was upgrading him. He was my man.

My visa was up and, after five months, it was time to go home. Ron had to stay to work and so I reluctantly left him to the eager clutches of the other woman impatiently waiting in the wings, and headed back to New Zealand for three months to run track and enjoy the summer with my Kiwi running friends.

Back home I found that I had been labelled a marathoner and whenever I was mentioned with regards to track in the newspaper it was with the caveat that I had performed well for one not endowed with speed, that is, a marathon runner. It seemed my track past had been erased.

These races were of not much significance and I had not specifically prepared for them. I had come to divide races into Races for Learning and Races for Winning. Races for Learning, such as these, were for experience only, and could be classified as a facet of training. They were a valuable way to discover my shortcomings under pressure so that adjustments could be made to ready myself for Races for Winning. Races for Winning were worth putting myself on the line for, so needed to be carefully selected. I was beginning to understand how important this discernment was.

International athletes Grete Waitz from Norway and the beautiful Natalia Maracescu from Romania had been invited to New Zealand to compete. Grete was the current world record holder for the marathon, and a very fast track runner. Natalia was more of a 1,500 and 3,000 metre track specialist. I, along with my friends, served as filler for the races with them, for we were quite simply in a league below these champions. While we ran around nine minutes and some change for 3,000 metres and felt we had done well, these two women turned in times in the low 8:30s, with the Romanian able to outsprint the Norwegian at the finish every time.

These being Races for Learning, I observed as much as possible. What was the difference between these fast women and me? Were they just born faster or did they train differently? Natalia Maracescu, it turned out, was banned for a positive steroid test a year later, so the inequity with her was easily explained (although she blew my idea of the effects of steroids — they don't necessarily make you ugly or masculine). But with Grete it was a different story. She was so well trained that she could quite effortlessly run six-minute miles in her daily training runs. Her aerobic efficiency obviously was the key but how come she could do it and I couldn't? I needed to train faster or harder or longer, I told myself, but I wasn't sure which. Getting back to Ron was the answer since he understood it all better than I. I needed him, I told myself, more than ever.

At the end of the track series a party was held for the athletes in the Logan Park Hotel across from Cornwall Park. I arrived with my girlfriends, all dollied up in our best dresses and high-heeled shoes. Without Ron I could dance and drink and flirt without inhibition.

Suddenly I heard screams. Geoff Capes, a British hammer thrower, egged on by the other heavies, had thrown one of my friends over his shoulder and tossed her into the swimming pool. This was sport at its finest for this giant bully and he foraged for more young ladies to dunk. His heavy mates had blocked the exits; there was no escape. One by one, plonk, plonk, plonk, in they went.

He grabbed me and tossed me over his shoulder like a hand-bag. "Let me down!" I screamed as I flailed my arms at his back. Unfazed he headed for the pool. *To hell if I am going to get wet*, I thought. I swung my head to the side of him and bit down on his arm. Not a little bite, I figured this was a one-shot deal so I had mustered a full-throttled chomp.

"Bitch!" he yelled as he dropped me on the floor. He twisted his arm over to survey his wound. It was clearly indented. "She bit me!" he whined as his friends clucked around to gawk like force–fed Christmas turkeys at feed time. I had hurt him and although I felt a twinge of remorse, I knew that this was an excellent time to make my exit.

A few years later I saw him on TV, pulling a tanker truck with his teeth. He was now hailed as "The Strongest Man in the World."

I wondered if he would remember me.

Ron broke up with me. He wrote me a letter explaining that while he loved me, he was too old for me. He had had kids and wanted no more, and did not want to deny me the opportunity of having children by being stuck with him. I cried. I was touched by his noble reasons and wanted him all the more. I was also suspicious that Tessa was lurking in the background, urging him on. I wrote back, explaining that what I wanted in life was my decision to make, not his. If he was to break up with me for his own sake then I would accept it, but breaking up with me for my own good without my input was unacceptable from someone who claimed to love me. I had bought my ticket back, I explained, but would not come if that was what he really wanted. All he had to do was say, "Don't come."

I might have received such word but a little accident tipped the scales back in my favour.

When I arrived back in March, Ron picked me up in his 'customised' car. From the back it looked like the same blue car I left. The front, however, told a different story. It was red and rusted out. The headlights were suspended in empty sockets by metal tape and swung as we drove, beaming a hypnotic light show all over the road and occasionally high in the air when we hit a bump. He turned them on and off by twisting two wires together under the dash. It was freezing and icy rain was coming in through the cracks in the welding. "We now have air conditioning," Ron declared. When we got to the house my clothes had rusty water spots all over them, which never came out.

Ron took great care to explain this customisation. While I was away his ex-girlfriend had come over one evening to talk. "It was late," Ron emphasised, "*and rather than have her stay the night*, she borrowed the car to go to her *own home to sleep* — and, well, she crashed it." So to save her money, he went to a junkyard and bought a 'matching' front end for $50 and welded it on himself.

It all reeked of fishy business but I said nothing. I was happy to be back to reclaim my rightful position in his house and life. As far as I could see, Tessa had had her chance to get him back and had blown it by crashing his car. Good deal!

We settled back down to training, racing and remodelling the house. The car was an embarrassment to me, but not for Ron, who revelled in its curious appearance as a symbol of his individuality. He was flattered when the neighbors called the city officials to complain that he was keeping a junkyard. I cringed when he eagerly explained to the powers-that-be that the junk was in fact his vehicles, which he used regularly.

The vibe was out. Ron got a call from a man who had a car that he was considering junking and wondered if Ron would like first dibs. Ron was excited. A free car, what luck! Immediately we drove to the outskirts of the city and the deal was made, "You take it and don't bring it back." Ron eagerly seized the wheel of a droopy mint-green junker and fired it up. It sounded like an 80-year-old man with pneumonia. For once I was happy to drive the two-tone beast.

Sure enough, within a few miles the junker died. I coasted alongside. "You'll have to give me a push." Ron instructed. "Drive around the block and come up behind me." The block was about quarter of a mile long; not sure of how to do what Ron asked, I inched towards him from about 300 metres away.

Suddenly his hand flew out of the window and he was gesturing for me to hurry up, his arm waving wildly in a big circling motion. I knew then that I was doing it all wrong, so I took this cue and floored the accelerator. I hit the back of him at about 20 miles per hour and gaining. Whack! I saw his arms fly above his head and his neck snap back, and in that moment I knew I had really done it wrong. I got out to check. His head was still attached, it was articulating and it was livid.

"What the hell do ya think you're doing?!!" He yelled.

"Giving you a push?" I murmured.

"You rammed me. Whaddaya trying to do, kill me?"

"No, I just thought you wanted me to go fast."

"Jeez, you idiot," he muttered. He was okay.

Suddenly it all seemed funny. I started to giggle and couldn't stop, which infuriated Ron all the more. I finally composed myself enough to give him the gentle nudge he needed and we got home, with one more car to add to the junk pile in the backyard.

CHAPTER 19

Queen

The first virtue in a soldier is endurance of fatigue;
courage is only the second virtue.
— Napolean Bonaparte

AUGUST 1980

Ron became my coach. I consented because it was one step closer to commitment. I reasoned that he was already receiving the accolades for my marathon effort so he might as well officially be given the job. Besides, I was dubious about beating him in races — but I was getting awfully close. I worried that he would take it as an affront to his masculine superiority. If I enlisted him as my coach, I reasoned, my improving performances would be seen as a testimony to his coaching, rather than highlighting his decline as an athlete. I was willing to sacrifice the credit for my wins to him to keep him on board with me.

Ron threw himself into the coaching role with unbounded vigour. "Oh man," I heard him proudly declare to some runners, "she was running so fast that even *I* couldn't keep up with her!" My plan was working.

I was invited to run the 1980 Avon International Women's Marathon in London. I was keen to see London but not to run a marathon. Ron insisted. He had considerably more respect and enthusiasm for the marathon than I did, and set about planning the perfect training programme for the event. He spent hours at it in deep concentration, poring over his old running diaries from 1967 and 1968 (his favourites) and extrapolating, comparing and filling in the calendar like a crossword puzzle until he was satisfied it was tailored to perfection for me. I thought it was all rather tedious, after all, marathon running had to be fairly simple: run long and hard enough to get stronger, but not long and hard enough to get weaker (and only the runner could know the difference).

Ron was not fazed by my simplistic opinions. Finally he showed me his masterpiece with the air of a Michelangelo unveiling a David. The Avon programme was titled The All-Purpose Foolproof God-sheet. I looked it over. It had no rest days, 100-mile weeks and 28-mile runs every Sunday. I told him it looked like too much, that I didn't want to do 28-mile runs.

"You have to do over-distance training and if you are running the marathon, over-distance is twenty-eight miles. If you can't run twenty-eight miles in training how can you run twenty-six miles in a race?"

"But I didn't do them for Grandma's and I had no trouble going the distance."

"Do it your way then!" he yelled and tore the Godsheet out of my hands and into shreds. He threw it in the trash bin and stalked off. He refused to talk to me for the rest of the day.

It was not so much the programme that was the issue for me; but I could see I was fast losing the right to allow my own judgment to be the final authority when it came to my running. Ron was claiming that position, and I knew that if he did, he would own me.

However I couldn't stand the silence, and my desire to belong out-stripped my prized independence. I pulled the tatters of the Godsheet out of the bin, pieced them together with sticky tape, and pinned it up on the wall. Then I announced to Ron that I was prepared to do whatever it took to be a champion. He liked that. The All-Purpose Foolproof Godsheet ruled.

Each Saturday evening, Ron meticulously added up the miles of the week to enter into his training diary, the marriage partner of the Godsheet. He used a sketch pad, each page ruled into squares marking the daily training sessions for a month. He made one for me, and I was expected to follow suit.

I was sloppy with my calculations, as I always had been, rounding out the miles and squeezing an extra one in here and there to boost my weekly total. As my coach, Ron took issue with my accounting and claimed I was cheating. He had discovered that on three of my runs I had, in fact, been a half mile short, making my weekly total 98.5 rather than 100. Since the Godsheet called for 100-mile weeks he demanded I put on my running gear and go out for a one and a half mile run.

"Who's cares?" I shot back. "No-one will know. It makes no difference to my fitness."

"No, you're wrong! YOU know. Your body knows. You're on a Lydiard programme and it has to be one hundred miles a week!"

"But Arthur never told me to do a hundred miles a week."

"That's 'cos you were a girl running track. You want to run a marathon, you have to train like a man!"

"But I still don't get it. A one and half mile training run doesn't add anything in the big scheme of things."

"Wrong again! It's a matter of principle. It's the difference between a winner and a loser!"

"Well, I think it's dumb," I mumbled as I skulked off to change into my shorts.

In the ensuing months I clocked precise 100-mile weeks, through thunderstorms, snow and sweltering heat. I ran weekday mornings on my own while Ron was at work, then I slept most afternoons, going out again for some bashing run with Ron in the evening. And every Sunday I ran 28 miles as The All-Purpose Foolproof Godsheet mandated.

One Sunday midsummer in Minnesota as the temperatures rose quickly into the 100s I headed out for my 28-mile run. After about 18 miles I was so dehydrated and weakened that I knew I could not finish. I stopped at a public bathroom, drank a few sips of water from the wash basin and dry-retched for about ten minutes, then headed for home.

Ron admonished me for being a quitter and demanded that I do this key work-out the next day. So Monday I set off again on another 28-mile safari. It was just as hot and I still felt queasy from the run the day before, but this time when I dry-retched it was in mid-stride and I did not indulge myself with a stop until I was done. I walked into the living room and collapsed on the floor. I could not move and lay there for hours, too exhausted to have a drink or change my sweaty clothes.

I knew that I had done well. I remembered Ron telling me that when he had trained for the Olympics, his Sunday runs were so challenging that he would come in and lie down on the living room floor, just as I was now. The first week, when the phone rang he could not rouse himself to make the ten feet to get the receiver. Two weeks later he was lying on the floor after a 28 mile run, and this time when the phone rang he managed to crawl to get it. This, he announced, signaled to him that he was making progress.

He wanted nothing less from me. I knew that if he could see me now he would be proud.

He was. "When you line up in London," he said, "you will have the confidence that none of the others trained as hard as you did." *No kidding*, I thought. *If they trained harder than me they would be dead.*

Six weeks before the London race I went off to Grandma's again for my second marathon. This was to be a training run, to be run comfortably with a two-mile warm-up and two-mile cool-down to make it a 30-mile over-distance run. I won again comfortably in 2:38. It felt downright easy. I was ready for the Avon International Women's Marathon in London.

Under the direction of Boston Marathon legend Kathrine Switzer, Avon gathered together the best women marathoners for a World Championship. Because it was not an Olympic event for women, it held little official status. In the interests of providing opportunity and parity for women, Kathrine created an historic event; the first time the streets of London had ever been closed for a sporting event. Besides providing an occasion which rightfully needed to exist, Kathrine hoped to sway the old boy network of the Olympic committee, persuading them that women could run marathons of quality and that the marathon should be included in the Olympic Games. At that time the longest distance running event for women in the Olympics was 1,500 metres, less than one mile, whereas the men had contested the Olympic Marathon since 1896.

Ron and I had first met Kathrine in person in New York for the Avon press conference a month before the race in London. A fine-boned effusive woman with an outburst of dark hair, beautifully groomed and sleek in her tailored Avon red suit and jangling with several gold bracelets, Kathrine was the consummate PR woman, taking the lead, and tending to ten things at once while making you feel you were special. She talked enthusiastically in big words: great, terrific, and fantastic; and when extra-excited their superlatives: greatest, really terrific and absolutely fantastic. Ron thought she was a bit too flashy, a bit too 'on' in a New York kind of way. Coming from a country that values the modesty of understatement, I was inclined to side with Ron, except that I was in awe of her, admired her, wanted to be confident like her, dress like her, and have her like me. She was the one who dared to do what she loved to do: run a marathon when it was a no-no for women to do so. I had to admire that kind of spirit. I had finally found my role model: athletic, savvy, intrepid and attractive, a trend-setter with no apology for having it all.

1980 Avon International Women's Marathon — London, England

The Knightsbridge Hotel in Kensington London was race head-quarters for the Avon Marathon, and also home to an unfathomably rich Saudi family who lived on the top floor, reputedly paying thousands of pounds per week.

I was waiting for the elevator after my training run. In skimpy shorts and singlet I felt like I was standing in my underwear and was anxious to get up to my room. The elevator arrived, the doors opened. As I went to embark, a wave from behind swept me aside and several Arab men strode aboard with an entourage of veiled women, who dutifully took their place at the back of elevator. I embarked last and stood near the doors, only to be elbowed to the rear. I found myself facing the backs of the imperious men and surrounded by the shrouded women, who hissed at me like mother geese, presumably unhinged at my scandalous state of undress in the presence of their men. I stared at my feet and covered my thighs with my hands. Back in my room, I took a few deep breaths, waking up from that nightmare where you go out confidently in public and then realise you have no pants on. For the first time I appreciated living in a world where women were relatively emancipated.

Race day. I stood on the start and knew that I would win. In my mind marathoning was easy, for under Ron's tutelage I had run 28-milers on Sundays and clocked up 100-mile weeks. He was right. None of the other women had done that kind of work.

Ron was busy whispering all his favourite running adages into my ear: go out easy; seconds given away in the early miles translate to minutes saved in the last few; the marathon is a ten-k race with a 20-mile warm-up; drink water early and often. He was also convinced I would win; after all I had followed the programme as laid out in The All-Purpose Foolproof Godsheet.

I looked across at the other runners and they all looked either porky or puny and worn-out. My arrogant and erroneous perception was of a bunch of has-been distance runners without my track credentials. So I set off to win, obediently following my race instructions.

The day was warm with temperatures that would climb into the high eighties, and muggy too. After my retching, Minneapolis, summer-run disaster I had become wary of the heat and knew the importance of taking water early. As I trotted with the pack past the first drink station, I grabbed for a cup. Slosh! It was spilt before I could get it into my mouth. At the next stop I grabbed for another. The first gulp went up my nose. The second went over my shoulder. Until then I had no idea that drinking while running is an art form which one must practise to master. There was one sip left so I stopped dead in my tracks to down the last precious ounces. The pack didn't wait. I had to hustle to catch them. From then on it was a run composed of three-mile repeats with walk intervals: stopping at each water stand, walking a few paces between sips and sprinting to catch the pack again.

As the race progressed, the pack dwindled. By about 20 miles there was no-one left to sprint off, save the long-legged, red-haired American, Nancy Conz, who had a sizeable lead, having broken away from the pack to make her bid for the win. Mentally I hooked a line into her back and step-by-step reeled her in. *Pass strongly, pass strongly*, I muttered under my breath, knowing that once she conceded a gap to me the race was mine. Next thing I was clearly in the lead and there were just a few miles to go.

The heat and distance were taking their toll and I was feeling nauseated. I looked up at the press truck in front of me, a classic red double-decker bus packed with reporters and photographers gabbing and rubber-necking excitedly like turkeys unwittingly on the way to the slaughterhouse. Kathrine stood out: an elegant centerpiece in her Avon red and white, nodding to me. I took it she was pleased that I was winning and this spurred me on.

Draped across the top of the bus was a banner, heralding the parade that I was leading: *Avon, the beauty of women in motion.* It was starting to bother me. I had the stitch, water was sloshing in my stomach, nausea was overwhelming me, and now I had the added responsibility of representing the elegance and loveliness of all sporting women while a staring camera broadcast my face to the world. I couldn't hold it down any longer and, barely missing a stride, I threw up in the gutter. Rather than hurl, I attempted to place it on the ground as beatifically as possible, but I spewed on my feet and I could feel stomach acid seeping through my socks.

I pressed on. I was weary, my legs began to drag and I was not sure how far I had to go. A horde of cyclists was following the race and one yelled at me that I had a clear lead and there was only a mile left to go.

I turned a corner to see the finish line seething with a sea of reporters and photographers. The bells of St Laurent's were chiming my arrival. "Queen Lorraine!" they announced on the TV. I walked through the tape. I didn't want to collide with any of the mobbing media and besides I was just too tired to run another step.

I had won the Women's World Championship. Ron ran over. He was grinning proudly and stood by my side as Kathrine ushered me to the cameras of NBC and BBC Sports for interviews. *No big deal*, I kept reminding myself, *it is after all only a marathon; only good as training for the track. No-one back home will care.* But secretly I was pleased.

That night I dressed in a violet cocktail dress for the awards. Beaming with a winner's confidence, I held my elbows out in defiance and pushed my way to the front of the Arab cluster, to embark first on the elevator.

Ron insisted that camping was the only way to travel around Britain. His backpack was loaded with his clothing, tent, and lightweight 30-below sleeping bag that he was eager to snuggle into in a cold Scottish campground. I carried my suitcase and his old sleeping bag, which was about 20 years old and made of kapok. My muscles were stiff from the marathon and my bones creaky with broken cells and dehydration. I had thought that Ron might offer his sleeping bag to me, but I was dreaming.

We headed up to Edinburgh on the train. The area was so magical that I did not mind braving the campground or lugging the sleeping bag from town to town along the Welsh border and down the coast back to England.

It was in a campground in Salisbury that I lost it. It had rained during the night and Ron's tent had leaked like the spout of a watering can. My sleeping bag was soaked which doubled its weight and I was miserable from lack of sleep and the chill in my bones. Ron was refreshed and happy after his snuggly sleep in his 30-below, and had no sympathy for me. I dragged the dead sleeping bag along the street, trailing Ron, as we hurried to the bus that would take us to the train station. My shoulder had knotted up along with my temperament.

At the train station we saw our train pulling away. Ron was exasperated and blamed me for lagging. That did it. I dumped the sleeping bag into the nearest rubbish bin.

"Hey, that's mine," Ron protested.

"If you want it then you carry it," I retorted.

Ron was using my pen, my favourite felt-tip as he waited for the train. He launched it like a missile onto the tracks.

"Hey," I yelled, "that was my pen."

"If you want it then you get it."

I started to cry. "It's not fair," I whined.

Suddenly Ron was climbing over the rail towards the tracks.

"Don't, don't, don't!" I yelled, certain a train would flatten him, if he wasn't electrocuted first.

He took another step down.

"I don't care about the pen, please don't!" I pleaded. I ran to the bin and retrieved the sleeping bag.

Ron swung his leg back over the railing onto the platform, and plonked himself back on the wooden bench, with a smug grin on his face. He had won.

A few minutes later the train came whizzing into the station and we embarked. It was such a relief to get out of there.

"Hey, where's the sleeping bag?" He looked around anxiously.

"Oh dear!" I faked a quick look-see. "I must have left it on the seat at the station."

1980 Nike Oregon Track Club Marathon — USA, August

Six weeks after London I ran and won my fourth consecutive marathon, in Eugene, Oregon — the Nike OTC Marathon. While the course was flat, the temperatures soared into the high seventies but I was unfazed. Marathons seemed far easier to me than track races. When people talked about 'the wall' that hits you at 20 miles, I had no idea what they were talking about. A marathon to me was a long run, like any other Sunday run, just a bit faster.

1980 Maratona Atlantica Boavista — Rio De Janeiro, Brazil, December

I wound up the year with my third marathon in less than three months. This was the first ever marathon in Brazil, held in Rio de Janeiro. Both Ron and I were excited at our good fortunes – another free trip in exchange for a fast long run from me.

When we arrived in Rio, Ron was coming down with a cold. Ron had a theory about colds. He would fry it out of his system by wrapping himself up very, very warmly in multiple layers of clothing: tights, pants, sweaters, a coat, three pairs of thick socks and a woolly hat and scarf. It seemed to work but it annoyed me intensely since Ron often felt on the verge of a cold and I hated being crowded out in bed by a sweating mummy.

Now here we were in summer on Copacabana Beach, enjoying the exotic paradise packed with gorgeous bodies bursting out of their thongs, and Ron was wearing a turtleneck sweater, long pants, scarf and a knitted hat with a pom-pom on the top. Every few minutes a boy would run up to him proffering suntan lotion, "You no burn, only one dollar!" Ron took to swatting them away like sandflies. "Why don't they leave me alone?" he whined.

The Maratona Atlantica Boavista, named after its newspaper sponsor, had 1,000 entrants in its first year. All of these were men, save three: me, Sissel Grottenburg, the unfailingly cheerful Norwegian who could drink any guy under the table, and Raymonde Cornou, the statuesque French 50-mile National Women's Champion with the elegant bearing of a snowy egret.

It was evident from my training runs that people here were not accustomed to women running. They stared rudely as I ran along the beachfront. Often a bronzed mesomorph would sprint by for a hundred yards or so, then, satisfied that he had just proved he was faster than I, would stop at a chin-up bar and pump away, showcasing his superior upper body strength, while I kept running on to demonstrate my superior endurance, and to convey that I really didn't care.

The race was held on a Saturday evening ostensibly to beat the heat and the traffic. Traffic is so congested that cars are parked two and three deep. People leave their brakes off and their cars out of gear so that if somebody gets parked in, the offending cars can be rolled aside and they can leave. Since we ran on the road they had traffic control for the first ten miles to get us through a tunnel and out of the city. After that we were running in open traffic, which was suffocating and something of a dodgem gala. I ignored all this as best I could and hunkered down in the middle of the pack, running the race I knew I had to, pacing myself according to the heat and allowing the runners around me to form a safety barrier.

The field took off fast. Too fast. There were so many inexperienced runners, and so many macho men who signed up with great bravado and no idea how far it was. And there was me, one of the few women, pitter-pattering in mid-pack, there for the long haul.

As the race progressed I began to pass runners. A pattern emerged. From his peripheral vision, Mr Machismo would spot the outline of breasts, a modest pair but breasts nevertheless, do a double-take, then sprint. I would catch him about 100 metres on, whereupon he would sprint again. After about the third sprint he was done for and I would not see that particular runner again. This happened so often it kept me amused and time passed quite quickly. When the race statistics showed that only 500 of the 1,000 starters finished, I felt personally responsible for many of those 500, all men, who dropped out.

Steadily I worked my way to the front of the field. Around 20 miles I came upon a horde of cyclists following the leaders — not part of the race but they thought they were, for they went through and depleted the water stops before we runners got there. My mouth was parched and I could feel the roughness of salt on the undersides of my arms as I swung them back and forth, but I trundled on stoically.

After completing a 20-mile-plus loop, we merged with the Saturday-night traffic on the popular frontage road along Ipanema and Copacabana Beaches. My steady pace was interrupted as I ran into a swarm of revving cars pushing up against the red stoplight. As I prepared to slow to a stop, the light suddenly changed green and full-throttle they all raced to the next red light as if it was the finish line of the Indy 500, leaving me spluttering through a cloud of exhaust. Patter, patter, patter, *Here I come, please change light so I don't have to stop*, I prayed. Green. *Thank God.* Vrrroom! Patter, patter, patter. Red. Screech!! Green. Vrrroom! Patter, patter, patter. Red. Screech!! I was caught in a new marathon rhythm: violent and staccato with a hint of samba.

And so it went until I approached the finish line and the course moved onto the pavement. The way ahead was blocked by the thick, cheering crowd which miraculously parted like the Red Sea for Moses. For the last few miles, a swarthy guy rode on his Harley hog, in front of me, joining in the race and waving triumphantly to the cheering onlookers as if he was beating me. As soon as I got close he sped up. The fumes from his shiny chrome tailpipe fed my stream of air intake but I was thankful for the path he created. He drove through the finish line and threw both his arms in the air, in a full-fisted victory. The crowd cheered as an official gestured at him wildly to keep going and not come back.

I crossed the line as first woman and in eighth place behind the invited male runners. A doctor rustled me to the medical room to take my temperature and body weight. He was doing a scientific study on marathon runners and dehydration. I had lost ten pounds in two hours and 39 minutes in 80 plus degree temperatures, and yet I did not feel too bad, just a little thirsty.

Almost precisely an hour later the third woman came in. Ray Cornou commanded a rousing cheer as she blew kisses to the crowd. At six feet tall, with her long blonde hair, full make-up, and snow-white running shorts and singlet with matching gloves, she looked as pristine as when she started. She told me before the race that her gloves served to hold her sugar cubes which she sucked on when she needed energy, whereupon she pulled down her cuff to reveal a little white cube that perfectly complemented her outfit. Rumor had it that she stopped in at the hotel on Copacabana Beach with a few miles to go to freshen up for the finish, with a shower, a clean set of matching clothes, and new make-up.

When the awards were given, Ron stepped up with me on the podium. As my coach and man, he considered my win a shared honour. They put a gold medal around my neck. A little guy stood in the front row of the audience. For an hour he had been watching me and continued to shake his head. His concept of what women were about had just been blown apart and he was still reeling.

But it was Ron who seized the crowd's attention. He grabbed my medal, still attached to my neck, and bit it. I shrank down with embarrassment.

"Why did he do that?" the reporters asked. The race director's wife, an Englishwoman, was quick to cover for him.

"It's an American custom for good luck," she explained in Portuguese.

"Why?" I asked him later.

He shrugged, "It didn't look real, so I was just checking." Then pointing to the silvery teeth marks in the gold metal, he added triumphantly, "It isn't."

CHAPTER 20

Breaking Times and Tissues

The time is always right to do what is right.
— Martin Luther King Jr.

The 1981 Pacific Conference Games — Christchurch, New Zealand

That winter Ron took leave from work and we headed down to New Zealand in what was fast becoming an annual ritual. It made sense to leave the brutal Minnesotan winter in favour of the sun and beaches of my homeland. Besides I could get back to my first love of running, track. I did not run track in the USA. There it was an entirely different sport to road-running that I was not tapped into, whereas in New Zealand, road running, cross country and track all came under the same umbrella of the Amateur Athletic Association.

The five-nation track competition, the Pacific Conference Games, were coming up in Christchurch and I was selected to run the 3,000 metres.

Ron directed me in a gruelling schedule. For a month I ran three sessions a week of hill training from the bottom of the gully at Khyber Pass to the road that went through the Auckland Domain, followed by four weeks of interval work at Mount Smart Stadium. When this was completed, Ron declared that I was ready to take the title.

The fastest woman in the field, an American from Wisconsin named Cindy Bremser, was noted for her withering sprint over the last 200 metres. My race instructions were clear. To beat her I had to make a break with two laps to go. That was far enough out, Ron surmised, that she would not be willing to go with me. With my marathon endurance I could and must get a big enough lead so that she could not catch me in the last 200 metres.

I did exactly that. With 800 metres to go I jumped to the front and ran off, gaining a sizeable lead on my stunned competitor. She was catching me towards the end but my lead was too great for her to bridge and I won convincingly. The element of surprise had won the day for me.

Ron was now known as my coach and a smart one at that. I had re-established myself as a track runner, which augured well for the Commonwealth Games in Brisbane in 18 months' time.

Kathrine called me from the USA. She was breathless on the other end of the line.

"They just voted. The women's marathon is in the Olympics!"

The dam of possibilities had just been cracked open. The Olympics were still three years away and I had been thinking that I would run track. I twirled the possibility of running the marathon around in my mind. Maybe. Of one thing I was certain: that I would be in Los Angeles running in the 1984 Olympic Games.

On my way back into the USA, I was taken by immigration into the little back room and interrogated. I had been spending way too much time in their country on a visitor's visa, they said sternly. They let me on through but I knew I was on their radar. Ron suggested that we get engaged, and marry before my next trip to New Zealand. It was a practical no-nonsense proposition.

We were getting married! I was inwardly triumphant. This was my dream come true.

They say, be careful what you wish for, for the gods may grant it to teach you a lesson. I was in love with my fantasy and although the truth was right in front of me, my delusion prevented me from seeing that I was headed for disaster.

1981 Grandma's Marathon

"Dehydration is the biggest cause of injury," Dr Alex Ratelle explained. He was an anaesthesiologist and a nationally ranked master's runner. "When I see dehydrated tissue on the operating table, it just disintegrates like tissue paper when it's cut." He rubbed his thumb and forefinger together until the imaginary tissue evaporated into the air. We were on a run, training together for Grandma's Marathon. Well matched in pace we had just made a bet as to which of us would be the first to break two hours 30 for the marathon. Alex had bottles of tea stashed at regular intervals on his runs, and was continually dashing into the bushes to retrieve them. After those words I eagerly shared his refreshments.

Allison Deed, now Roe, had won the Boston Marathon a few months earlier in two hours 26, to become one of a handful of women to have run under two and a half hours. I was genuinely thrilled for her. Her win had bolstered my confidence that the goal was within my reach.

Alex and I strode together at Grandma's Marathon, sharing the pace and drawing on each other's strength of focus. When Alex dashed to the drink station for his tea at 20 miles, I thought, *to hell with it, I don't care if my tissues break I'm not stopping for anything*, and ran on. I won again, this time in a new course record of two hours 29 minutes and 29 seconds. I had my under-two-and-a-half-hours credential. Alex ran just over two hours 30, unable to gain back what he had lost at the drink station, and I won the bet.

1981 Cascade Run-Off — Portland, Oregon, USA

One week after Grandma's, Ron and I were off to Portland for the Cascade Run-Off. Although it was generally a no-no to race again so soon after a marathon, we were keen to see Dick, Sue and Allison once again, and we both found it hard to turn down the expenses-paid trips. I knew Anne Garrett (now married and going by her new name, Audain) would be there also, itching to give me a thrashing. Ron said it didn't matter and that I should race easy as I was still recovering. I did not realise that by going there I was running right into the middle of a revolution.

The night before the race we attended a rabble-rousing meeting, where amateurism versus professionalism was passionately debated. There were great inequities in the sport. After two seasons of racing in the US, it had became obvious to me that there was money to be had, but with the amateur rules barring payment to athletes of any kind, and which were strictly enforced by lifetime banishment from competition, its trickle into the athletes' pockets came only by way of an underground channel. This created resentment and suspicion amongst athletes. Rumours abounded at every race, about who was supposedly getting what to run. It became obvious to many runners that somebody else was getting paid handsomely at their expense, and, they suspected, that was somebody they beat. I only had to look to other sports, like tennis, to see that professionalism worked well, and there seemed no good reason why runners should be prevented from earning a living. Clearly it was time for a change.

Nike had given a $60,000 purse as prize money to the runners. Their goal was to recruit enough runners willing to take the money, in the belief that en masse we would have a much better chance of bearing up under the ensuing showdown with our federations and the International Amateur Athletic Federation who ruled the sport. Now we were faced with the decision of laying our amateur status on the line, flouting the rules and signing up to receive the prize money or remaining as we were: unpaid entertainers.

We came out of the meeting all charged up. I believed that we needed to change the system — but at the risk of being banned for life? That was pretty heavy. — Anne Audain was clear. She had her eye on the $10,000 first prize. That was quite an incentive, but I knew that just a week after a marathon, I had little show of winning.

Allison was gung-ho, motivated more by the cause than the cash. "Just think of it, Lorraine," she gushed, "we'll be like the Christians riding off to the crusades!" I didn't quite see it that way; perhaps more like the wives of Henry the Eighth going to the chopping block. But her enthusiasm was infectious, and knowing both that with Anne and Allison I was not alone, and that we were in the company of big names such as Bill Rodgers and Frank Shorter, bolstered me to find the courage of my convictions. I was in.

Anne, Allison and I all declared ourselves racing for cash, and lined up for this landmark race. Anne finished first, collecting ten grand; Allison second, taking five; and me, third for two thousand dollars: a Kiwi sweep. New Zealand should have been proud. As it turned out, Bill Rodgers declined to take the money and Frank declared that he had not really run in the race because he had run on the sidewalk the whole way which earned him the nickname amongst the runners of 'Sidewalk Frank'. While I was miffed that they had led the charge to the starting line but seemingly hid for the battle, I was later grateful for their participation as both were soon to play vital roles in securing professionalism for the sport, and I would personally benefit greatly from the actions of each of them.

The race director, Chuck Galford, had become a friend of mine and had helped me with setting up an investment account for my earnings. Now he suggested he hold this 'hot' money in trust for me until I got a sense of what was coming down. In turn, I suggested that Allison do the same, which she did.

"How does it feel to be a professional?" the Olympic runner-turned-journalist, Kenny Moore, asked in the elevator as we made our way back to our rooms after the race.

"Well," I mused, "it's kind of like losing your virginity. Scary at first but then when it's done you realise, hey, there's a whole new world out there!" Kenny was jotting my words down furiously in his notebook. This became the closing quote for his story on the event, published in *Sports Illustrated* the following month.

When I arrived back in Minneapolis all hell broke loose. The New Zealand media began calling night and day. People were trying to comprehend what we had done.

The New Zealand Amateur Athletic Association (NZAAA) was not proud of our performances. It took no time in revving up the bureaucratic steam roller to crush this revolution. This was the old boys' club who had ruled the sport for eons; the ones who, unchallenged, invalidated our performances for various technicalities like having the wrong numbers of stripes on our shorts. They saw this uprising as nothing short of insurrection, and a menace to be quickly squelched.

An emergency meeting was called in Wellington, the home of the NZAAA. My brother, Gary, got wind of it and hurried along to represent my interests. When he arrived he knew it was going to be bad news. The front rows were taken by old ladies knitting while the guillotine was being sharpened. Even though it was a public meeting, he was asked to leave and the doors were closed in his face. He sat out in the hallway eavesdropping.

The charges against the three women were presented. When it came to my name, the *Sports Illustrated* quote was read out as evidence of my guilt. Not only was I no longer an amateur, I was also no longer a virgin! My brother says at that point he heard a collective gasp from inside the room, along with a few sniggers from the press at the back. Shortly thereafter I was be-legged. The Association banned me for life from amateur competition, along with Allison Roe and Anne Audain. As far as they could help it, our careers were finished and we would never race again.

Fortunately public sentiment was with us. The media had portrayed us as three brave girls crucified for standing against hypocrisy, and much debate ensued.

The situation continued to heat up. The 1982 Commonwealth Games were coming up and New Zealand had just cut the top (or the bottom, depending how you want to look at it) off its women's distance contenders. The general public, the majority of who were avid sports fans, were not pleased. Even the Prime Minister, Robert Muldoon, spoke in our favour.

Back in the USA, away from the ruckus, the ban did not affect me and my legs continued training and racing underneath my torso as they had always done. Ron was proud of me. He hated the system and likened the International Amateur Athletic Federation (IAAF — the parent organisation to each country's respective governing body) to the mafia who promised not to break your legs if you joined them and gave them all your money.

Meanwhile back in New Zealand Allison was in the hot seat, taking the brunt of the Association's outrage and the barrage of media questions. Her case was quickly managed by her attorney whose mission was to save her career. Allison, he said, did not take the money but left it in the care of the race director.

With increasing criticism the Association became anxious to make a popular move, and Allison, still hot off the press with her Boston win and a daily media focus, was the ideal candidate. A deal was struck: on the basis that Allison had not taken possession of the money, she was reinstated. Her $5000 prize money was handed over to the Association for their safe-keeping and shortly thereafter she was awarded a $10,000 Sports Foundation Training Grant. (A grant that Allison says she never received. It was later found that the chairman of the Sports Foundation had been embezzling the funds and was eventually incarcerated for it.)

I felt betrayed. After all the hoopla about our solidarity as crusaders against hypocrisy Allison had seemingly recanted to save her own skin. Our winnings were in the same account. But while I quietly fumed at the perfidy of my friend, I was also hopeful. The Association was relenting and had shown that they had the power and the willingness to reverse their decision.

Meanwhile I ignored my ban and continued to compete in road races around the USA.

1981 The Bobby Crim Ten-Mile Road Race

When I arrived at the Bobby Crim ten-mile race in Flint, Michigan, I was pleased just to be racing. The New Zealand Association had not succeeded in snuffing out my career; indeed, my running activities since the ban were not curtailed in the slightest.

My sense of security was short-lived. The night before the race, the race director told me I was no longer permitted to take part. Three of the top male English runners had complained that there were pro-fessionals in the race and that if they raced against them they would be in danger of being banned by their own federation. It was against the athletic mafia rules to compete against professionals, and doing so made one a professional by association. This was known as the 'Contamination Rule' and had rarely been tested. Now, rather than face a showdown and test the absurdity of this ruling, the English asked that the offenders (me and Domingo Tibaduiza from Colombia) be ousted from competing.

I was astounded, not so much at the race director but at the willingness of these other runners to kowtow to their federation and sacrifice their own kind for their own sakes. I had banked on there being solidarity among runners, and now I was finding there were two groups of runners: individual players, and individual players with a team spirit.

Amongst the Americans was a solid core of the latter. Many of the top names in American road racing had been competitive in the Cascade Run-off and laid their careers on the line. Now they were here at this ten-mile race.

Unlike the NZ Association with its knee-jerk response, the USA Federation had so far failed to censure the outlaws. They had quickly seen that they could not ban a slew of their top road racers without throwing the entire lucrative road racing circuit into jeopardy. So they did nothing while looking for a workable solution.

Late Friday night in Flint, Bill Rodgers, Don Kardong, Jon Sinclair, Herb Lindsay, Greg Meyer, Patti Catalano, Benji Durden and others met in a hotel room to discuss this new development. Those who had taken the money at Cascade were adamant: they would stick by us. But it was Bill Rodgers, one of the biggest draws in American road racing at the time, who clinched it. Criticised for his fence-sitting at the Cascade Run-Off, he now made a bold declaration: if Domingo and I did not race, neither would he. With that, I believe, he tipped the scale to our side. The sport of running had changed its course.

The news they delivered brought tears to my eyes. It was said by the keepers of the old system that running as an individual sport is basically selfish and because of that runners could never organise a revolution. They were banking on it. That evening I knew that to be wrong. These were my people, good people with conscience, and my comrades in the crusade.

The race director capitulated. The race could not go on without Bill. So Bill ran, I ran, and so did Domingo and the American runners. The three Englishmen sat on the sidelines, keeping their rapidly depreciating amateur status untarnished.

I had to laugh. The contamination rule presented an exponential problem. Every time I raced, every other person in the field was theoretically infected, who passed it on in turn to everyone they in turn raced against. By their own rules, professionalism was a socially transmitted virus that was fast causing an epidemic. They could ban us, but without the means to quarantine us, their cause was lost.

Meanwhile, Frank Shorter had been negotiating for a system that would resolve the amateur/professional stand-off between runners and federations. Thanks largely to his efforts, the trust fund system was about to be born. Runners would soon be allowed to receive money for professional services, including prize money, put it into a trust fund and withdraw it for training and living expenses. It would be a face-saver for everyone.

My father wrote congratulating me on my win and offered some advice. "The Prime Minister, Mr Muldoon, approves and admires you," he wrote. "Those little guys who have made big jobs for themselves must be apprehensive as they can see their little systems may collapse. Stick to your guns and keep your aquiline nostrils in the air and sniff disdainfully when questioned about the super God of these times — money."

I ran two more marathons that season. The first was in Rio again for a repeat win in slightly cooler temperatures since they had wisely moved the race to the winter. This time no cyclists took our water and we ran, not in open traffic but on the beachfront footpaths.

In Rio, Ron and I selected a ring. "If you want it, you buy it," Ron declared when it came time to part with the cash. To secure my participation in this event, Ron had negotiated for an equal share of money with me for 'clinic fees'. After years of not collecting his due as an Olympian, author and brilliant coach, he was not about to spend his long-awaited rewards on something as frivolous as a ring. So I bought the ring and preciously hoarded it for my wedding day.

About five weeks later I ran the Nike OTC Marathon in Eugene once again. Marathons were easy and the competition offered by the fast-rising American star, Patti Catalano among others, meant little to me. I ran with the confidence that my victory was a foregone conclusion, and so it was. This time Nike had given a $100,000 dollar purse to consolidate the professional movement. I won my third marathon in ten weeks, and collected $20,000. *The NZAAA can rub their noses in that*, I thought. They could no longer control me. I was my own runner.

Dick Quax had taken a job as coach with the Nike-funded elite running club, Athletics West, and was now living in Eugene, Oregon, with the very pretty, vivacious Sue Jowett, who had represented New Zealand in the sprints at Montreal. I was so happy to be with some Kiwis, a chance to let loose a little, tell some silly jokes, and not have to repeat everything I said to foreigners who could not understand my accent.

My heart missed a beat or two when I saw Ron mashing a brownie into his mouth. He had bypassed the snacks laid out on the kitchen table and gone foraging for goodies in the kitchen. There he had found our secret stash, the ones laced with marijuana. His hand reached for a second one. I knew I was in big trouble.

We were celebrating post-race with a party at Dick and Sue's, Kiwi style: a few snacks and lots of beer for the blokes and wine for the chicks. Sue had enlisted my help to incorporate her herbs into brownies. This was not something I had done before but I threw myself into the project and together we made two lots, one with, which we hid at the back of the kitchen counter, and one without, which was put out on the table with the other snacks. We shared our secret with just a select few: not Dick, who preferred his beer, nor Ron, who was very anti-drugs.

I snatched the second brownie from Ron's hand. "Don't eat that one, have one of these." I grabbed the pan of duds from the table and waved them in front of him. He swiped the brownie back off me, indignantly. "I happen to like these," and he moved back to the counter and took another, just to show me. Then he went back to the sofa to talk more running with Jos.

"Sue, Sue," I whispered, "Ron is making a pig of himself on brownies."

"How many?"

"Three — at least."

Sue laughed and shrugged. *She's right*, I thought, *nothing I can do now. Perhaps it will loosen him up.* My mind flipped between my being damned forever in hell for doing this to him, and that it served him right for making a pig of himself in someone else's kitchen.

We went to watch Ron. The brownies were gone. He was jabbering with Jos Hermans, the Dutch runner and longtime friend of Dick's. Jos was a captive audience, laid up on the couch after leg surgery. I cringed. Ron was such a groupie and I wished he would loosen up and not bore everyone with running talk every waking moment. Ron suddenly stopped talking to survey his half glass of beer, "Wow, what's in this stuff?"

Later, as we lay in bed, I confessed to Ron that the brownies were laced. He was furious, in a much mellower way than usual. "You slipped me drugs! Why did you do that?"

"I didn't. You stuffed them in your mouth without asking first."

"You could have warned me! You deliberately drugged me! I can't believe it!"

I tried to point out to him that it was herbal rather than pharmaceutical, that it would probably have less effect than all the preservatives and food colourings he had been consuming for years, and was akin to the alcohol he drank on occasion. But he was uncheered. In his mind, his drug-free body had been sullied forever more.

After that, for as long as I knew him, whenever he had the entrée, Ron would bring up the time that I drugged him against his will, insinuating to whomever would listen that I was an evil woman.

CHAPTER 21

Wedding Presents

Love is the irresistible desire to be irresistibly desired.
— Robert Frost

OCTOBER 1981

A week before the wedding day I realised that if we were to get married I would have to organise it. While Ron was at work I caught the bus to the shopping mall and bought a wedding dress. Now to the delicate matter of getting Ron appropriately outfitted. If I played it wrong he would show up in some stupid get-up, like his lederhosen or a hippie outfit with one of his Cossack shirts that an old girlfriend had embroidered for him. I decided the best approach would be reverse psychology.

"Ron," I appealed, "everyone expects you to dress down for your wedding. Wouldn't it be such a surprise if you showed up in a suit? Now that would just bowl them over!" He fell for it and that evening we went to the outlet store and bought him a black velvet suit. When we got home he paraded around in it all evening, frequently dashing into the bathroom to check himself in the mirror.

A friend offered up his house to use for the wedding. It was on Lake Powderhorn and we could use it as a base. Ron wanted to get married on the little island in the middle of the lake. His plan was to canoe everyone over there. There was a hall on the shore of the island we could rent for a nominal charge. Now all I needed was a minister to marry us and a band for the after-wedding dance. I found both in the yellow pages. We were all set.

A few days before the wedding, Ron was driving over the bridge at Lake Nokomis in rush hour when a gust of wind lifted the bonnet of his car off. It flew up and landed behind him, whereupon the following three cars ran over it. He salvaged it, but this beaten washboard no longer fit. Ever-resourceful, he got the sledgehammer and did his own panel beating job and then tied it in place with rope. The car now resembled a float of a gnashing alligator, but Ron didn't care: it had a very good engine.

While Ron was doing business with the sledgehammer I got a phone call from Tessa. She did not want to talk to Ron, but to me.

"Congratulations. I am leaving to live in California. You may have won the battle," she hissed, "but you have lost the war. Ron is no prize. I'm not the only one he's had while you've been here. Ask him about Suzanne and Patty and …" she reeled off a list. I suspected these names were thorns in her side before me. I took careful note and ran outside to tell Ron. "Sour grapes," he replied. "Ignore her." I could understand her grumblings. She had lost and I had won. I pushed it out of my mind. There were more important things to think about.

Dick and Sue arrived from Eugene for the wedding: Dick to give me away and Sue to be my bridesmaid. My dad did not come. He was too busy, which meant my wedding was low on his priority list. My mother, on the other hand, braved the 30-hour trip from New Zealand, pleased to see me finally marry this classy American.

On the morning of the wedding it was pelting with hard, driving rain. Sue and I went early to the house to prepare, leaving Dick and Ron to make their own way. Halfway there, Ron's car broke down. Dick, not stupid enough to wear his suit to sit in that rust box, was dressed in the only thing he could find: a pair of Sue's yellow sweat pants that came to mid-calf, his pristine white shirt and dress shoes. Ron was in his groomly attire and needed to stay dry. And so it was that Dick pushed Ron to his wedding. Later, Ron would say his car was trying to save him from my clutches.

When they arrived — late — Sue and I were upstairs in the house waiting for the call to make our entrance. Ron stationed himself over at the hall, as instructed.

Dick knocked at our door.

"Ron says you can still get married on the island."

I yelled through the keyhole. "Tell Ron it's too wet, we're getting married in the house."

Dick ran off. Five minutes later, he was back.

"Ron still wants to get married on the island."

I looked out the window; waves were lashing on the island's shores, the trees bowing to howling winds. "Tell Ron we are getting married in the house. Everyone is waiting, tell him to hurry up." I was getting exasperated.

Dick ran off again. A third time he arrived at the door.

"Ron says it's okay to get married on the island."

"Tell Ron we get married in the house or not at all."

Dick ran off and reappeared again. "Ron is downstairs and we are ready to go."

It turned out the minister, Reverend McLean, was a minister of Satsang yoga. He had a long ponytail and a beard to match and turned up with his guitar in hand. Our friends and family were all waiting expectantly. He struck up a chord, and we all launched into 'Michael Row the Boat Ashore'. I guess he had expected us to be getting married on the island and had not had time to change his repertoire. Our vows were said, and friends read excerpts from *The Prophet*, a few poems about love, and then we all sang 'Kumbaya'. As our families and friends thronged towards us to offer their congratulations, Ron's mother cornered her newlywed son, with her sister backing her up. She spoke confidentially and earnestly — and somewhat too loudly because she was deaf. "Ronnie, are you sure this is legal?"

We then sprinted through the pelting rain across the road to the hall. It was thundering down and at times drowned out the piano accordion in the dance band that looked and sounded like they were performing at an evening out at the old folks' home. They had been inexpensive and available at late notice. Now I knew why, but I didn't care. I was finally married.

As a present to myself I bought a car. I no longer wanted to ride in Ron's monstrosity. During the course of the year his car had been hit by all sides, making it a most peculiar shape. The back seat had popped up on a diagonal and moss was growing on the floor. And then of course there was the bonnet. Ron was pulled up by a cop for running a stop sign. "I didn't see it," was his excuse. The policeman walked around Ron's car. "There is more metal in that sign than in your car!" he said, whereupon he wrote Ron a ticket.

My car was, by contrast, intact. It was a canary yellow VW runabout, not only cute but in full working order. It cost me $3,000. Ron liked it too and pretty soon he was driving it in preference to his own.

I felt a little more secure now that we were married. One night I lay on the bed naked, waiting for Ron. He walked in, took one look at me and screwed up his face. "You make me sick." Then he walked out.

My innards shrivelled. I berated myself for being so stupid as to expect it to be any different. I was still ugly – and lucky to have him. Just three weeks into our marriage, it dawned on me that it was my running he had married. I should be grateful because now I could stay in the USA and run.

Within weeks I filed for a green card. We were interviewed by INS. All went well, as they asked us sundry questions about our life and love for each other and whether or not I had communist affiliations or had solicited sex for money. We were almost done when Ron leaned forward to the guy and said, "You forgot to ask about cannibalism." I laughed through gritted teeth and punched Ron a little harder than playfully on the arm. The agent looked blank, then coughed and said, "I think that is all we need for now, Mr and Mrs Daws."

CHAPTER 22

Rough Crossings

Pay heed to the word of your mother
as though it were the word of a God.
— Anonymous, 3000 BC Mesopotamia

DECEMBER 1981, NEW ZEALAND

My new husband was sulky. Ron hated being in New Zealand. He was especially disgruntled because they did not serve ketchup or pickles at hamburger bars or in fish and chip shops. Such cultural oversights ruined his meal. As far as he was concerned the whole country was just too 'goddam backward'. He talked constantly about how he felt like 'a nobody' and didn't like getting around on my shirt-tails. When anyone asked him about my running he would launch into mile-by-mile detail of his own training, followed with a litany of sad excuses for why he was not a world-beater.

Dad wanted to have a 'little talk' with me. Sigh. This time he did not mince any words. "The way Ron carries on about his running is embarrassing and you should talk to him about it. And don't walk behind him like an obedient Japanese wife," he barked. "Hold your head up and be proud. This is your show, not his!"

"But he coaches me," I whimpered back.

"To hell with the coaching! You do it, not him! Any idiot could coach you! He struts around like an imperious bastard. Tell him to lay off. He looks silly."

I dared not say a word to Ron. I figured if I could just run faster,

164

he would feel more successful by association and not have to seek attention.

Ron rallied temporarily for our meeting in Wellington with the New Zealand Association. The professionalism affair had become an embarrassment to them and now they were willing to patch things up and give me the same sort of deal given to Allison. My brother Gary had brought to their attention that my money had technically stayed in trust also. It appeared that Anne, who had taken the money outright, would remain the sacrificial lamb.

With the collaboration of Frank Shorter and his associates, the American Federation had established a runner's trust fund with the approval of the IAAF. Runners could now deposit their winnings and withdraw training expenses from this account, thus were able to collect money from races while retaining their amateur status. This would be the blueprint for federations across the world. If I agreed to partake of the trust fund and deposit my winnings from the Cascade Run-Off into it, my amateur status could be reinstated in time for the Commonwealth Games.

I didn't see why we could not earn money and spend it as we pleased, without an intermediary, but, as Ron pointed out, this was a halfway house on the road to athletes' autonomy, and a face-saving device for the losing side. I accepted on condition that the same offer be extended to Anne. After the example of solidarity shown to me by the Americans, I felt compelled to act in kind, even to Anne. The Association conceded. Shortly thereafter I was reinstated and not long after that Anne had a similar meeting with a similar outcome.

Ron and I were happy when we headed back to Auckland for the New Year and for races to prepare for the National Champs in early March, the results of which would weigh heavily for Commonwealth Games team selection. But as with many athletes, Ron's humour was only as good as his last race.

One evening there was a veterans' track meet at Mount Smart Stadium and Ron decided to enter the 5,000 metres. As he belted out his warm-up, stretched, and did strides on the track, I already knew that this was not going to be good. He was way too tense and I was glad my dad was not there to witness what was about to happen.

When the gun went off, Ron launched himself like a wind-up toy cranked to capacity and rapidly wound down, slower and slower with every lap. As the other runners passed him one by one, I could see that same strained look on his face as when I had first saw him — the Sneetchy look.

I sat with my friends in the stands and loyally cheered him on with each painful lap. When he finished Ron wandered over to collect his training shoes. His eyes were downcast and he did not look up as I handed them over.

"Good run," I lied.

"Like hell. It was pathetic." He was chiding not only himself but also me for my dishonesty.

"Well, it wasn't as bad as you think. You did fine, now forget it, it's only a race. Come on, we're all going to the ice-cream parlour."

"I don't deserve ice-cream," he glowered and he set out to run the four miles of penance back to our house.

A group of us sat in the ice-cream parlour slurping our sundaes and along trudged my husband. We waved cheerily, but he didn't look up. He was hypnotised by the ground two feet ahead of him, legs turning wearily, his face a glazed mask. His shoulders heaved from side to side and his fists jabbed the air in front of him. As he lurched off into the night it dawned on me that the ice-cream parlour window had separated us into parallel realities. He faded from my view like a character on a television show that had just finished its season. *I don't even know who this person is*, I thought to myself.

In the Auckland Domain, Ron introduced me to Clint: a fellow American, tall, blond, blue-eyed and very, very, good-looking. I was always suspicious of beautiful people. I assumed they would love themselves to excess and only be interested in other beautiful people. Clint told me later he thought I was snotty to him. But I was busy training and didn't want to be bothered with any beautiful person looking for admiration from the lesser-looking. Clint was on sabbatical from his job, and an avid runner. He had read Ron's book, *The Self-Made Olympian*, and was thrilled to have met him by chance, that day. Ron was flattered. They arranged to meet the next day.

The three of us began hanging out together, going to races, running and sharing meals. They timed me for workouts and cheered me on at the track. My build-up of 100-mile weeks has been completed, and in this phase of my training approaching competition, my workouts were shorter but more intense.

Clint came back to Putaruru with us for a weekend and met my parents and even went running in the Pinedale Forest with my dad. As perverse and morose as Ron was, Clint was cheerful and positive. Ron seemed happier around him and so was I. And so we invited Clint to take the three-day drive with us to the National Championships in Christchurch in a few weeks' time.

One night after a track meeting we were invited to a hot tub party. It was still early and Ron got up and grabbed his jacket.

"Where are you going? I asked.

"I'm tired. I'm going home."

"Oh don't, why do we have to go so soon?" I pleaded.

"No, not you, just me, I can walk home, I need to rest for my long run in the morning. You stay, with Clint. He can bring you home." And he turned and walked off.

I was stunned. I could feel the anchor of disappointment sinking to the bottom of my belly. We never went to bed this early, and besides, I was the one training — where was his concern for my sleep? But the overwhelming perplexity to me was that my new husband just abandoned me to another man. I knew it: Ron was having second thoughts about being married to me.

I hung around at the party for another hour, jollying myself along with the company. I sat near the hot tub, talking to Clint. He was witty and attentive and I enjoyed talking to him. Suddenly he leaned over and kissed me: a full slurpy kiss on the mouth. I was astonished. I didn't know what to do so I did nothing except cross my fingers that no-one had seen us. I had not thought of him in this way and the implications were too mind-boggling. Clint told me later that my gaze was lingering and he had taken that as an invitation. When he walked me home I iterated to him that I was married and that we had to forget that this had ever happened.

But it had happened. One kiss and my destiny was changed.

Clint offered to opt out of the South Island trip. He thought it might be awkward. I put it to Ron, failing of course to mention that I had locked lips with the guy. I told him that Clint was concerned that 'two's company, three's a crowd'.

"Nonsense," said Ron, "tell him I want him to come."

We pooled our money for the trip in the ashtray of my old Vauxhall Viva and set off on a journey that became more perilous as we descended further south.

Our first stop was my home town. Dad was rankled to see Clint with us. He did not think it was right. "Trouble," he muttered. I ignored him.

Every morning we went for an easy run. It was our standard routine, one that we could all do together and I did not mind sacrificing my pace for the company. I did my harder, more specialised training, on my own in the early evening. Ron started to find excuses not to run with Clint and me. Early into the run he would stop to tie his shoelace, or nip off to the bathroom and leave us to run alone. Once near the end of our run we spotted him hiding behind the bushes, watching us. It was disturbing.

When we arrived in Wellington to stay with my brother, things were strained. Ron was silent and moody but would not 'fess up to what was bothering him so I gave up asking. Meantime Clint was pleasantly engaging, and I have to admit, flirtatious.

The three of us started out on a morning run. Ron slowed down. I slowed down, Clint slowed down. Ron slowed down some more.

"What's wrong?" I asked.

"I just want to run slow. Go on ahead."

"No, I'll slow down with you."

Ron went even slower, ridiculously slow so that he was running with pin steps. My patience wore out and I ran on, Clint in tow, leaving Ron to inch his way along. Clint and I finished the run and went about the day.

I was in the kitchen reading the newspaper and Clint was washing up the dishes when suddenly Ron dashed furtively by the window.

"Did you see that?" Clint asked. "Ron is spying on us."

"This is ridiculous," I declared, and went to find him.

Ron slipped in the back door and went and showered. I cornered him in the bedroom.

"Ron," I asked, "what is going on? Why are you spying on us?"

"I wasn't."

"Oh come on, we saw you."

Ron averted his gaze. He did not want to talk about it.

"Is it Clint? He says he is quite happy to cut loose and travel on his own. Would that make you feel better?"

Ron turned front-on for an attack. "And what do you want, eh? Do you want to sleep with him?!"

I was stumped. I went to say, 'Of course not', but the truth was that that one kiss had ignited something in me and I was finding him very attractive in a way that made absolutely no sense. The idea of kissing him again was consuming me and I was beginning to understand what my Auntie Christine had meant some ten years ago when she said, 'Love makes you ache inside and causes you to do crazy things.' As I weighed up the right answer against the true answer Ron threw up his arms.

"Your hesitation is a good enough answer for me," he said and he stormed off. He was back in a few minutes with his bag and began to throw things into it furiously.

"Ron, Ron," I pleaded, "Let's talk about this."

"There is nothing to talk about!" He stomped out with clothes trailing from his bag.

I sat on the bed and cried. I could hear the car screeching away.

Clint came in. "What was that all about?" he asked.

"Ron asked me if I wanted to sleep with you."

"Oh ... and what did you say?"

"Nothing."

"Hmm ... well ... he rushed in while I was eating breakfast. He said, 'I have some bad news and some good news. The bad news is I am taking the car. The good news is I am leaving you with my wife.' And then he took off. So do you?"

"What?"

"Want to sleep with me?"

I paused again. I had already been caught out once on this question. "Yes," I blushed, "... but I'm not going to."

Clint arranged to go his own way. The ferry left for the South Island in the morning.

When my brother and sister-in-law arrived home for the evening, the situation quickly became a family affair. Their consensus was that I would reconcile with Ron as soon as I could figure out where he had gone.

It did not take long to track him down. My brother got a phone call from Dad. Ron had driven directly to my parents' place and had burst into their house crying, "My wife ran off with that guy!" My brother talked to my father then my mother, all the time giving me a look that said, 'You're in deep doo-doo.' Finally I got to talk to my father.

"What the hell's going on?" he demanded.

"I didn't do anything."

"What's going on with this Clint guy?"

"Nothing."

"I knew he was trouble."

"Nothing's going on!" I emphasised.

"I'm taking Ron up to the beach to settle down for a few days. He says he's leaving for America next week. That will give you time to get back here and sort it out with him. Just behave yourself. Now I'll put you onto Mum."

"Mum here, what's going on?"

"Nothing." Pause. "Honestly nothing. It's all in Ron's head."

"Well, he's very upset. Now listen, what are you going to do now?"

"I'll get a bus back and go back home with Ron next week."

"And what about the Nationals?"

"Guess I'll just have to miss them."

"Why?"

"Because Ron's leaving. I'll have to go back with him."

"Forget Ron. He'll get over it. Go run your race."

So it was with my mother's blessing that I left Ron to stew in his own juices for a week and made plans to catch a plane to Christchurch to run the National Championships.

Next morning Clint and I caught a taxi, first stop the inter-island ferry for Clint, and second stop the airport for my flight. As the taxi was nearing the wharf I was thinking, *It would be so much fun to travel with Clint. Ron has been such a poop-head, I deserve to have some fun. Besides I have been judged for a crime that I have not yet had the pleasure of committing.*

A sign on the pier said, "Crossing Conditions today: Very Rough". It was a warning, interrupting my dangerous train of thought. I knew that if I did this I risked every ounce of decency I owned and if found out I would be branded a harlot in the eyes of my husband, my family and probably all of New Zealand. I would be outcast, condemned, and possibly stoned to death. I knew without a doubt what I must do.

CHAPTER 23

Roller Coaster

I generally avoid temptation unless I can't resist it.
— Mae West

MARCH 1982

I first committed adultery in a cheap motel in Blenheim. It was also the first time I had ever felt beautiful with my clothes off. I was so grateful for the attention that I almost mistook it for love. By the time Clint and I reached Christchurch, I had colour in my cheeks for perhaps the first time.

Furtively we checked into a motel room in Christchurch, making sure to enter separately. We had just started unpacking our bags when we heard a familiar loud voice outside the room. I peeked through the curtains. Arthur Lydiard was moving his gear into the room next door. With as much stealth as possible we moved motels.

I ran well and qualified for the Commonwealth Games in both my events, the 1,500 metres and the 3,000 metres.

When people asked me where Ron was, I told them that he had preferred to go to the beach.

"You slept with him didn't you?" It was Ron's first question when I met up with him in Auckland. He had not flown back to the USA as he had threatened to do, so I figured there was still hope for us working it out. Clint and I had parted ways with no plans to meet again. It had been unspoken that this was a romantic interlude and now I must get back to my real life. But facing Ron, I was nervous. He looked me up and down, searching for emanations of Clint in my aura. He knew all right and I knew he knew. But I could not bring myself to own up. Ron was explosive and an affirmative answer would have been an invitation for him to blow.

Besides, I always thought 'sleeping with someone' was a silly expression to describe having sex. We had hardly slept at all. So when I said "no" I almost felt like I was telling the truth on the grounds of a technicality.

We struggled through the next days. He badgered me for details of my affair. I was not complying. Ron was terrified. He hated to fail and now he had made a big mistake, the biggest mistake of his life, he said. He blamed me and considered that I had wronged him terribly after he had made the tremendous commitment of marrying once again.

"You have a double standard! You've been having an affair with Tessa the whole time you've been with me!"

"Where'd you get that from? You're just making stuff up."

"No, I'm not. I read all her letters."

"Bullshit!!"

"Yes, I did, they were under a box in your office drawer. I read them all."

"You had no right to go through my stuff."

"You had no right to lie to me."

"But that all happened before we were married. I gave her up when I married you."

"You might have given her up, but you never came clean with me! Don't you think I am important enough to be honest with?" I cried.

"Apparently not," he retorted. "You have just proven yourself to be untrustworthy!"

"I'll never talk to you again if you do anything funny," I threatened. The Nike Roller Coaster was a ten-kilometre race held the following weekend along the coastal road on Auckland's North Shore, named because of the pitching and rolling terrain. I knew there was a good chance that Clint would be there, and Ron was threatening to kill him if he saw him. As we were leaving the house I paused at the door. I had a sense of foreboding. For the third time I made Ron swear that he would not pull any stunts, otherwise I would not go.

"For chrissake I said I wouldn't! Whadda ya want me to do? Cross my heart and hope to die?"

I nodded.

"Listen goddammit, I won't do anything!!"

So off we went. I should have known better.

My heart sank. Anne Audain was at the start. I just could not face another battle. She sidled up to me with a warm smile. She was quite endearing when she wanted to be. "This is just a training run for me," she confided.

"Me too."

"Then how about we run together, save ourselves?"

"Sounds good."

I welcomed the collaboration with her and was relieved for the licence not to race. We ran side by side, finishing first equal in a few seconds over 33 minutes on this treacherous course. For all the emotional upheaval, I was surprised at how easy it felt.

The finish was at a big grassy park in Brown's Bay near the ocean, where the runners gathered for the after-race festivities. This was no rinky-dink affair; the stage was dotted with dignitaries and celebrities, and there was a crowd of a thousand or more. As the awards got underway Ron and I stood waiting. I was happy. My race had gone well and I mistakenly thought that perhaps the tide had changed and that everything would work out fine after all.

I was being called to accept my award and was about to step up to the stage when Ron pulled on my arm from behind. I swung around. His eyes were blazing with the hell-bent focus of a Messiah about to lead his people into the apocalypse. "I've just seen that bastard you've been fucking!" His whole body was quivering and he was not whispering confidentially, he was exploding in my face with all the force he could muster. He wanted the whole world to hear of my transgression against him.

With that, he stormed off into the sea of faces. I wanted to run after him to avert a murder but in a flash he was gone. All eyes were on me and I was temporarily paralysed, like a deer in the headlights. From the stage I felt like I was watching a bad movie. Ron charted a beeline through the sea of bodies to Clint who was standing with others watching the awards. He did not hesitate; he announced himself to Clint with a shove from the side and stood there snorting with his fisty-cuffs raised. My heart was pounding. I knew that shortly I would have to renounce my New Zealand citizenship. Then as quickly as it had flared up, the fracas defused. Clint turned and walked away, leaving Ron posturing to thin air. I was filled with relief — and gratitude. Clint was a lover, not a fighter. I shook hands with the mayor, accepted my award and waved numbly to the crowd. Underneath, my whole body was shaking.

Ron arrived back still snorting like a bull.

"I would've killed the guy! What a coward!" He was punching at the air as he spoke.

I could not speak back to him, I was so livid. I wanted to kill him. *How could he have done that, how could he, how could he?*

My running went flat after that. Anne Audain set the world record for the 5,000 metres a few days later. John Davies had asked me to pace her, which I did early on but any hope I had of stealing her show dissipated after the first few miles, and I finished it out as a shadow trailing the spotlight. Ron berated me on the finish line for not keeping up. I had embarrassed him. He ranted like I was a little kid, extra loudly so that others could hear: if I had just listened to him and done what he said I would have run better. I didn't care. I felt beaten down, and defeated. I knew in my heart of hearts that our marriage was over. Ron had crossed a line that could not be uncrossed.

But I stayed with him. I felt responsible for his pain.

CHAPTER 24

Beyond Repair

A man must be able to cut a knot, for everything cannot be untied.
— Henri Frederic Amiel

1982 London Marathon — England

"Goodnight," I whispered timidly.

"Goodnight whore."

I lay there silently. It was late on the eve of the London Marathon. Avon had provided the blueprint for this new event and the organisers wanted me, the reigning champion and undefeated in my eight marathon starts, to race. For the first time I was being paid an appearance fee: £8,000, plus expenses for me and Ron and Ron's best friend, Phil. We were all to run the marathon and then Ron and Phil planned to stay on to sightsee afterward. I was emotionally exhausted and physically flat. I wanted out but I was the boys' ticket for a British holiday and Ron was hell-bent on extracting his dues from me.

"So how many times did you say you fucked the guy?"

"I didn't."

Suddenly Ron was on his feet, prowling around the bed like a tiger at mealtime.

"How does it feel to be a whore? Was it good, huh? How many have there been, then? You've been fucking around all this time, haven't you?" His questions were falling off his lips in a fury. He wanted full disclosure after which, I was certain, he would tear my flesh off with his teeth.

176

"Ron, this is pointless. I need my sleep, so do you. Please get into bed. We have to be up early."

"You lie in bed thinking about him, don't you? Fucking whore! I can't believe I could have been so stupid."

I lay there with my eyes closed and my jaw clenched shut until he finally gave in to my silence. I barely slept.

Early on the race morning, we were escorted to the start line at Greenwich Park. Ron, playing the coach, barked the usual litany of race instructions. I didn't want to hear it and let him parrot on, my mind and body turned off, tears just around the corner.

When the gun went off I was all action and no heart, like the tin man, tagging onto the back of my main competition, the British runner Joyce Smith. Joyce was a versatile runner with considerable talent. In her early forties she had turned her sights to the marathon and won this race a year ago breaking two hours 30. Such a fast time didn't faze me. In our one race against each other in the Avon Marathon, I had won. (I failed to consider that she had chicken-pox at the time.) But by halfway, Joyce was clearly pulling away and I was struggling. My string of wins was about to be broken and it was all Ron's fault. Tears were choking me and I was reduced to a walk.

I stopped. Joyce quickly disappeared out of sight. My mind wrestled: *Should I bale out or get back in?* The Child of Instinct wanted to crouch and hide. Miss Rational couldn't stand such displays of cowardice. *Don't even think about quitting. Pull yourself together. You still have a chance to get second.* She could be stern, and I felt obliged to start running again. I plugged on resignedly, just so I did not look like a poor sport.

With eight miles to go, Ron raced past me. I was walking again. He flew on by without a word. *How can you do that?* I wanted to yell, but he was gone. Heaving sobs grabbed my chest, overwhelming me like a sudden wave on a silent shore. I stopped and bent into the pavement, pretending to tie my laces. Suddenly an undertow of rage welled up inside me. I started to jog, then run. Fuelled now with a grudge, I decided to chase Ron down. Already he was out of sight.

I pressed on, mile after mile. Harder and harder I ran. I desperately wanted to pass him the way he had passed me, without acknowledgment. I had to show him I couldn't be beaten. There was only a mile left when I finally caught a glimpse of his swaying form up ahead. The gap was closing. Then there was just 100 metres to go, a kiddie-sprint, and I was Little Lorraine once more, hurtling down the grass track at Glenshea Park. Without looking back, Ron sprinted too; a mad, furious, head-waggling, body-lurching thrust for the line. He crossed it just ahead of me and then turned to confirm that it was really me he had successfully fended off. I burst into tears. Confidentially he leant into my ear, I thought to comfort me, and I moved towards him so that we were almost hugging.

"You always get upset when I beat you," he sneered.

The next day Ron and Phil helped me with my bags to catch a cab. I was leaving to go back to Minneapolis. They planned to stay on, camping of course. I had £8,000 stuffed in my back pocket and Ron wanted his cut. I counted out £1,200 and held it out.

"What's this?" His face was crestfallen.

"Agent's fee. Fifteen per cent."

Ron shook his head. "Aw, come on, I got you that money. I deserve half."

"But I ran the damn race!"

"Well, so did I."

"Yeah, but they didn't pay for *you* to run. That's all you're getting. I gotta go." He took it and stood watching as the cab pulled away. *Take a good look*, I thought. *This is the last you'll ever see of me.* Already I knew where I was going.

Walking back into Clint's arms was luxurious. He had finished his stay in New Zealand and had returned to his Westwood apartment in Los Angeles.

For two weeks we played together. It was the life of Bacchus: fine restaurants, wine, and languid nights making love. At first I felt sophisticated and sensual but soon I was tiring of it; my senses were satiated:

the restaurants served too much food, the wine was too acidic, the air was too smoggy and the bedroom a little too claustrophobic. I wasn't doing anything useful. I missed the freshness and trails of the Twin Cities. What's more, I knew Ron had returned home and did not know where I was. I have to admit, I felt very, very guilty. I could not just walk away. So I went back.

I lied to Ron about where I'd been and steadfastly refused to elaborate. Nor was I interested in hearing about his trip. There was nothing to say to each other. We lived in silence, barely tolerating each other's presence and going through the motions of daily living like two zombies.

1982 Avon International Women's Marathon — San Francisco, USA

Still we ran together. The Avon International Women's Marathon was coming up again and I was the defending champion. This time it was held in San Francisco. Kathrine had succeeded in securing the Golden Gate Bridge for the start, the first time in history that this icon of architecture had lanes closed for an event. Sporting women were making inroads into the institutions and largely because of the drive of this one remarkable Switzer woman.

It was less than two months since London and I was tired, but I needed to redeem my first marathon loss. It was pride that ran that day, over the bridge, out and back along Fisherman's Wharf, and then up the hills, around Lake Merced and back to the finish in a small stadium in Golden Gate Park. For me it was formula running. Hold back early, take the lead at about 20 miles, and win.

I ran into the stadium, a clear leader. There was a crowd gathered around the track, watching expectedly. An impulse grabbed me and I did something that I would have been jeered at for in New Zealand. *What the hell*, I thought, *this is America*. I waved. They cheered. A surge of power went through me. Wow!! I waved again, and again the crowd cheered. *What a trip! I am commanding all these people.* So I waved once more and again the cheer went up. I was getting addicted, but I thought better of pushing my luck and finished the last few metres with what modicum of Kiwi dignity I still owned.

Ron disappeared some time during the awards. When it was over I walked in ever-increasing circles around the parking lot looking for him. Then I spied him through the trees, deep in conversation with a dark-haired woman. An intimate tête-à-tête. I recognised the woman. It was Tessa.

I did not mention it. I no longer trusted him enough to fight with him. Besides, I could see nothing left worth fighting for.

Back at the house the atmosphere was so toxic all our houseplants died. For my twenty-fifth birthday, Ron and Phil had conspired to give me a book of cut-out nose disguises. They thought it was funny. I was sad. A cocktail of anger, guilt and worry was eating me up inside and I fretted that I would get cancer. I took to checking my temples in the bathroom mirror, searching for grey hairs, and every day it seemed that I found more. I was sure that they were losing colour in compliance with my seeking but I could not stop myself.

Shopping became my therapy. While Ron was at work I went to the mall and bought myself beautiful and expensive clothes, eschewing polyester and nylon in favour of silk and fine linens. I imagined I was Kathrine Switzer shopping on Madison Avenue. My new rule was that if I wanted something and had the money, I would buy it. When I spent $80 on a designer blouse I was thrilled with my daring. I left it lying out on the bed so that Ron could see the price tag. I knew that would drive the cheapskate nuts.

One day we drove to the post office. I did not want to go inside, preferring to sit wistfully with my own thoughts. Ron did his errands and returned to the car. A woman emerged from the post office soon after. There was something in her aura that transfixed us both. Perhaps it was her tall, svelte figure, shown off by a cotton dress belted at the waist, which exuded an Audrey Hepburn confidence and femininity, or her cascade of wavy blonde hair that bobbed with the swing of her skirt as she walked, or a freshness and joy in her step in contrast to our gloominess. We were hypnotised as she approached her car. She looked at Ron and flashed a bright smile. I felt him draw her cheerfulness into himself and his being lift. "There," I said, "That is the woman you should be with." Ron blushed. He was caught in the act of a venal sin, and yet I was not judging him. I meant it.

The next day, a strange thing happened. Ron was at work. I was on the bed reading my Seth book, *The Nature of Personal Reality*, learning how we all create our own experience though our belief systems, when outside it began to hail. I could hear the stones pattering on the roof, then it seemed they were getting bigger: the thumping grew deafening. I fell asleep. When I awoke the room was full of stones: smooth round grey ones like from the bed of a fast-flowing creek. The weight of them had collapsed the roof and I could see sky through the hole. But I was trapped. There was no way out but to crawl on my belly, wending my way through the debris of roof and stones. I could not find the phone and made my way out the front door. The neighbour's house was untouched. Perhaps I could call Ron from their phone and let him know of the damage. Then I woke up.

I should have known that things were too far gone, that the marriage crucible had collapsed beyond the point of repair and that I should just quit. But I didn't and I had no counsel.

What if I get ripped off? What if she is a fake? What if she isn't and tells me something I don't want to know? All this went through my mind as I pressed the stop buzzer on the bus. I had seen the sign 'Psychic Readings' from the bus window many times but had been too afraid to stop, until now. I was desperate. Next thing I was sitting in the parlour of a cute little house, across a table from a motherly woman named Carol. With a tarot deck in her hand, she turned the cards. "It is over," she said. "Every door that was open, he has slammed shut. There is nowhere to go now but apart." She looked at my downcast face, put the cards aside and took my hands. "Listen," she said, "if you want an honest marriage then you must be honest. He then has the opportunity to rise to that level of honesty. Whether or not he does is hardly the point. You will be on your way towards what you are looking for."

It was the most sense anyone had spoken to me.

I went home and declared to Ron that I was willing to come clean and tell him whatever he wanted to know. It was a sordid cross-examination and I was on the witness stand with my hand on the Bible. At the end of his questioning, Ron pronounced his verdict, "Guilty!" Without another word he strode to the bedroom to scoop up armloads of my belongings and throw them on the street.

I pleaded with him to stop.

"At least give me the keys to my car and let me get some boxes for my stuff."

"No." He held the keys behind his back, "It's my car now. You owe me."

I left to stay with my one girlfriend in the area. Alex was an artist who loved to run. She lived with her husband of ten years who was a plastic surgeon. When I confessed to Alex that I thought the ultimate source of all my problems was my big nose, she organised with her husband's colleague to get me a nose job. He was willing to do it tomorrow and at a cut rate. *Do all surgeons have cut rates?* I wondered.

The surgeon asked me to look through a pile of magazines and find a picture of the sort of nose I wanted. I found one, an Italian model with a biggish nose but not too big — handsome, one might call it. I showed it to the surgeon. "I don't know what you want me to do then," he said, "your nose is just like that."

I was embarrassed. "Like that but a little smaller, then."

Within a few days of leaving Ron I was in surgery.

I had opted for a local anaesthetic since I could not stand the thought of being anaesthetised and I loathed hospitals. This way I would be treated as an outpatient and would remain conscious. Should the worst happen, I could always run away, or so I reasoned.

Waiting for my turn, I began to have second thoughts. I didn't want people to think I was vain, and I was terrified about getting a little pug nose. Holding my thumb and index finger just a few millimetres apart, I reminded the surgeon once again to take just a little bit off.

When the nurse administered the intravenous valium, my fears dissipated. It was like a cloud of plush velvet that I sunk into from the inside-out, nerves first laid down to rest after a lifetime of slavery, and the other tissues following their cue. Such luxury. "Do anything you like," I heard myself saying dreamily.

The surgeon went about his business with files and saws and hammer and chisels; a regular little road-works on the centre of my face. I was having a mighty good time somewhere between reality and fairyland while he chipped and snipped away. I felt two hands cradling my head. Then, wham! My nose was hit so hard with a hammer that I felt my head snap. Nah, didn't hurt.

Once home, the valium wore off and my head swelled. My nose was stuffed with wads of cotton and caked in dried blood. I had to breathe through my mouth and my head was throbbing. *What on earth have I done to myself!* I cried. But underneath the pain I was pleased. I wanted a new start and I wanted to be beautiful with it and if this temporary inconvenience was all it took I was willing to suffer through it.

Ron was distraught and lonely, and Alex, feeling sorry for him over the phone, invited him for dinner. Since my arrival at their house, Alex and her husband had announced that they too were divorcing.

When Ron arrived and we all sat down to dinner, it was a sombre occasion, I with my silly nose cast on and two black eyes, and we two splitting couples doing our best to maintain our manners. We sat quietly as Alex served the first course. Barbara Streisand was warbling in the background, *"Mem'ries ... like the corners of my mind ..."* I noticed big clear drops falling from Ron's face into his soup. We all watched, our eyes transfixed by each regular little dent in the pumpkin puree. *"Misty water-coloured memories ... of the way we were ..."* Ron had become the mock turtle.

"Somebody do something," I appealed.

Alex leapt up and snapped off the music. Our dinner was eaten in silence.

As I walked Ron to my car that he now claimed as his, he apologised to me for being a blithering idiot. We both knew that the next step was divorce, a process, he said, that felt like DNF-ing in a thousand races all at once. I felt sorry for him. I thought of the first time I met him and the premonition that I could crush him underfoot. Now it was done and it was all my fault.

CHAPTER 25

Vivaxis

"Forget guys and focus on your running," my new coach advised. The Commonwealth Games were looming in just two months. Cast adrift from Ron, I needed some grounding and direction. I would have liked to reconnect with John Davies and have him resume coaching me. He knew my running history and I liked and respected him enormously. But, Dick Quax informed me, while I was with Ron, Anne Audain had recruited John to be her coach. I was out of luck. So I asked Dick to help me, who by now was an experienced and noted coach in his own right. Like the big brother he had undertaken to be seven years earlier, he took me under his care and gave me a training programme for the Commonwealth Games. Dick was now my coach and would guide me on and off for the next 14 years through four Olympic Games.

1982 Commonwealth Games — Brisbane, Australia

A vivaxis is an energy beam that connects us to the earth. According to Frances Nixon, who named them in the 1960s, our birth vivaxis is established when we are born; it's a sort of geographic umbilical cord emanating from the place of our birth that grounds and nourishes us. Long before I had ever heard of such things, I instinctively felt home pulling me back to her when I needed healing. I longed for that little owl's nest in New Zealand; to put my feet on the dirt tracks at

Pinedale Forest and to breathe in tree air, to hear my dad puffing away at my side and feel the occasional drop of his sweat flick on my skin as we matched strides. I needed to regenerate after the worst year of my life, and Putaruru, as backward as it seemed to me then, with its forest, parochial town and rambling house that I grew up in, was my reliable fireside armchair that I could sink into and relax. I headed home for my final preparation.

I waited for my family to say something about my new profile. No-one did. Finally I could stand it no longer.

"Do you notice anything different about me?"

"You have a new dress?"

"No, something else, not clothes."

"Um, you're happier?"

"No, no, look here," and I turned sideways. My mum and dad, two brothers and my little sister looked quizzically at each other.

"Uh, we give up," my brother offered.

I could not believe it. "My nose, I had a nose job!"

"Why?" they queried, almost in unison.

My brothers thought it was silly. My mother exclaimed, "Oh Lorraine!" as if I had done something admirably outrageous. My dad was disappointed and let me know it. He regarded my previously aquiline nose as a family heirloom denoting a certain aristocracy, and that I had needed only to bear it proudly rather than to cut it off. I felt as if I had let him down. It was never mentioned again. I swear that over the ensuing years the genetic blueprint won out and my nose did somewhat grow back.

Nobody mentioned my impending divorce.

Putaruru rejuvenated me. I felt settled there; enough to focus on running rather than Ron, and by the time I got to Brisbane for the 1982 Commonwealth Games that awful last year was in the periphery of my awareness.

In my first event, the 3,000 metres, Anne Audain won a fine victory, out-kicking Wendy Smith of England on the final bend. John had worked well with her. I was not in the contest with those two but was content to pick up the bronze medal. Our third black-shirted team member, Dianne Rodger, was fourth, and together we carried Anne around the track on our clasped hand throne for a victory lap. It was a New Zealand day and I was downright happy for us all.

The next day I could hardly move my arms. Carrying Anne had its price. What's more, my throat was sore, my glands swollen, and the heats of my next event were just four days away. I laid low and drank my concoction of lemon juice, garlic and honey every hour until race day. It worked. I won another bronze medal in the 1,500 metres, an astonishing feat for a marathon runner, some said. They did not know what Arthur Lydiard had taught us — that marathons did not take one's speed, they enhanced it. I ran personal best times in both events.

The royal ocean liner, the *QEII*, was docked in Brisbane and I was invited along with a few others to afternoon tea aboard the ship with Her Majesty Queen Elizabeth and her husband the Duke of Edinburgh, Prince Philip. To get from the dock to the state room meant negotiating several narrow and steep steel ladders. "Ladies first," the male leaders of our group indicated. I would have expected nothing short of such chivalry aboard the Queen's ship. As I ascended I became crucially aware of my short skirt and of the gathering at the bottom of the stairs smiling up at me.

High tea consisted of sausage rolls and tiny cucumber sandwiches. A waiter filled our glasses with orange cordial. When the Queen arrived, she milled around the guests and we bowed and curtseyed as we were introduced. I had forgotten how petite she was.

Suddenly there was a loud bang.

"Are we at war?" I asked no-one in particular.

A voice beside me replied, "The Australians fire their cannon at the end of each day of competition."

"Whew, that's a relief. I was about to hit the deck and wait for Her Majesty's Royal Navy to start firing back!"

Bang! Bang! Bang! The cannon fire continued in regular succession.

"One shot for every gold medal," the voice beside me explained.

"Well heck, the Aussies are cleaning up, it must be hard for folks around here to get any sleep." I turned to face the voice.

"Too true," the Duke laughed.

After the Games ended I didn't really know what to do with myself. I returned to California and stayed with Clint, but even with his amorous attention I felt homeless in the US — cast adrift amongst aliens.

I returned briefly to Minneapolis. Ron had found a do–it–yourself divorce place where for $500 all papers would be correctly filed, and that's not all folks, it also included up to two bonus divorces should either of us ever need them, at absolutely no additional cost. The catch was that there could be no dispute and so I signed everything over to Ron: car and house, and paid the $500. Ron refused to split the fee and since I still felt guilty I forked over. It was just 14 months after our wedding. Ron told me he was now dating the attractive woman we had seen at the post office. I think he wanted me to feel jealous but the news made me feel better. He was sobbing when I left. That was the last time I saw him alive.

CHAPTER 26

Breathing Space

1982 — 1983

I returned to New Zealand for four months. Clint followed me out. He wanted me to live with him. I felt suffocated but I had no energy to resist. And he was a good-looking palliative. We returned to the US and set up home together.

I chose Boulder for a few reasons. I heard it was a good place for runners. It was a world unto itself with its innovative body therapies and New Age culture.

There was one other compelling reason I chose Boulder. Anne Audain had followed me to the road races of America and moved to Denver. We had met at the Freedom Trail Run in Boston. She won. I couldn't even keep with her past the first mile. I put it down to a bad day and went back to Minneapolis determined to train harder. We met again some months later at the Bloomsday Race in Spokane. Again she trounced me so convincingly that I then knew something was up. The only thing I could figure was that she had altitude and I didn't. Now that I had left Ron, it was time for me to have altitude too, but Denver was not big enough for both Anne and me. So I chose Boulder, just 30 minutes' drive away.

1983 World Championships — Helsinki, Finland
   I was selected to run the 3,000 metres in the World Track and Field Championships in Helsinki, based on my Commonwealth Games

performance. I was happy to be on another trip regrouping with my fellow Kiwis, and to have some space from Clint after six months of cohabitation.

I had convinced myself I was in love and that that in itself justified my actions and exonerated me from guilt over my failed marriage. After all, history is not only forgiving but full of accolades when soul-mates find one another despite difficult circumstances. Take Anthony and Cleopatra, for example, and Queen Guinevere and Lancelot. Who would fault them? I asked myself. I should have known that it was romantic poppycock on my part, for now and then I was seized with the familiar urge to flee. But I didn't. I reasoned that I just needed 'breathing space' before I committed myself to marriage and children with my new one true love, Clint.

Clint loved me too, I was sure. It perturbed me a little that he spent hours of his time on his top-ten list, ranking my running competitors in order of attractiveness.

Finland seemed so light and spacious. Perhaps it was because I was on my own and I had the freedom to please myself. It was summer and the sun set about 11 p.m. and rose again at 4 a.m. I slept little and filled what seemed like endless days running, shopping, hanging out with my team-mates and resting in preparation for the champion-ships.

One evening in the dining hall, a new team arrived and seated themselves at the long table beside ours. They were Eastern European women and obviously 'heavies', which in athletic lingo means throwers. I had never seen a group of people so unattractive. They had the musculature of gorillas: heavy-set Neanderthal faces with large jaws and brows, bone-crushing hands, and chests that qualified as continents. We were nudging one another, whispering things like, 'Steroid queens' and, 'Is it a he or a she?' They knew all eyes were on them and kept their gaze on their plates, sombre and introverted. There was none of the banter and high jinks that permeated our team's interactions.

The next day they arrived again for lunch but this time the 'burly-girls' were wearing frilly blouses, make-up and jewellery. I supposed that the command from their handlers had been to pretty themselves up, but it just made things worse. Lace and testosterone, rather than cancelling each other out, serve by contrast to accentuate each other. There was nothing in this world that would make me want to be like them: no world record, no medal, no fame. Even though I regarded them as cheats, I knew they were pawns to a greedy regime and I felt sorry for them.

I called Clint one evening. "It is so wonderful here," I enthused, "I miss you, I wish you were here." It was lover's sop and a little insincere but it seemed safe small-talk because I was here and he was there, penniless after his world travels. Besides, I was having a good time without him. I had a promising flirtation going with a charismatic young distance runner from South America who had flashed me a cheeky smile across his perfect white teeth one time too often.

However, Clint took me at my word and within a few days was on his way to Finland to watch the games and see me. What annoyed me was that somehow he had convinced the local bank manager to release the funds from my account to pay for his trip. "Well, you wanted me to come," he argued, "and you knew I had no money, so what was I to do?" *Stay home*, I thought, but I bit my tongue and feigned delight at his presence, although to me it all seemed rather pointless. I was living in the athletes' village and he was booked in a hotel in town (which I apparently was paying for) so I could not see him often.

When I lined up for the heats for the 3,000 metres I was nervous: a familiar feeling, but one that I knew readied me for the task ahead. As I stood on the curved line I scanned the legs on either side of me. It struck me that there were two groupings: the velveteen, tan legs of the western runners, and the hairy, white legs of the eastern bloc runners. That struck me as funny and I laughed out loud when the starting gun went off, which brought me back to the task at hand. I settled into an easy rhythm behind Mary Decker and company, running strongly through the last lap to qualify for the final in a personal best time of 8:51.7. Now that was easy.

Back at the village after my performance, I made my way to my South American friend's quarters to share my happiness, only to find that he had failed to qualify for the final in his event. Three other young athletic women were hovering over him, one holding his hand, another rubbing his shoulders and the third giving the other two the evil eye. He was blubbering like a big baby, totally inconsolable. *Geez,* I thought as big tears rolled down his smooth brown cheeks, forming rivulets which trickled onto his now soaking T-shirt, *it's only a race.* I wanted to tell him that if he had so desperately wanted to make the final he should have run faster, but I would have had to take a number for my turn with him, so I slipped away and called Clint, who was endearingly enthusiastic about my race.

Forty-eight hours later I approached the final with great confidence, believing that I could run with the best. But this time on the start line I was not amused, and the jaunty stride of a few days ago now had the texture of molasses. I had not yet recovered from my last race. Mary Decker won with German Briggitte Kraus second. I struggled home somewhere back in the field in around nine minutes.

"Why can't I keep up with them? I don't see how I can go any faster. I train hard on a programme I believe in, I'm tough and yet these women run so much faster! I run 8:51 and they run 8:30. Are they really that much better than I am? Am I under some sort of delusion that I can be at the top? What do they have that I don't?" I was crying my frustrations to Dick.

He looked me straight on as he considered my questions and weighed up his answer. I prepared for the awful truth: I was not good enough.

"Steroids," Dick finally said, shrugging his shoulders resignedly. "They give an athlete about a two per cent increase in performance. You're very talented. Don't doubt that. The only woman I have met with more athletic talent than you is Mary Decker."

It was an awful truth that made perfect sense. Unless I was prepared to cheat, I would never be a world track champion. I was not exceptional enough.

Dick was not advocating I take drugs nor was he suggesting that the competitors ahead of me all took drugs. I knew that. He was giving me his honest opinion.

"Besides, Lorraine, your blood count is always a bit on the low side. I wonder if at times your particular biochemistry is not suited for a series of anaerobic races in a short space of time, such as the Worlds require."

"Do you think then I could be the best in the marathon?"

"Yes I do. Here's why. Aerobic conditioning correctly applied over time can make an average runner into an international marathoner, and a talented runner into a superb marathoner. And while steroids give the advantage of quicker recovery and lower fat-to-muscle ratio, I believe the same effect can be achieved with years of conditioning. You've already got a head-start, Lorraine. You've been training since you were fourteen. And you've already shown you can be the best in the marathon."

"Do you think I could win the Olympics?"

"Let's just say you have a better chance than most."

I had to believe him, or retire.

Clint and I returned to our home. Much as I felt attuned to Boulder and loved its ambience of mountains, quaint little coffee shops and off-beat industries, I was not happy. Underneath I was still reeling with the emotional fallout of nuclear divorce.

Over and over in my head I replayed the many ways in which I was trespassed upon until I developed a watertight case against Ron: he had robbed me, betrayed me, set me up and fleeced me. I was convinced he had skewed the account of events to make it look like I was the adulteress and he was just a poor unsuspecting bloke who got caught in my treacherous web. As dedicated as a prosecuting attorney, night and day I shaped my argument for my redemption and Ron's condemnation into a granite sculpture of monumental proportions skilfully etched with the chisel of outrage. I had become an angry woman.

I was particularly peeved that from guilt I had handed him my car and the property that I had just spent $30,000 of my winnings on remodelling. The piece de résistance of this remodel was a triangular custom-made window that Ron had originally nixed because it was too costly.

"It'll look great. I'll pay for it!" I had insisted in a romantic fit of generosity.

At night my insomniac mind was running and rerunning the vision of returning there by cover of night, throwing a rock through the offending window and flying back to Boulder all in one day. But being of civilised upbringing, I could not carry it out. I decided there was only one satisfying way to get revenge. Win. Big time.

"What are you thinking?" Clint asked.

"Oh, nothing," I replied.

CHAPTER 27

Scrabble Squabble

Well behaved women rarely make history.
— Laurel Thatcher Ulrich

1983

Anne Audain was training for a marathon. I heard it from Dick, who heard it from John Davies. She had a physiological test with Nike, her sponsor and her predicted marathon capability was purported to be around 2:23. I rankled at the thought. She had a habit of muscling in my territory. Every time I thought I had carved out a niche for myself, along she came ready to hijack it away: teenage running prodigy; pioneer woman on the US roads; now she had taken my coach and wanted the marathon as well. I could hear her singing to herself, Annie Oakley style, "*Anything you can do I can do better, I can do anything better than you!*"

I watched with feigned disinterest for her debut result in the Chicago Marathon. She ran out of gas and fizzled, wobbling to the finish in second place after being passed in the last 800 metres by the upcoming Portuguese runner, Rosa Mota. Her time was 2:32-ish.

A few days later I got an unexpected call from New Zealand. It was John Davies. He couldn't figure out where Anne had gone wrong and wanted my advice. While I was glad that he considered me knowledgeable enough to be a resource, and flattered that he should seek my help, I was caught. I would do anything for John, but help Anne to trump me in the marathon? Not very likely.

"Perhaps she did not eat enough the night before?" he wondered.

"Could be," I agreed. "I personally have never had that problem."

As far as I was concerned there was only one basic mistake to be made in the marathon, besides being untrained: going too fast too soon. I told John so, but he disagreed. The treadmill test indicated that she was well within her limits, he said. I felt heartened. I knew then that Anne would never be a great marathoner for she lacked an essential skill; she ran by the numbers instead of tuning into her body. My best advice would have been to tell her to stick to the 10-k. She was good at that and it suited her aggressive style. The marathon was better left to the silent, brooding type like me, who could sit and stalk, not the bashing runner like her who gained confidence from being in front. But I said nothing.

I headed home to New Zealand at the beginning of December, fit and healthy and confident of making the team. After all, I had won every marathon I had contested, bar one, and the only New Zealander to have run a faster time was Allison Roe. Even though I had posted a qualifying time, it was a month outside of the selectors' guidelines and they wanted me to run another. No problem — or at least it seemed that way at the time.

I stopped in Hawaii on my long flight home. Dad was running the Honolulu Marathon and I wanted to cheer him on. Stepping off the plane, I joined Dad in a ten-mile run to preview the course. I had forgotten to pack my orthotics.

I had run my whole life without orthotics, much of it barefooted, but once I was given a contract with New Balance, it included the bonus of a treadmill bio-mechanical analysis of my form, and a consultation with a renowned podiatrist. He diagnosed me with one shorter leg by about a quarter inch. I now know that such discrepancies are most often the result of stress patterns carried in the body, and given the right conditions, are mostly self-correcting. But I did not know that then, so followed the standard course of action and allowed him to set me up with a hard pair of plastic platforms in my shoes to even me up. I hated the things. The joy of barefoot running was fast becoming a relic as I found myself becoming trapped by sponsors who touted science with their indisputable graphs and statistics and technology that took the fun out of it. The orthotics had taken some getting used to and now here I was without them. I ran anyway.

The next day I could not walk for the pain in my knee. So I rested. When I got to New Zealand four days later, it was no better. I rested a week then two. Weeks became a month and still each time I went out my knee was so painful I could not manage more than a few steps. Dick got me out riding a bike to keep my fitness. Physiotherapy did not help, nor did new orthotics. I began to feel panicked. Time was running out and with it the opportunities to race.

It was the end of January when I visited Andrew Wilson, a friend of mine in Tauranga, who is an osteopath. "Let's have a look at the knee of yours," he volunteered. With expert fingers he did what no-one else had ventured to: meticulously palpated my knee until he found a grain of scar tissue on the front of my kneecap. "This will hurt," he warned. "I don't care," I replied with all sincerity. He ground on the nodule with his thumb for about 30 minutes, then put an icepack on it. It was fire-generating, spine-churning, four-letter-word pain and the chill afterwards was welcome. Every day, twice a day for five days, Andrew repeated this procedure until the knot on my knee had disappeared. In a few days I was able to run, completely pain free, and, I decided, orthotic-free. After eight weeks off I now had to quickly whip myself into shape and find myself a qualifying race.

Meantime Anne competed in another marathon, this time in Los Angeles, hoping to gain a faster time and consolidate her place on the team. Again she ran in the low 2:30s but, I noted smugly, was out-sprinted by a much slower 10-k runner than herself, the Canadian, Jacqueline Gareau. My point was proven. Anne's speed was useless to her in the marathon and she could not even pull off a win.

Finding a timely marathon was no easy task. There were simply no marathon races for which I could be prepared before the cut-off qualifying period of 1 April. Allison Roe was also recovering from injury, as were several of the top men. That meant that four of New Zealand's fastest marathon runners were scrambling for selection.

(The 'professionalism affair' had blown over. I now understood that the glare of the New Zealand spotlight was harsh and that Allison had not had the shadows of distance to shield her that Anne and I had. All was forgiven.)

The Boston Marathon was just two weeks later so we appealed to the selectors to extend the qualifying period to 15 April. This proposal met with virulent opposition, which surprised me; it was spearheaded by John Davies, of all people. Since John was my friend I was rock-certain he was put up to it by Anne. Three women had made the qualifying time already (one of them Anne), three would be selected, and should Allison and/or I qualify, one or two of them could be bumped. The two-week extension was granted. The selectors made it clear that to be chosen for the team, our performances would have to be exceptionally better than those of the other qualifiers.

I now had that extra motivation. *I will make that team come hell or high water and bump Anne right off her little perch*, I thought to myself when the announcement was made.

Clint was now my constant companion and we filled the days between training sessions with Scrabble games. What started out as occasional easy-going time fillers, quickly became edgy blood sport, supposed to prove who was the smarter. It was obvious that I could run faster than Clint, and since he was not working, I earned more money. But Clint would often point out that there were two great levellers: one, he was a decade older than me, and therefore much more worldly-wise; and two, being well-read in English literature and being erudite with sesquipedalian expressions, was more intelligent than me. This latter fact, he reasoned, would be borne out by his superior Scrabble talents. I did not quite see it his way and was not willing to concede wisdom or intelligence points to him, but had he asked, I would certainly have given him a vastly superior score on looks.

Sometimes he won, often I did, in which case he would insist on a rematch. There was one factor on my side which he had not considered. Call it luck; I call it the magnetism of focused intent: the ability to draw to oneself that which one requires. Clint frequently complained that the lights on Canyon Boulevard near our home were deliberately timed so that he always hit one red light after another, and yet whenever I drove on my own I could sail the length of it through successive green lights. The same principle was at work with Scrabble. I consistently drew high scoring letters in favourable combinations while Clint wrestled more often than not with a tray of e's and i's. We played game after game after game like this, until it superceded most other pastimes except running. But, I must confess, I was by now spending my runs thinking up good words.

The competition reached a feverish pitch in Los Angeles on a stopover on our way to the Boston Marathon. Our board and tiles were sprawled across the dining room table in the apartment of Clint's friend, Al.

I had been winning too often and Clint was getting exasperated. He deduced that I won because I cheated: feeling the letters in the bag and choosing the ones I needed. I agreed to place the letters face down so that the possibility that I might be selecting by Braille was removed. When I won again I expected to be vindicated but Clint concluded that his intellect did not stand a chance when Lady Luck had handed me the 'x', the 'z' and the 'q' with a 'u'. So he devised an equaliser: the letters were divided into two piles of matching values: his pile and my pile.

When I won again, Clint said it was because I was taking too long on my turn. This time he said we were to play, still drawing letters from our separate piles, but with a one-minute time limit. I drew first turn. Clint, the self-appointed timekeeper, started the watch before I had drawn tiles.

"Time's up!" he announced.

"But Clint," I lamented, "I've hardly had time to look at my letters."

"Too bad." He plonked down his word and restarted the watch on me.

The next minute was spent scrambling for a word.

"Time's up!" Clint proclaimed once more and put down his second word and promptly commenced my third countdown.

I was stonkered. "Wait, wait!" I stammered. Not one one-minute word save 'it' was presenting itself.

"Forty seconds," he counted.

"But I need more time. I don't have a word."

"Thirty seconds."

"You took my time for your own word. It's not fair," I grumbled.

"Twenty seconds."

"Wait, wait, wait. This isn't working out."

"Ten seconds."

"This is ridiculous! I don't want to play any more."

"My turn."

His third word, conceived on my time I might add, was hatched onto the board and once again the stopwatch was on me. I sat there not moving, staring blankly at the table.

"One minute …" Clint started.

"I said I'm not playing any more!" I yelled, jumping to my feet, grabbing the board and tipping the winning words on the floor. Clint was tsk-tsking at my poor sportsmanship; his friend Al craned his neck from the kitchen to see what wild emotion had been unleashed upon his dining room. I was not done. I shredded the board like a strongman tearing telephone books at a sideshow. Then, all done, I gathered up the pieces and threw them in the bin.

"Hey, you can't do that!" Clint protested.

"I just did," I replied, wiping my hands in the gesture of fait accompli. That was the last game of Scrabble I ever played with him.

1984 Boston Marathon — USA

I was in fine warrior mode for the Boston Marathon. The women's race was tipped as a match between Allison Roe and me: the two Kiwis duking it out for Olympic berths. Being a past winner, Allison was hyped up by the press as the favourite. I was grateful for that. The attention of the media squeezes many an aspiring champion to make mistakes. I was betting on Allison going out too fast, but this time I did not caution her. The trick for me today was to stay centred, tune in, and focus on making that team. This was a much easier task as the underdog, away from the media microscope.

I stood on the start line confident that I could win. I remembered how Ron's eyes would sparkle as he regaled others with his stories of the Boston Marathon and how excited I had been to watch Allison win here a few years back, and now it was my turn.

The day was cold and a little rainy, with quite a stiff breeze in our faces. I liked that kind of weather the best: not the headwind, but the briskness that gave me goose-bumps on my limbs when I stripped down to my shorts and singlet. I felt a frisky nervousness, like a yearling at the races, my lean limbs hungry to stretch out over the pavement and carry me to the victory, and on to the Olympics.

The race was predictable. I did what I had been taught by Ron to do; I went out at the pace at which I felt comfortable and then deliberately slowed down. That always made good sense. The adrenaline one feels on the start line often gets a marathon runner committed to a pace that cannot be maintained. I chuckled as I saw Allison clear off into the distance ahead of me. *See you on Heartbreak Hill*, I said to myself, for I knew that she was running too fast and would be running low on precious glycogen reserves somewhere after the 20 mile mark.

Sure enough, as I ascended the famous hill I could see Allison quickly coming into focus with my every stride, and she was flagging. I drew alongside. I wanted to be encouraging, and so I muttered, "Come on, Allison," hoping she might find some strength from me, but not too much. I thought it would be neat to go to the Olympics together. But my passing was not the encouragement she needed. She pulled out shortly thereafter and I went on to win, breaking two hours and 30 minutes on this cold, windy day. I had won the Boston Marathon, but more importantly I had my exceptional Olympic qualifying time.

Early the next morning I was taken to NBC Studios for *Good Morning America*, along with the men's winner, the British aircraft technician, Geoff Smith. This was my movie star moment and my sponsor, New Balance, insisted I wear a rain-suit. I felt silly walking into the studio zipped up for inclement weather and rustling with every movement. Swish, swish, swish.

As we were leaving the studio, Geoff asked me, "Hey Lorraine, what did you think of the medal?"

"What medal?"

"The winner's medal."

"Yeah, okay."

"Don't you know it is gold and the diamond inset is real?"

I rushed back to the hotel room and crawled under the bed to find it where it had fallen in the after-marathon mêlée. This was the last year that Boston held out as an amateur race so this was my prize. I made no money.

When the Olympic team was announced a few days later the committee had selected the fastest three times for the women's marathon. I was in and so was Anne. Mary O'Connor filled the third spot. Glenys Quick was bumped out of the places. I felt sorry for her.

A few days later I received a letter from the White House. It is customary for the winner of the Boston Marathon to receive a congratulatory message from the President of the Unites States of America.

> Dear Miss Moller:
>
> I'm happy to take this opportunity to congratulate you on your strong victory in the women's field at the eighty-eighth annual Boston Marathon on Monday. Your come-from-behind effort in adverse weather was eloquent testimony to your rigourous preparation and to your determination. You can be very proud.
>
> With my best wishes.
>
> Sincerely,
>
> Ronald Reagan

PART FOUR

Olympian

Elation after winning the Boston Marathon, 1984. (John Kerry, former US Presidential candidate, in the background.) *Courtesy of New Balance*

CHAPTER 28

The Messenger

Women have the right to mount the scaffold; they should likewise have the right to mount the rostrum. — Olympe de Gouges, author of *Declaration of Rights of Women,* 1791, France.

1984

Mercury, the wing-footed god of communication, arts, commerce and trickery, introduced himself to me during the 1984 Olympics in Los Angeles. I do not presume to say that I found him, for though I have often been guilty of hubris, I know that when it comes to deities, celestial powers and forces of nature, they find us and not the other way around. I also know that he found me long before I was aware of him; indeed, it is most likely that he has always been with me.

Mercury is the guardian of the crossroads, and as trickster, is renowned for turning the signposts when you are not paying attention. The unsuspecting candidate, such as I, sets off down an unfamiliar road and next thing she knows she is engaged in unforeseen and challenging circumstances that stretch her beyond her limitations and break down her ego structures. It is no wonder to me now that at the same time I became an Olympian, my awareness of my alliance with Mercury began and a new era of my life was ushered in.

Olympian is a heavy title for any mortal to carry. When it was first bestowed upon me in 1984 I grabbed it greedily, without knowing the real prize that was being offered. Back then I was just a kid who wanted a gold medal. But in the next 12 years, spanning four Olympic Games, Mercury tampered unabashedly with my signposts so that, like it or not, the pursuit of gold was a shaping process that required me to face the burdens of the past that I carried: my petty jealousies, my projections upon others, my self-doubt, my anger, and finally my sadness. In the magical way of alchemy, I gradually became what I aspired to.

Mercury can always be counted on to catalyse monumental change and his presence at the inaugural women's Olympic marathon was by celestial design. The time had come for the participation and performance of women in endurance sports to take a huge evolutionary leap forward.

When the Olympic Games were first recorded in 776 BC, it was said that women were not allowed to compete, indeed were not allowed to watch: under penalty of death. This leads to the current misconception that women back then were not given their due as athletic creatures. But the truth is that Greek women in ancient times had their own games, called the Herarea, held in the name of Hera, the goddess counterpart of Zeus in whose honour the Olympic Games were held. In my opinion, women and men did not compete in the same games, not because of inequality, but because they were seen as having different roles that were complementary rather then competitive. It is suggested by F. M. Cornford, who wrote a chapter in the book *Epilegomena to the Study of Greek Religion* by Jane Ellen Harrison, that both these games stemmed from ancient rituals where foot-races were used to select both the male representative of Zeus (the Hero), and the female representative of Hera (the feminine version of the word Hero) whose consummation ensured a superior genetic legacy.

If we compare ancient times to the modern Olympics perhaps women back then had a better shake. Modern women were not even included when the Olympic Games were reinstated in 1896, and no corresponding female version was even considered for this festival. However, from the outset, various heraic women gate-crashed the modern Olympics, forcing the issue of feminine inclusion.

One woman, on her own volition, ran the marathon course the day after the men competed in the 1896 Olympics in Paris and completed the final lap outside the stadium. Officials could not remember her name so she was dubbed 'Melpomene' after the Greek muse of tragedy.

From then on a smattering of events, such as ballooning, golf and tennis were included for women, and often just as quickly excluded. By 1928, the eighth Olympic Games of the modern era, women competed for the first time in five track and field events. The 880 yards, two laps of the track, was a bold inclusion for women, considering that the prevailing sentiment was that such an exhausting distance would render the participants masculine and leave them barren. These expectations were borne out as women collapsed around the track. It was concluded that the female body could not tolerate such strenuous activity and the event was banned and not reinstated until 1960, when for the first time in 32 years a distance over 220 yards was offered again for women. The 1,500 metres, just less than a mile, was finally added to the women's programme at the 1972 Olympics in Munich.

Now, 1984, the marathon had finally been added to the Olympic programme. It would be just another four years before the 5,000 metres and 10,000 metres would also be included and women could claim to have parity with the men. The modern Olympics would finally recognise Woman as Runner.

What I knew was that this was time to get serious. I mean really serious, not just trifling around with World Championships or Commonwealth Games. This was Olympic serious.

Suddenly Boulder was teeming with runners preparing for the inaugural women's Olympic marathon. Priscilla Welch from England, Rosa Mota from Portugal, Jacqueline Gareau from Canada, and Ingrid Kristiansen from Norway, among others, all became Boulder imports. We met socially but rarely trained together. I didn't want the other women knowing my secrets and I suspect they felt the same about me.

In the high, dry summer of Colorado I followed my schedule to the letter, putting in my long runs as written, and my two-a-day runs of varying tempos on the other days. As Ron would have done, I added layers of clothing to simulate the humidity of Los Angeles. Boulder was hot enough in the summer but it was a dry heat, so wearing a pair of rain pants and a long-sleeved shirt a few times a week did the trick of firing the sweat glands into full working order. I trained in the middle of the day which also helped. It was the usual habit of mine, not for the acclimatisation, but simply because I hated getting out of bed early.

As I ran along one day, heavily clad in the madness of the midday sun, I crossed paths with Jacqueline Gareau, dressed in shorts and singlet, with her fine, tanned limbs. We bid our cheery 'hellos'. My state of dress had been discovered. The next time I saw Jacqueline running she was sweating it out in full body cover.

I added freshly squeezed vegetable and fruit juices to my daily dietary routine: apple, orange and pineapple first thing in the morning and carrot, cucumber and beetroot before dinner. This was part of my clean-living routine where junk food had no place and my body had ceased to be my playground but was prepared as a high performance engine. This time I went one further, forgoing restaurant food for a non-fat diet prepared by my friend of gourmet culinary skill, Allison Richards. The benefits were instantly noticeable and I could feel my body kicking into a higher gear; I was becoming mentally clear, sleek and very, very fast.

Clint was a good sport about it all, delighting in having our own personal cook. It seemed that all of Clint's Hollywood friends had adopted the Pritikin diet, and he eagerly called to tell them that we had joined the fray. Like them, he knew our arteries would become plaque-free and not only would I run faster but we would both remain young and sexy for the rest of eternity. I was not so convinced. I had always done well in my Saturday meets in New Zealand on a Friday night feed of fish and chips and I missed them. As the fat-free weeks clicked by I began to dream about the crispy bits lying at the bottom of folded, grease-soaked newspaper. This hankering was occasionally satisfied by potato chips which I sneaked at social gatherings when Clint wasn't watching.

Clint and I drove from Boulder's mile high altitude to Los Angeles, leaving so that we arrived for a carefully timed ten days at sea level before competition. According to the exercise physiologists, such an interval would best ensure my complete adaptation to sea level while I retained the advantage of my altitude-enhanced red blood cells. In those days I followed such protocol to the letter. In my later years, as I became more experienced and confident, I would become more cavalier with the 'rules'. Clint dropped me off at the Olympic village in Westwood where I joined my team.

Our team captain, Graeme McCabe, was from my hometown and his presence made me feel comfortable. He showed me to our quarters. It was an apartment with two twin bedrooms, a bathroom and a living room with a small kitchen. There were six on the women's team so bunk beds had been erected in the living room to accommodate us all. I abhor bunk beds. They give me claustrophobia; and besides the thought of having a stranger, or worse still, a rival, breathing into my personal space while I was sleeping gave me the willies.

I checked the bedrooms. Three of the beds had been taken. I put my gear on the fourth bed, thankful that I had arrived before the other two. But no. My roommate informed me that this bed had been reserved 'in absentia' for none other than my arch-rival, Anne Audain. I would have to move to a bunk bed as she would be arriving in two days' time. I declared that I would sleep there for now and sort it out when she arrived. But I had absolutely no intention of budging.

When Anne showed up, Graeme told me I would have to move. I point blank refused. As far as I was concerned, I was there first.

I discovered that possession truly is nine-tenths of the law. Anne had no choice but to sleep in the bunk. Not a word was said but in the undercurrent we both knew this victory was mine. An order had been established. In a week's time we would be competing against each other. At least one thing was clear: I was not moving over for her.

The next day I went down to the track to run a 12-lap time trial, approximately three miles.

The Olympic training track is a tricky place where big races are won and lost. Runners watch one another train, secretly timing their rivals and often feeding their own insecurities as they do so. There is a temptation to show off by running too hard, taking the edge off one's condition before competition. This is where a good coach can be invaluable, pulling the runner back and giving reassurance. But, as with most championships, our personal coaches were not included on the team and we were relying on team coaches who often lacked the overview of our individual conditioning.

But I was not in danger. My programme was sound and my faith in it was absolute. This was my last blow-out, with a week to recover. Dick had advised me to run it in my clunkers (bulky old training flats) rather than in my lightweight racers. Psychologically it took the pressure off. I ran fluidly from the outset. 75, 75, 75, each lap clocking the same seconds as the last, I strode like a metronome, clicking away until I finished right on the dot of 15 minutes. Five minute miles. Easy. I was elated. I was in my best shape ever.

When I arrived back to the village after my training, the courtyard was abuzz with reporters and television cameras. Zola Budd, the teenaged, barefooted South African who had gained controversial citizenship to Great Britain so that she could pursue her dream of Olympic participation, had just arrived armed with her stuffed animals. I craned my neck to get a gander. She stood shyly amid the swarm, which was forbidden to inquire about the sports politics of South Africa, so were now asking her to elaborate on her pet ostrich named Sydney.

CHAPTER 29

The Anointed One

*In the name of all competitors I promise that we shall take part in these
Olympic Games, respecting and abiding by the rules which govern them,
committing ourselves to a sport, without doping and without drugs, in the
true spirit of sportsmanship, for the glory of sport and the honour of our
teams.* — The Athletes' Olympic Oath

AUGUST 1984, LOS ANGELES

The opening ceremony was magnificent. As I marched around
the stadium with my team-mates under the New Zealand banner, a chill of excitement shimmered up my spine and tears filled my
eyes. My chest swelled with Kiwi pride and I was lifted with good
spirits. Not only was I was here at the centre of this grand stage but
I had been elevated from my station in life. I bore a tag which meant
I was one of the privileged few who could enter the Holy Village of
Olympians at will while the ordinary mortals thronged at the gates,
begging for autographs and hoping for a sprinkling of Olympic gold-
dust from one of us: The Anointed. I was thrilled with this new status
conferred upon me, a feeling that surpassed even the pride of being a
first-year university student.

I was eagerly anticipating the showdown between America's dar-
ling, Mary Decker, and the barefooted South African teen, Zola
Budd, as much as everyone else. Unlike Zola, Mary was staying away
from the village and the media's glare, in the same hotel where Dick
and Sue were staying, at Nike's expense. A pretty-faced woman with

211

golden eyes and dark hair, Mary is feisty and emotional. The word from the Nike camp was that Mary was touchy about the attention given to Zola as her rival and felt it undeserved. She was ready to set the record straight.

I watched Zola and Mary from the stands in the final of the 3,000-metre event a few days later. Mary ran on Zola's shoulder, her eyes bearing down on the bare heels in front of her. Suddenly Zola leapt into the air as Mary's descending spikes caught the rising leg, ripping a long gash. Zola regained her stride and they continued as before. Mary was not using her outstretched arms to mark her space and balance herself as a trailing track runner does; instead her foot caught Zola's heel again, and this time Mary lost her balance, tripped and tumbled. She lay on the infield, wailing, as the crowd booed the bewildered, bleeding Budd, who ran on. Maricica Puica from Romania won, Wendy Sly, the British runner who had won the same event in the Commonwealth Games two years earlier, was second, and the Canadian Lynn Kanuka-Williams finished third. My rival from the Pacific Conference Games 3,000 metres, Cindy Bremser, sprinted into fourth place.

Dramatic as the Decker/Budd showdown was, it played out like the Greek tragedy one might expect at the Olympics. It was the realisation that blood-doping was rampant that I found most jarring. I had heard that during their Olympic build-up runners would arrive from overseas, often to Boulder, train in the rarefied altitude for a period, thus forming red corpuscle-rich blood, have it extracted, spun in a centrifuge to increase the concentration of red blood cells, and re-infused before the big event. It was easy to pick them. They travelled in teams of three: the athlete, their coach and a doctor. This extra blood-carrying capacity enabled endurance runners to laugh all the way to the podium, where they could read *War and Peace* as they waited for their competition who sweated it out for the forgettable places.

Since the Finns had blitzed the distance events in previous Olympics, rumors of their blood-doping were rampant. If the grumblings were true then they had robbed our Dick Quax of a gold and Rod Dixon of another bronze. Now it seemed that at this Olympics the practice was widespread. Members of the USA distance-cycling team admitted to it, after the fact. After all, they said, it was not illegal and was still their own blood. While secret blood transfusions may not have been against the rules at the time, they were hardly ethical. (The rational mind will readily issue licence for bad behaviour, which is precisely why I continued to demote mine over time in favour of the ethical mind. Besides, she eventually became way too bossy.)

I was annoyed when I had read of a European doctor who recommended blood-doping as a prescriptive measure for anaemia for athletes. I frequently had anaemia but ethically such an option was not open to me. Later I was told by one of our Olympic cyclists that this same doctor had a reputation in the elite cycling world as 'Dr Forty-Nine Percenter'. Since a haematocrit level over 50 per cent was deathly dangerous and cycling rules required that any athletes with such levels be sidelined, this guy was touted to be the expert who could get you right up to the line but not over.

Anyhow, all this blood-doping bugged me. I took some consolation in the thought that dehydration from the heat of mid-summer could render the dopers' blood to sludge. In my fantasy I would smirk as they failed, mid-race, to remove the cap from their vials of rat poison — meant to thin the blood before their hearts gave out. Not that I would, in reality, wish such a fate on anyone. Many athletes have tragically died from too much of a good thing.

But until they developed a test to combat such cheating, I would have to be content for them to stew in their own conscience, for the rest of eternity.

Steroids were rampant too, but these were not news to me. Over the years I had become jaded at their mention, and took some comfort from the fact that they were tested for. Runners got caught now and then, and steroids were perhaps less relevant to the slow-twitch muscle events such as the distance races than the fast-twitch sprints. Perhaps. The coach of a European athlete confided that it was a relatively easy matter to get around the steroid issue: she was issued with a medical certificate declaring her an asthmatic, along with a legal prescription for steroids to treat it.

"But does she get asthma?" I asked.

He shrugged. "Does anyone?"

"I do, and I don't take steroids."

He shrugged again as if I was a fool.

"I think I'm good enough without them," I added.

He shrugged a third time.

His charge went on to become a multiple Olympic medallist.

When Martti Vainio, the lanky Finn, got pulled from the heats of the 5,000 metres for a positive drug test, I was pleased. I had suspected him in the 10,000 metres where he won silver and in protest had refused to cast my eyes on him as he circled the track ahead of everyone else. I believed the real race, the honest race, was three places back and I applauded those runners as if they were the winners. He pleaded that his drinks had been spiked, and anything else he could think of in a pinch, but he had been well and truly nailed and was later banned.

The story that circulated among the athletes was that his amazement at a positive steroid test was genuine. After all, the steroids had been taken months before in his build-up phase, and discontinued on a schedule that would guarantee they had circulated out of his body before competition. What he did not count on was that his old blood, transfused into him before the race, still contained detectable traces of those steroids.

After watching this race I was even more determined to do my damnedest to beat the cheats, whoever they were, even with my puny haematocrit levels and my sometimes asthma. Perhaps naïvely, I believed in the magical pathway of the hero.

Our women's marathon team was called for a press conference: I, the seasoned marathoner; Anne Audain, the newcomer to the marathon scene; and Mary O'Connor, whose dedication to the Lydiard method over the years had turned her moderate speed over shorter distances into a force to be reckoned with over 26 miles. But when it came to this race, thoughts of Mary did not even enter my consideration. It was Anne who engaged my attention.

Now at the press conference Anne took centre stage from the outset, not shy at all to declare herself a gold medal prospect. "To win," she declared, "you have to make a move" — implying that she had the winning move in her possession. I couldn't believe her audacity. Did she have no respect for the company she would be in? Like Waitz and Kristiansen? And me?

I had thought that top billing was something conferred on you by the press who had done their homework. But Anne had just stridden in to seize the 'favourite' banner and wrap herself in it while I was waiting politely for my due. She had trumped me. Certainly I had no race strategy to announce, nor words to imply, that I was a gold medal aspirant. That would be very un-Kiwi. I was just hopeful. The media was mesmerised and in Anne's presence I had become invisible. It seemed the bulk of questions were geared to her.

Then before I could modestly allude to my excellent prospects, the conference was over. They had their story, and it was Anne. I wanted to yell to the press, "Wake-up! She is not the Marathon Queen, I am! I have won more marathons than any other runner in the field, re-member, and she has not won one. She has cast a spell on you. She's an imposter!" but I held my tongue as they slipped away. I was pipped.

"Don't worry," Graeme whispered as we left, "let your legs do the talking."

1984 Summer Olympics — Women's Marathon, Los Angeles, USA
Anne. Wherever I was, I felt her. My arch-rival radar was humming. Even when she was out of my field of vision I knew if she was to my left or right or sitting on my shoulder.

Joan Benoit had taken off with what looked like a Kamikaze stunt. She had had a knee operation just two weeks before the Olympic trials, and although she won, she had looked stressed on the TV. In my mind, and everyone else's, she was not a contender. We just let her go. I could not understand her confidence after all she'd been through, and expected her to run tentatively. But no, after three miles she just took off. I felt much more secure in the company of the Norwegian stars, Grete Waitz and Ingrid Kristiansen, around whom a comfort pack of about 12 had formed.

The race started in the morning and it was warm and getting warmer, but nothing unbearable: mid-seventies going into the eighties. Focus changes reality. In any other situation I would have felt it was too hot to run — and it would have been. Here I didn't even consider it.

We climbed onto a freeway for a few miles, a lonely stretch with no spectators, and as had been the prediction, the leading bunch broke apart into a stretching line of chasers and stragglers. Anne dropped off my radar. I hesitated. With Anne gone I had suddenly lost my focal point. My Rational Mind sprang to life. She had been waiting at Mercury's crossroads, determined to make sure I didn't do anything rash. *This is the hard part. Everyone says so,* she chimed into my ear, *and it's so hot.* Yes, now that I thought about it I could feel the heat in my head. *Let them go, you've beaten Anne. You can relax now. Don't kill yourself in this weather.*

So I trundled along with the stragglers for about five miles, telling myself how doggone hard this was, when Miss Rational tapped me on the shoulder again.

My gosh, Lorraine! What are you doing? There are only three miles left. This is the Olympics! Get a move on and salvage what you can.

She was right. I woke up from my weary, thigh-lifting sighs and suddenly found I had energy to haul in the runners ahead.

When I finally passed Priscilla Welch from England in the last mile before the stadium, I didn't know what place I was in, but I could see Ingrid way ahead of me and I assumed that Rosa Mota and Grete Waitz were in front of her. I wondered if Joan Benoit had pulled out. I had plenty of running left in me but the race was running out and I was not gaining on Ingrid fast enough.

Suddenly I was passing the Nike mural of Joan Benoit breasting the tape. I remembered that mural well. I had run with Joanie just after it had been erected, at the time of the US Olympic trials when I had come here to scout the course. A woman was lining up to take a photo of the mural just as Joanie and I ran by. She swore at us for blocking her photo and we laughed to each other. She did not know that she had just got a shot of the real thing. *Isn't that how it is?* I thought as I rounded the turn towards the tunnel. *We constantly think we are short-changed, only because our perspective has insufficient distance.*

And then I arrived. I ran down the shute into the shadows of the tunnel and out into the stadium as my name was announced: "Lorraine Moller from New Zealand". A resounding cheer went up. Although it was hot I shivered all over with pride and felt like weeping with gratitude, as I had in the opening ceremony. I felt as if I had sprung from the birth canal after an arduous labour, but this time I was being hailed rather than slapped.

Joanie was running around the track with an American flag, blowing kisses. Obviously she had won. Grete and Rosa were running and waving too. Second and third. Ingrid was just finishing.

As I was striding out on the final lap, trying to take it all in, the loudspeaker announced, "Anne Audain from New Zealand." *Anne! How did she get there?* I had left her a long time ago but she must have been hauling to come from behind and pass Priscilla. I knew she could not catch me, but just the same, I put on a little spurt. I was surprised that I still had something left. When I crossed the line with a modest half wave befitting my placing, the first thing I did was turn to look. I was relieved. It was Priscilla coming in and not Anne. Merely a case of mistaken identity.

I had just run my fastest time ever and finished fifth in the Olympics.

When I got back to the village, I felt empty. No medal dangling from my neck, no thronging crowds jostling for my autograph. Just the number five next to my name.

It was late afternoon when Anne arrived back to our quarters. Graeme supported her into the living room after collecting her from the hospital. She looked tired and her face was wan but I wasn't sure if it was stress or if her make-up had been washed off. The backs of her hands were taped.

She looked up at me, with a certain urgency.

"How did you do?"

She didn't know. I would have given anything to say I had won.

"Fifth," I mumbled, casting my eyes down.

"Good job! You must be very pleased with that!" she exclaimed with annoyingly good cheer.

With what? That I exceeded your low expectation of me? Most certainly not. I shrugged ungraciously.

"And what happened to you?" I asked, feeling compelled to cloak my scorn in fake sympathy.

"I just got out of hospital. They put me on intravenous."

"For what?"

"Dehydration."

Dehydration?! We are all dehydrated.

With no further prompting Anne launched into the tale of her demise. "I was just behind you at twenty-two miles, about to make my move when I felt all dizzy," she started out.

Liar, I muttered under my breath, the heat rising in my head. If I had held one ounce of hope that Anne would admit that I had her beaten this time, that I had played it better, that the self-professed Queen of the Marathon had just been dethroned, it was dashed in that moment, for I knew that she was not conceding me one point of up-man-ship.

The explanation continued in detail, all of which whirled around in my head like ball-bearings in a pinball machine, zinging all over my brain, lighting off my emotional hot spots: she had become delirious, she searched for help, finally collapsing at the wheels of an ambulance, blah blah blah. My ears tuned in; I was hearing not her words but the underlying message: *I would surely have won had not Fate singled me out for this great misfortune.*

Suddenly she stopped talking and looked at me. But I was off-line, quietly fuming. She was waiting for me to say something. It was my turn to fire a ball.

"Well, Anne," I offered, as I looked her up and down, acknowledging her sorry state. "The marathon does not begin until twenty miles."

The next day I scoured the *New Zealand Herald*'s Olympic Report section. With shades of the 1928 Olympic Women's 880 yards outrage,* the lead story was titled 'Athlete's Agony in Marathon Angers

Doctors'. The strenuous misfortunes of Anne and the wobbly finish of Swiss runner Gabrielle Anderson-Scheiss were discussed in detail. The performance results of this momentous race in history, in which I was mentioned as fifth, rated only as a follow-up story.

Queen Anne reigned. Once again she had sliced the cake and taken the biggest piece for herself. And for the life of me I couldn't figure out how she did it.

---

* In 1928 the women competitors in the 880 yard race collapsed and the Olympic Committee ruled that the race was too strenuous for women. A decision that was led, interestingly, by Harold Abrahams, the runner who was immortalised in the movie, *Chariots of Fire*.

CHAPTER 30

Squares into Wheels

1984

Fifth. Solid, strong, commendable, others said. Fifth this time was, in a twisted way, not even better-than-Anne. It was stuck fifth. A little-bit-chicken-fifth. I knew that I was in the shape of my life, and had the ability to win. I knew that I was in the company of extraordinary talent, and that the four ahead of me would be hailed by many as the greatest runners of their era, but I was still fifth. At 17 miles the pack I was running in had broken apart and Grete, Ingrid and Rosa fled in pursuit of medals. When it had come time to lay it on the line, I had played safe. I let them go, focusing on my petty competition with Anne and readily accepting Miss Rational's excuses about the heat, the distance, and my ability. I knew they were excuses, but it was as if my mind played tricks on me. Yes, just a little bit chicken.

My team-mate and long-time friend, Diane Rodger, had seen a little jewellery store in Westwood. "Let's go shopping." she suggested. It sounded like a good idea. After all, this was America. If we had not won gold medals, why not do the next best thing and go and buy some? That was where Mercury found me. He was embossed on a gold pendant: lithe, naked and in stride, presumably through the heavens. This was my guy.

Funny thing, this: Mercury's number in numerology is five — the number that occurs when we take a square and add one more facet to form a pentagon — unstable, wheel-like. You see, when Mercury visits, your safe little box starts turning, things move, life becomes unpredictable, everything is turned upside down, and pretty soon your box is falling apart. That's what happened to me the moment I donned his image.

Once back in Boulder I did a lot of soul searching. 'Fifth' buzzed around in my brain, like a bothersome blowfly that could not be ignored. I knew I could do so much better, but how? What was my stumbling block? What was I afraid of? If I couldn't answer my own questions, what was I hiding from myself?

First of all I had to turn down the volume. I had recruited so many people to tell me what to do that I could no longer hear my own voice. I started with a deliberate social cleanse, beginning with my outer circle and gradually working my way in. I stopped going to chiropractors, acupuncturists, massage therapists and aura fluffers who aligned my energies.

But that wasn't enough. I wanted total separation. First I wrote to Dick, telling him that in the interests of 'finding myself' I wanted to coach myself for a while. I told him I was no longer interested in a coach/athlete relationship that resembled that of a father/child situation where orders are given and obediently followed. I asked him if we could evolve to a relationship of equals where he would act as my friend and mentor and give me advice when I felt I needed it. He was fine with that and although I did not call on his coaching services for the next two years, our relationship developed into a friendship which we have to this day.

Clint was not so easy.

1984 Avon International Women's Marathon — Paris, France

A few months after the Olympics I was invited to the Avon Women's Marathon once again, this time in Paris. Paris was Clint's scene: romantic, late-night, eight-course dinners that stretched into the wee hours, with a fine beaujolais to boot, lingering sleep-ins in a plush hotel with room service of croissants and hot coffee, press conferences and official functions where I could play 'star' and he 'star's consort' — all on Avon's ticket. I had a grand time, but it was hardly a week of the sort of sharpening that hones a champion. With all these cafés beckoning I barely had time to run. By the end of the week I was fattening and starting to look like the kind of girl with breeding potential. I didn't give it a second thought. I was confident that the race was mine. After all, I was the Avon Queen.

The course circled the Bois de Bologne with two 13-mile loops, and finished on the Champs Elysées with the Arc de Triomphe as a backdrop, another coup for Kathrine Switzer. It was the first time this famous avenue had ever been closed for a running event, and as with the London Marathon, Kathrine's legacy would provide the blueprint for the Paris Marathon. Added to this, Kathrine had persuaded Avon to become the first women's race to give prize money: a handsome purse that offered $20,000 for first place.

I started off conservatively, as I always did, and tucked in with the lead pack. Shortly after halfway I considered the pace a bit pedestrian, pooh-poohed my competition with a snootiness that would have made Parisians proud, and took command of the race, leaving the rabble behind me to sort out the minor placings.

With less than two miles to go, I was climbing the last long hill before an easy coast down to the turn that would take me onto the finishing straight, when I spied a figure to my far right, in front of me. It was a runner, the Dutch national champion Carla Buerskins, and she had passed me and now had a 20-yard lead. I was dumbfounded; so self-assured had I been that I had it in the bag, I hadn't even seen her overtake me. A wave of panic spirited the wind out of my pipes, and now she had 30 yards on me and was going away. I could see the press truck up ahead, whizzing to the finish line and Carla's coach was hanging off the back, flapping his arms like an albatross about to take flight.

The sight spurred me into competitive overdrive. *The audacity of her*, I thought, as I assumed the spirit of Elizabeth the First, and Carla became Mary Queen of Scots racing away in her underpants. *How dare she aspire to my throne!* Down the hill I careered, eating away at the lead and passing her as she slowed to round the corner. I was now sprinting. *Please, dear God*, I prayed, *don't let this straight be longer than I remember.* I have to confess that in my cockiness I had failed to do due diligence, as normally I would run the last five miles of the course to gauge from what point I could sprint home, and now I had no idea how far it was to the finish. It stretched out considerably farther than I had banked on and memories of Morocco flashed across my mindscape. But I was committed now and only one task mattered — to get to the finish faster than her. My dash was dwindling as I scuttled across the line in one of the fastest finishes I ever had in a marathon.

I had won my third Avon title. Kathrine was beaming and wrapped her arm around my shoulder as a horde of reporters thronged towards me, cameras flashing, pens poised to notepads, microphones searching for my mouth.

"Kathrine," I whispered urgently, "tell them to get out of the way. I'm going to be sick." While my legs had abruptly come to a stop, my stomach contents were still travelling and bile spewed from my mouth as if I was in the starring role from *The Exorcist*. The reporters, who had been scrambling for proximity, were doing a merry tap dance as I splattered their shoes with my stomach acid. Kathrine grabbed a space blanket and canopied my head as I heaved away.

"No photos, no photos!" She shooed them off then huddled under the blanket with me while her helpers took over as tent poles.

"All done?"

I nodded. She produced a tissue and wiped the residue off my face and shirt, then combed my hair off my face with her fingers, with the caring touch of a mother to her teen on a first date. She stepped back to check that I had no suspicious chunks lodged on my vest.

"Ready?"

"Ready."

She threw aside the blanket as if unveiling a masterpiece and in royal form I thrust my arms into the victory pose as the lights flashed and the cameras whirred. Third time Avon World Champion.

The next day, the Paris newspaper, *L'Equipe*, published a cartoon showing a prostitute standing on a street corner as a skinny woman, presumably me, whizzes by. "Twenty-thousand dollars pour ça," she scoffs, "C'est scandaleux!"

With my winnings I bought a townhouse. Wooden shingled, with heaps of windows, and numerous rooms, it was both close to downtown and the running trails along the western foothills of Boulder. I knew instantly that it was mine.

It was then that Clint presented me with an engagement ring; a large diamond solitaire that was a family heirloom. I was now engaged for the third time and Clint had just consolidated his place as my partner and equal in all things. I accepted with reservation.

My new home came with two mortgages, over double of what I had been paying in rent. I used to run with no thoughts of money. Now it was necessary I race often and well to cover our combined expenses. Clint had become job-resistant. He argued that after a skin cancer scare and ten years of working close to computer screens, the radiation was an occupational hazard he could do without. I could not argue with that one. Other jobs, he said, did not pay enough and he needed to be free to accompany me on trips. Besides, he reasoned, women have been sponging off men for centuries so his financial reliance on me was repayment of the karmic debt that modern women have incurred. As a case in point he declared that a woman had once lived with him for four months and he had paid all her living expenses. Unfortunately my philanthropy did not extend to clearing the liability of his past girlfriend and I resented being landed with the debts incurred by all females since Eve, and Clint appointing himself the recipient for all those duped males since Adam.

Holding on to the win from American Cindy Bremser in the 3,000 metre race, 1981 Pan Pacific
Conference Games in Christchurch, New Zealand. *Waikato Times*

Passing Julie Brown, 1986 Osaka International Ladies' Marathon.
Courtesy of Osaka International Ladies' Marathon and Sankei Sports

Finishing line, 1986 Osaka International Ladies' Marathon.
Courtesy of Osaka International Ladies' Marathon and Sankei Sports

The statue of Mercury,
downtown Osaka, Japan.

First samurai warrior helmet, 1986.
Courtesy of Osaka International Ladies'
Marathon and Sankei Sports

Start of 1987 Osaka International Ladies' Marathon. Wearing number '2'.
Courtesy of Osaka International Ladies' Marathon and Sankei Sports

Coach and trainer, brothers Gary and Gordon, Osaka, 1987.

Winning the 1989 Osaka
International Ladies' Marathon.
Courtesy of Osaka International Ladies'
Marathon and Sankei Sports

In third place and giving chase, 1992 Olympic Games, Barcelona. *Harlan Smith*

Dick Quax, friend, coach and mentor.

Victory lap at the 1992 Barcelona
Olympics. *Bruce Ulrich*

Standing on the steps of Parliament with the Rt Hon. Helen Clark, Prime Minister, then Minister of Health, along with brother Gary and other Commonwealth Games medallists, who gave their support to the Tobacco-free Sport Funding Bill, 1990. *The Dominion Post Collection, Alexander Turnbull Library, EP/1990/0521A*

With greatest running mentors, Kathrine Switzer and Dick Quax.

With Norwegian runner Ingrid Kristiansen and Diana, Princess of Wales, London Marathon, 1993.

With Harlan, our 'First Wedding',
1 August, 1993.

'Second Wedding' with fake cake,
Sapporo, 1993. *Studio Hayama, Sapporo*

'Third Wedding' in Boulder, Colorado,
4 September, 1993.

CHAPTER 31

New Channels

There are more things in heaven and earth, Horatio,
Than are dreamt of in your philosophy.
— From *Hamlet* by William Shakespeare

1985

Andy changed my life. I met him at a Seth Conference in Austin, Texas. I had seen a small ad for it in a magazine and without consulting Clint, I booked my ticket. *To hell with him,* I thought. *This is for me!* And in a few days I was off. It was early 1985.

I was out running every morning and so was Andy. "Great legs," I yelled at him as I flashed past. He was a presenter at the conference and I wanted him to remember me. He knew stuff I wanted to know. Actually, he did have great legs, tanned and muscular, evenly supporting a barrel of a body and a substantial face. He looked like Dick Van Dyke. Definitely a dog. And a Circle. Afterwards he sought me out and we quickly became friends.

That week we took many walks together while Andy explained to me the nuts and bolts of how we create our reality through the focus of our beliefs.

"Don't limit yourself," Andy urged. "You are no less than a creative, loving process in a realm of unlimited probabilities. But first you must learn to love yourself unconditionally."

"How do I do that?"

"Whenever life stops being fun for you, you're experiencing one of your limiting beliefs, a belief that you are something less than a creative, loving process. Life is giving you an opportunity to change that belief, a chance to love yourself where you previously haven't."

Once back home, I phoned Andy regularly. His talk energised me. Clint resented my conversations with him; I was way too enthusiastic. So next time Andy called I apologised and told him that I could not talk for long.

"Why not?"

"Clint doesn't like it. He thinks we're having an affair."

"Did you explain that we're not?"

"Yes. But he doesn't believe me."

"Well, that's his problem, not yours."

"But I still feel bad."

"So let me ask you this. Whose phone is it?"

"Mine."

"Who pays the bill?"

"Me."

"Do you want to keep talking?"

"Yes."

"Are you an adult?"

"Yes."

"So why do you give him the power to make the decision about what you do?"

"You're right."

We talked for another hour and apart from twinges of guilt I felt my resolve to run my own life strengthening. When I got to bed Clint was livid. I told him it was my phone and I would talk to whomever I liked, whenever I liked, for as long as I liked, and if he didn't like it he could get his own phone.

In the ensuing months I read and talked Seth constantly. At my insistence, Clint attempted to read *The Nature of Personal Reality* but could not get past the first chapter. This presented something of a problem for me. How could we get married if we didn't even agree on a common life philosophy?

I visited Andy whenever I was travelling close to where he was, eager to escape my home and delve deeper into the mysteries of life. Clint was jealous but I ignored him, and shared little of my new interest with him. Andy never disappointed. "If you're not having fun, don't do it," was Andy's favourite Seth quote and he lived his life by it. Dedicated to pleasing himself, he had the most unusual lifestyle of anyone I had met, breaking all the rules of conventional living. He stayed awake until four in the morning, usually messing with some new electronic gadget, and slept till midday; he drank Diet Pepsi constantly and ate an extremely high fat diet such as double cheese burgers and baked potatoes with all the fixin's, to which he would add a quarter-pound stick of butter. And yet he looked surprisingly healthy and stayed dedicated to his daily exercise routine and three-mile runs. "It's the ideas that are all-important," Andy emphasised, "the rest is props."

It was with Andy that I first became aware of my 'feeling-tones'. Andy told me that we all have them — the sounds of our own unique resonance. If I were to lie down quietly and tune in, I would become aware of them.

They started off as a hum in my ears, like being inside a seashell. The more I listened and felt for them, the louder and longer they became, rolling like waves in and out of shore, lengthening until I could feel them surging throughout my torso. It became a ritual for me to take a few moments on the start line of each race to catch the wave.

The moment I saw Harlan I wanted to be with him. I was visiting Andy in Los Angeles and taking an afternoon rest. I was marveling at the new discovery of these energy waves when Andy stuck his head in the room.

"Hey, Lorraine, there is someone from Florida I want you to meet."

Another head appeared, sandy haired, clean-cut, vital.

"Hi, I'm Harlan."

Ms Rational (she had become something of a feminist and now insisted on being addressed as Ms rather than Miss) butted in. *He's too good-looking for you so don't even think about it. You're already taken and don't doubt he is also. He's probably dashing off to meet a beach chick, before he gets back to another one, or two, in Florida. You know, blonde, big boobs busting out of a tight leather dress, great tan…*

All right, enough, I get the picture. Pity, I thought.

I put out my hand to introduce myself. The handshake: an invitation to read another's blueprint, palm to palm, universe to universe, the consolidation of a first impression. Harlan took it. "Pleased to meet you." His were large, useful hands: practical yet pliable; firm but kind; charming and straightforward. I liked his hands.

He stayed only a few minutes then was off. He was on a tight schedule.

Blonde, Ms Rational whispered in my ear as the door closed behind him.

Back in Boulder, I joined a Seth group, and we took to meeting for a weekly meditation at the home of a skinny, bespectacled guy. David had oily black hair that hung down his back in clumps, and told stories with great flair, waving his arms like an Italian as he spoke. I liked him right away. At first I had no idea he was gay, having never met gay people before, that I knew of, but I twigged when I noticed that his bookshelves were crammed with homosexual erotica. One evening, David greeted us wearing a sequined cocktail dress, which looked absurd with his beard. My world was being stretched in all directions.

I was sitting in his living room after a very deep group meditation, waiting for the rest of the members to come back to earth, when I saw a burning blue light in the middle of the floor. It was a translucent Christ-blue, with a yellowish-white corona burning strongly like a chemical flame.

Flame! Someone had dropped a candle on the carpet and now it was on fire! Without a moment to waste, I leapt up and stomped it out.

When David languorously sighed, "Lorraine, what ARE you doing?" as I jumped up and down on the spot, it became apparent that there was no flame and that nobody else could see the blue light.

Blue lights appeared regularly after that, and still do. At first I wondered if I had a detached retina, or a brain tumour, but as they persisted with no ill effects to my health, I decided to take them as a sign that Mercury is around, and is giving me the cosmic confirmation that I am on the right path.

One day I read in the local newspaper about a 'channel' in Boulder. Now this I had to see. So I booked myself in for a session with Jonah, a non-physical being who on occasion borrowed the body of an earthbound soul, so that seekers like me might uncover the mystery of our existence.

I was a little nervous when I showed up at the mountain home where this inter-dimensional event was to unfold. A smiling middle-aged woman showed me into the room and I sat waiting for her husband, the channel, to arrive. When he walked into the room, he was, well … ordinary: a little portly, a little balding and a little reticent in his manner. He sat in a big easy chair, his wife at his side. I waited. He seemed to fall asleep and for a while nothing happened. Suddenly his breathing became shallow, quickly evolving into a series of short snorts which quite startled me. His body began to twitch randomly like a man in an electric chair and then his face scrunched and pulled from side to side as if the incoming entity was putting on a sweater five sizes too small. And then he opened his eyes and stared directly at me with his head tilted to the side and a presence so big that his eyes bulged. Jonah was in.

I was intimidated. I stammered around with long pauses, searching for the questions that I wanted to ask. I can't remember much of what he said. But I do recall him telling me that Andy and I were well connected and had been brothers several times in other lives. Hence our relationship this time would be one of assistance to one another as with siblings and much would come of it. He was not so enthusiastic about my relationship with Clint, saying that it had served its purpose. And he was adamant that my duty in this lifetime was to 'speak out', adding that this time I would not be burned at the stake, or have my head chopped off for doing so.

When I arrived home Clint declared I was 'an easy target for hucksters and pranksters' and that I had just been fleeced. But of course he wanted to know what Jonah had said about him — just in case.

Considering the content, I declined to talk any more about it.

Within a few weeks I had issued a challenge to Clint that he come to a session and judge for himself. At the risk of appearing closed-minded by refusing, he accepted.

During our hour-long session I asked again about our relationship. I wanted Jonah to tell him what I could not. Jonah did not disappoint. In a past life, he relayed, Clint had been a cripple and I had carried him around on my back. He looked directly at Clint. "What you need to remember in this lifetime is that you can walk."

That really pissed Clint off. Afterwards he denounced channelling as the sham he always knew it to be.

"My turn." In our Manhattan hotel, the night before the New York City Marathon, Clint was insisting that I massage his legs since he had massaged mine last week. I protested that my race at the front of the elite division was more important than his race in the midfield of the citizens' division, but he didn't want to hear it. He lay face down on the bed. "Fair's fair," he mumbled into the pillow. As my fingers pressed up and down his calves at his incessant direction, I realised that this was absurd and that the burden of carrying him was too heavy. I was better off without him. But I said nothing.

The next day, race day, I was chock-full of resentment. Somewhere around halfway, my calves went into what could be termed 'umbrage lock-up.' Like Beverly Hills chihuahuas they were pouting that they had not received their massage and were going on strike. I dropped off the leading pack. As I watched the leaders disappear, I blamed Clint.

I started to wish I would start coughing blood or get run over by a cabbie who had gone bonkers over the road closures. I would even have gone for the stray gunshot to the head but that one had already been used in this race, and the runner had gone on to finish. Failing is miserable but how to fail with minimal damage is an art I had not perfected. For a while I couldn't decide whether to quit or trudge into the minor places. There is no doubt about quitting. You will surely be accused of lacking in guts but your talent is less likely to be brought into question. DNF in the results is dismissible. A number, like eleventh or sixteenth or fifth, follows you around.

So I quit. Then I wished I hadn't. Stopping is easy. Pulling out is a problem. When you have just chosen non-action, next-action is now a dilemma. You become stranded. And cold. And embarrassed. You want someone to rescue you.

As I stood there stupidly, Eino came flying towards me. When he saw me loitering in the middle of Seventh Avenue he screeched to a halt. A Californian Finn, and a sculptor of renown, Eino is craggy, wild-haired and sinewy, with a fervent passion for people and art and running. Now in his fifties and still extremely fit, his ambition had stoked his engine too hot in the first few miles and meeting me was now the perfect excuse to stop.

"What's wrong with you?" His voice was deep and gravelly as if he had been born with a cigarette in his mouth.

"Calf cramps. Don't stop for me. Keep going."

"What are you going to do?"

"I don't know. Please don't stop for me, I'll be okay." As much as I wanted company, I didn't want the burden of his demise as well as my own.

"Which leg?" Eino had just appointed himself as my saviour from mid-marathon abandonment.

"You can do it!" spectators yelled to us. We ignored them. Hordes of runners wove their way around us while I lamented the unyield-ing protest of my lower legs to the only person in the world who seemed to care. Fortunately he knew the way back to the hotel, so we detoured off the course as people yelled, "Come back! This way! This way!"

We ran on, deaf, in the direction of the hotel. I noticed that my calf muscles didn't seem to hurt nearly so much, but feigned a little limp every dozen strides, just to let Eino see that I truly was disadvantaged. He was pushing the pace and soon we were running sub-six minute miles. Eino is a half-stepper: the type who can't help running a half-step ahead of you. Soon we were racing each other as we wove our way into Manhattan. We made it back to my hotel in a dead-heat sprint finish, in the nick of time to run up to my hotel room and see the winners finish on TV.

Clint was thrilled with his own performance and claimed his place as the hero of the day, which only compounded my resentment. "My turn for a leg massage," I reminded him. He gave my legs a cursory once-over, and then laid down for his turn again. It was two leg massages too many.

When we got home I returned Clint's engagement ring. I could not marry him, though I could not bring myself to break up. It was not love, but guilt over my extramarital affair with him that now bonded me to him.

CHAPTER 32

A Classy Affair

JANUARY 1986

The founder of the Osaka International Ladies' Marathon, Yuki, thought that the word 'Ladies' distinguished it as a classier, more genteel, race than the slightly more crass word 'Women's' that the other leading Japanese marathons used in their titles. Certainly this was a premier race, and arguably the most illustrious women's, ahem, ladies' marathon in the world. When I arrived in Japan I had no idea how prestigious.

They were giving me appearance money and were willing to bring both my mother and my aunt along for the ride, so I was happy to turn up and race. At the time I was training the Boulder winter away in the warm summer rays of New Zealand, as had become my yearly ritual. Clint was left behind, with the ultimatum that he get a job by the time I returned a few months later. I was now in the full thrust of my freedom phase of life, without a coach, trainer, agent or boyfriend in tow — just Mercury swinging around my neck, urging me to be open and trust in the process.

Bright lights and a television camera glared at us on the concourse as we disembarked from our flight at Osaka International airport. We were not yet cleared through customs. This was not at all usual. *There must be someone famous on the plane*, I concluded and started craning my neck to see if I could see Elizabeth Taylor or Michael Jackson. When I turned back the camera was in my face and a young lady bowed and thrust a huge bouquet of flowers into my arms. We were then whisked into a press conference. I came to the conclusion that marathon running was a big deal here and that the expectations of me were very high. My mother was thrilled to see that her daughter 'the star' was receiving the attention that she imagined I received wherever I went.

"Mum," I whispered, "don't think it is always like this." But I knew she was not swayed.

The Japanese, I have discovered, tend to ask three questions in press interviews. "What is your goal?" "What is your condition?" and "What is your impression of Japan?" My goal, I said, was to run my best. I waited for this to be interpreted. The answer seemed to satisfy.

"And your condition?"

"Yes, I am in good condition."

The impression of Japan was an easy one. "I have heard that Japan is very beautiful and the people are kind and gracious hosts. I have never been received so well as in this country." I meant it.

Quite often they will throw in a fourth question: "What is your slogan?" I since learned that some answers are better than others, for example, the slogan 'Fight the good fight' goes over much better than 'It's not over till the fat lady sings', but this time I was not prepared and couldn't think of a slogan. I was not to be let off easily.

"Some words for good race," the interpreter prompted.

"Go, go go." It was all I could think of in a jet-lagged pinch. The reporters nodded and wrote it down.

They wanted more: training times, race results, spreadsheets. What could I tell them? Certainly not that I was now being coached by Mercury and that feelings, not times, were my guidelines to gauging my condition. I answered with woolly, meaningless adjectives, like 'fine' and 'good' and let the interpreter dress it up as she wanted. She seemed to be inventing whole paragraphs around my cursory three-word answers.

Meantime Mum was sitting off to the side. I noticed that a young reporter had sidled up to her and with his pen to pad, seizing the opportunity to steal an inside scoop.

"Does Miss Morrer have a ruvver?" he queried.

"A what?"

"A ruvver."

"Ruvver?"

"Yes, ruvver."

Suddenly she twigged to the gist of his question and swatted at him with her passport.

"I am her mother," she replied indignantly, "and do not answer such questions!"

At the hotel we seemed to be in the care of Michiyo. Like all Japanese women she was immaculately groomed, and while it is near impossible to gauge the age of a Japanese person by the western standard of facial wrinkles, by demeanor she had the self-possession of one who had been in the corporate world for quite some time. It turned out she was the right-hand woman to the Mizuno family dynasty.

Mizuno was a major sponsor for the race and were paying me a few thousand dollars to run in their gear for this marathon only. They were the largest sporting goods manufacturer in the world, but running was just a minor branch of their business, and they had not to date had a sponsorship programme for runners, such as the shoe giants Nike, Adidas, Reebok and Asics offered. But here in Osaka, their international headquarters, this race was generating so much attention that they were considering whether to ramp up their running shoe and apparel manufacturing, and to sponsor a runner on a long-term basis. Little did I know that I was on trial and that this high-ranking woman had been assigned to me for this purpose.

"What is your training?" she asked.

I looked out and scouted the terrain. It was about five-thirty p.m. and already the sun had set and the street was lit by lamps, neon signs and the car lights of rush hour traffic.

"Nah, it's okay. It's getting dark and I don't know where to go."

But Michiyo insisted that my training must be done, and mindful that I do the right thing I agreed to a short run.

She turned to Mum and Nancy, my aunt. "Do you want to see her run?" They looked at me for the right answer. I shrugged. They would have much preferred scouting for shops. But they, too, wanted to do the right thing, so they nodded.

We met 20 minutes later for my training. Michiyo had commandeered a station wagon which I was to follow. I found myself face to face with a cameraman on his belly recording my evening training through the open hatch for that night's news broadcast. Mum and Nancy with our interpreter trailed me in a taxi. It was just a baby run to blow out the phoo-phoo valve after the long flight and I had not expected such a production. But since I was on TV I was mindful of showing a little spring in my legs, and out of deference to this formal culture forwent the one-fingered nostril snort that I had perfected in 15 years of running in favour of a surreptitious sleeve-wipe.

We encircled a three mile block and arrived back at the hotel. I had planned to run for about ten more minutes so continued on, while my entourage stopped at the red lights. Somehow I took a wrong turn. Next thing I heard my name being yelled and turned to see Michiyo in her flawlessly tailored business suit and heeled pumps dodging cars as she flailed after me, her stocky legs churning like egg-beaters. I was already heading down the on-ramp of a major freeway and, in the nick of time, Michiyo had saved me from being road-kill and someone else, possibly herself, from the social mandate of hara-kiri.

After my navigating misadventure we returned to the hotel to change and then were picked up by Michiyo in a chauffeur-driven car and taken out to dinner. Afterwards Michiyo took us by Mizuno headquarters on our way home. It was eight-thirty p.m. and yet the lights were on in the high-rise building and people were at their desks.

"How late do people work here?" we asked.

"Till six o'clock." Michiyo said.

"Then why are they still here?"

"No-one likes to be the first to leave. So they stay to show their loyalty."

The next day Michiyo introduced me to a visitor at the hotel. He was Akito Mizuno, the second son of the President of the Mizunos, a rather shy and sweet man, who had come on behalf of the company to wish me luck.

The day before the race I was again summoned to the hotel common room by Michiyo. This time I was introduced to Masato Mizuno, first son, the heir to the presidency. Masato, sporting what I came to know as his characteristically good-natured smile, had come to personally wish me 'Good luck'. He then took us to dinner, a meal that stretched out to 12 courses, presumably to ensure I was well fed before the race.

I was a bit of an anomaly to the Japanese. To begin with, I stood taller than most of them. Also, at 32, I was just plain old for a marathon runner. Most women retired in their early twenties once they got married. Then while the other runners showed up with their coaches, invariably males who tutored their every move, I had appeared with my aunt and mother. While they looked like unlikely coaches they were assigned badges in Japanese that, unbeknownst to them, titled them as 'Coach' and 'Trainer'. Our hosts were left scratching their heads when both my 'Coach' and 'Trainer' declined to attend any more of my training sessions and asked to be directed to the shops instead. What's more, they appeared totally clueless when interviewed about my training and racing strategy. Their standard answer was "I don't know", with a shrug of the shoulders; "Go ask Lorraine." Finally when I decided not to train one day, preferring to rest, I was besieged by phone calls from marathon staff who thought that I must be injured. To them a day off was incomprehensible.

As the week wore on I came to realise that I had stiff competition. American Julie Brown, the winner of the 1975 World Cross-country Champs in Morocco, on a similar career path to my own, had be-come a marathon runner, and with a career best of two hours and 26 minutes was considered one of the top women for the distance in the world.

I relished the one-on-one competition. Besides, with my new philo-sophy, I was now dedicated to the path that Mercury would present to me, and trusted that whatever the outcome it would be a good learning experience, even if it meant a thrashing from a better runner.

1986 Osaka International Ladies' Marathon — Japan

The day of the race dawned and we were bussed out to the stadium for a noon start. Mum and Nancy were as nervous as I was and twittered around until I had to tell them to buzz off and leave me to my own devices. Finally it was time to march out onto the stadium to warm up. I stripped down to my racing gear. Without my jacket, Mercury was flapping on my neck, impractical for the race, so I dashed over to Mum and gave the pendant to her to wear for luck while I was out on the streets. I needed my focus.

I stood on the start line and affirmed my new path. *This is the time to let go and do what I have trained for. Take care of each moment and let the outcome take care of itself,* I told myself. I tuned into my feeling-tones, and felt the familiar waves run up and down my body. *May whatever happens be for the good of all,* I entreated silently. And off we went.

The course consisted of a huge loop around Osaka City and finished back in the stadium. It was the cool of winter, perfect racing weather for me, and flat with long stretches of smooth road. The sidelines were packed with spectators, cheering, flag-waving, three-deep along the entire 26 miles.

Julie Brown raced out to the front quickly and established a sizeable lead. I paced myself as I knew I must. By half way she was so far in front of me that I could no longer see her. It seemed I would be second. I pondered second. *To be so clearly trounced and so early on. Perhaps Mercury is leading me astray, away from the winning way. Perhaps I need something along the lines of a coach with a bullhorn and a bamboo stick who will bully me into faster times, like some of the Japanese runners are rumoured to have.* Doubt, the great diluter of focus, was suddenly hitching a ride on my back, and slowing me up.

Ha! Should have stuck with what you knew! Ms Rational chimed in. As I debated with her whether my commitment to Mercury was a tactical error, I rounded the corner that took us into the central business district. There, in my direct line of vision, was a life-sized statue of Mercury.

My heart leapt. There was magic in the world! Mercury's finger was in the air, pointing to the high road, the path of higher consciousness. I was beginning to catch on that we're taken there by way of our shortcomings. *Do not doubt me*, Mercury transmitted, *I will never lead you astray.* This was the confirmation that I needed. I looked up and to my utter amazement Julie Brown was now right in front of me. It was as if I had jumped forward in space. Impossibly, I had instantly gained a hundred yards. It was not that I had defied the laws of physics; it was just that the laws had not yet been rewritten to take into account the hand of Mercury. Shortly thereafter I passed Julie and went on to win the race handsomely.

At the finish the press clustered around.

"When did you know you were going to win?" they clamored.

"When I saw the statue of Mercury," I answered. Nobody knew what I was talking about, so I stood up on the ball of my foot, my leg raised behind me and my finger pointing in the air, but drew a blank from my questioners. After putting it a few different ways, the interpreter finally gave up and moved on to my coach and trainer to see if they made any more sense.

With the press conference, awards and autograph-signing it was five p.m. by the time we arrived back at the hotel. The race had been over just a few hours, but on the news-stand was the evening paper with my winning photo on the cover.

That night, for the marathon party and more awards, I dressed up to the nines as I loved to do. Many of the runners chose to attend these events in their sweats but modelling myself on the style of Kathrine Switzer, I was prepared to put myself out as a trend-setter. I had come armed with a cocktail dress and high-heeled shoes, and a magnificent sparkly silk scarf that I could not have dared to wear had I not won.

The prizes were lined up on display: a rich array of trophies and cultural items. When I was called up on stage, the presentations seemed endless. I was given flowers, a camera, a tape player, a large silver cup, a gold medal, a framed ornamental fan, a replica of a Samurai warrior helmet with a large lacquered box to contain it, and the ribbon from the finishing line.

The next day we were taken to the Mizuno shop where they invited me to take anything I wanted. A model had been erected wearing my sweaty running clothes from the day before, my autographed shoes carefully arranged at the feet.

That afternoon we were invited down to the marathon headquarters where a committee was preparing a post-marathon tour of the quaint old city of Kyoto for me, Mum and Aunt Nancy. Mum and Nancy, who had come laden with New Zealand souvenirs which they had lavished on their hosts, now took the opportunity to present Mr Chigusa, the race director and a popular television show host, with some gifts. Being an artistic type, he distinguished himself from the sombre salaryman by forgoing the dark suit for wild, colourful clothing and perming his hair so that frizzy, thin, black twirls sprang out of his head. He sat at the table with his committee.

Mum handed him a gift bag, which back in her room had doubled as a laundry bag.

"For me?"

"Yes," we nodded in unison.

He pulled the first item out of the bag. Sheepskin slippers. He bowed profusely.

"Thank you, thank you, thank you."

He peered again in the bag. There was another gift. A handsome hand-knit sweater in bright colours. This time his bowing surpassed his last bout and he swung back and forth like a wind-up toy.

"Thank you, thank you, thank you."

He put his hand into the bag one more time and pulled up another item which he held in front of him. His body was bending into an automatic bow but his face was crinkled with confusion. He was gingerly holding my mother's petticoat. She looked up and swiped it from him with a sharp, "That's mine!" He looked as if he just been caught stealing panties off a clothesline. And then we all laughed so hard the tears ran down our faces. It was the ultimate gift.

That evening we were invited to a Mizuno press conference. A room was filled with Mizuno representatives, and we stood around tables eating cocktail food and raising our glasses as we all chimed, *Campai!* (cheers). I was then ushered to the microphone to give a speech for which I was totally unprepared. Once again I was being tested, but the interval afforded by the interpreters gave me time to think of what to say next. I thanked them all profusely, and attributed my win to my superior footwear. That evening I was invited to dinner with not just first and second Mizuno sons but with Mr Mizuno himself, the president of the company. I had won approval from the top. Shortly thereafter I signed a two-year sponsorship contract with Mizuno.

Later that year I finally asked Clint to move out. Jonah was right. Our relationship had served its purpose. Clint had made me feel beautiful but now it was time to move on.

I stayed unattached for the next three years, deliberately shunning men I found attractive.

1986 marked the beginning of my two best years of road racing.

CHAPTER 33

Love Beams

Whoso loves, believes the impossible.
— Elizabeth Barrett Browning

1986

I love myself. I lo-ove myself. I love myself!

I was repeating these words with all the conviction I could muster as I listened to the motivational tape Andy had made me. At first I could not say the words even though I was alone. I choked on them.

"The degree of difficulty you have with this exercise is the degree to which you don't love yourself. How much you love yourself determines how much you can love others and how much love you can accept back from them. So this is important because it sets the parameters of how you experience life. Promise me, no matter how hard it is for you, that you'll listen to it twice daily for a month. There's a time lag for things to be manifested in this reality, so you'll start to notice some really nice things happening for you after you've listened to it for a month."

"Like what?"

"Whatever you want."

"I want to win all my races. Will I run faster?"

"If you want."

This was not the answer I wanted. I was hoping for some sort of guarantee.

"So promise you'll listen to it?"

"Yep."

Because I trusted Andy I swallowed my resistance and listened to his tape faithfully, as promised. In three weeks' time, just as Andy said, some 'really nice' things happened.

The Norwegian super-star, Grete Waitz, won almost every race she ran. I had never come within spitting distance of her after the start line. Now here she was at the 15-kilometre Cascade Run-Off, ready to add another title to her large collection.

But Mercury was hovering and change was afoot.

At the pre-race press conference I was seated next to Grete in the front row facing the audience. As expected, the press mostly wanted to talk to her and the rest of us were just fillers. As she sat, patiently answering questions, a strange sensation came over me. I felt as if I was growing bigger, taller, and more powerful. As I did, Grete seemed to be shrinking into her chair, like a slowly deflating balloon.

When I left, the feeling of expansiveness was still with me and I felt a new confidence, as if I had just been remodelled from the inside out. I was walking with another runner, Sue Schneider, whom I had known from my time in Minneapolis.

"Is there any way you think you could beat Grete?" I asked.

"No, not a chance,' she replied, "What about you?"

"You know, for the first time I think it's possible."

As expected, Grete led from the start. The first five kilometres wound up through the hills, the second five kilometres scooted down the other side, and the last five kilometres were a level, straight shot along the riverfront to the finish.

I started comfortably, letting Grete go. I knew that if I had a show of challenging her my effort needed to be impeccably meted out, fast enough up the hill so that her lead was not insurmountable, but conservative enough that I had the energy left to take her on near the finish.

I climbed steadily up the hill, focused and intent on my task. As I crested the top I knew I was on target for a good one. But I had no idea how far ahead Grete was. I did know that she disliked downhills and ran them with the brakes on. Not me, I careered down. Free energy. My dad always took a free turn when driving, even if it went away from where he was going, because, he said, he could never turn down anything that was free. I guess it rubbed off on me when it came to downhills.

The terrain was flattening out and I was approaching the ten-kilometre mark when I saw Grete, her pigtails flying behind her and her escorts like bodyguards, flanking her.

I was at Mercury's Crossroads: that point where you play safe or take a risk. This was the cue Ms Rational had been waiting for. She jumped out and started quoting from T.S. Eliot's poem 'The Lovesong of J. Alfred Prufrock'. *Do you dare disturb the universe?*

She's right. I can't pass Grete. It's not right. Suddenly I felt guilty that I had had such sacrilegious thoughts. *What was I thinking?* Busy apologising to Ms Rational, I found that my momentum had now carried me to Grete's back and, short of stopping, I was on my way to passing her. Ms Rational cringed. *Now you've blown it*, she said, dramatically, assuming the crash position.

Taking her cue, I scrunched myself down, hoping to look smaller. Maybe she won't even see me, I hoped. But she did. Of course she did. For a moment I was terrified. *Now she'll put on her afterburners and blast me out of the atmosphere and, of course, I will be humiliated.*

But Grete graciously waved me through. She was not up for challenging that day and let me know it. I won. Grete finished second. The universe was disturbed.

Love, I decided after that, was the greatest force in the universe, the essence of life, and infinitely abundant. If I could project love I could run freely and effortlessly and as a result of this expression the world would be a better place. My priorities were probably not in the right order, and the sentiment, while sincere, was seeded by ambition, which is why I did not pause to consider that if I felt loving on all levels, then I would probably cease to have cause to compete.

From my regular talks with Andy I was convinced that my beliefs, propelled by the force of their attendant emotions, positive or negative, created the circumstances of my reality. When it came to racing, I knew that my anger, of the red-hot 'I'll show them' variety was often the thrust I needed for that something extra, and if I was riled up enough, I was a formidable opponent. It always helped to be written off by the press or someone whose opinion I cared about, or to have a grudge against one of my competitors, such as believing they were blood-doped or taking steroids. But I also knew that my anger stemmed from negative beliefs about myself and that if I wanted to take the big one, an Olympic gold medal, I would have to deal with those beliefs or be limited by them. It was still unclear what exactly I was angry about. I knew I was still angry at Ron, and definitely angry at the cheats I had to compete against, but I also knew it went deeper than that and I was not yet ready to mine for the source. Besides, I was not sure if I could give up my anger as my font of racing power. I still had good use for it — but I was willing to experiment.

I had a new strategy for my next race, held in Southfork, Dallas, home of JR from the popular TV series. The course consisted of a ten-kilometre loop around the complex, finishing in the grounds outside the mansion. Anne Audain would be there. Forgoing the marathon, she had gone back to her distance, the ten-kilometres, and now she was, arguably, the ten-kilometre ruler of North America. She would be the hardest, the perfect, challenge for the test of love.

As I waited on the start line for the gun to go off, I connected with my feeling-tones, this time assigning them the sweet waves of love. Bang! We were off. As usual I sat back for the first few miles, and once past halfway picked up the pace. One by one I lovingly passed women until, with a mile to go, there was just one runner ahead of me — Anne — confidently galloping for the finish line.

I knew I must pass decisively and powerfully so that I could gain a gap on her. I surged hard, barreling past her as I bombarded her with rays of love. "I love you, I love you," I repeated over and over to her in my mind. She mustered all she could but was spent. I went on to win, leaving Anne in my wake, just a little bewildered, I thought. Afterwards she was a good sport about it all as I continued to love-bomb her.

I was amazed. Love works! I had considered love as an emotional drive too soft and fluffy for competitive purposes, like trying to launch a pink cloud towards your goal rather than a poisoned arrow. But I had discovered when it came to the goal, the quality of the emotion, love or anger, did not really matter: it was the intensity of the focus that brought results. For sure, loving Anne had taken a much more sustained focus than I was used to and I had found it somewhat wearisome. But this was because I was not used to it. I had still won. I reasoned that if I could refine this harnessing of love, I would win my races, laughing all the way to the tape, my cells sparkling and continually replenished. This was now my goal.

On my way home on the plane, still high on both love and success, I made a pact with myself: if I had knowledge that would help someone else, I would share it freely.

I couldn't wait to call Andy and tell him of my success. Thinking of love brought up thoughts of Andy's friend, Harlan. Harlan had left the girlfriend in the tight leather dress and moved to Andy's house in Pennsylvania. Sometimes when I called Andy Harlan answered. He always pretended he didn't know who I was. "Lorraine who?" he would ask and I would have to go to great lengths to describe myself.

"The runner?"

"Yes. From New Zealand."

"Noo Zealand?"

"Yes. I live in Boulder."

"Boulder?"

He would keep repeating my answers back to me as questions until I finally asked to speak to Andy. At first I thought I rated less than a memory with him, but after about the tenth time I figured out it was his way of flirting with me.

My friends in Boulder thought I was wacky.

"What training are you doing now?" David Welch, coach and husband of the British marathon runner, Priscilla Welch, greeted me, "Sub-aqua?"

Usually I would reply to such questions earnestly with something like, "No, Dave I have discovered crystals and strap them all over my body." Dave would guffaw loudly, then tentatively ask a few more questions, just to make sure I didn't have something they might need. This time I told him in all sincerity that I had something so powerful it was mind-blowing.

"What?" He looked at me suspiciously.

"Love beams."

"Harrumph!" he snorted back, rolling his eyeballs.

CHAPTER 34

Killer Instinct

Do not wait to strike till the iron is hot,
but make it hot by striking.
— William Butler Yeats

AUGUST 1986

I was fairly confident that I could win the 1986 Commonwealth Games Women's Marathon. This was Edinburgh, the ancestral land of my mother's line, and I was tuning into those fearsome ruffians — the Gunns. Love beams were the furthest things from my mind. The only woman I considered competition was Lisa Martin, who had finished seventh in the Los Angeles Olympics. But could someone with a commonly decent name like Martin be a threat to a descendant of the war-mongering Gunns, especially one who had defeated the invincible Grete Waitz just a few months earlier? Not a chance.

One day I was on a training run along the streets of Edinburgh when I saw a quincunx of people running towards me. While the runners on the outside looked like rugby players, the central figure was more like the real thing. He had a familiar face so I waved with a big friendly smile and yelled, 'Hello!'. He responded in kind and we ran on, two runners doing what runners do, acknowledging the family. Only when I was well down the road did I realize that it was Prince Edward.

A few days after that I was invited with a select few athletes to join the royal family for lunch: her Majesty the Queen, her husband

248

Prince Philip and Their Royal Highnesses, Princess Diana and Prince Charles. They seated me next to Prince Philip, who talked to me as if we were old buddies, and I felt as if he actually remembered me. The discussion eventually led to the African boycott of the Games, which caused him considerable concern for the Commonwealth. He also brought up the issue of Daly Thomson, the English decathlete who had caused a stir by wearing a personal sponsor's logo in a pre-games meet, instead of the team's. The Duke made it clear he sided with Daly. When a fellow sitting across from us said that the Games sponsors needed to be considered, the Duke thumped the table. "Bugger the sponsors!" He startled me, but I took his candour as a compliment.

I raced the Commonwealth Games 3,000 metres as a warm-up to the marathon. Although it was my first track race for a year, I was in good enough shape to finish well up in the field, in the place reserved just for me — fifth. This augured well for the marathon a few days later.

On a crisp clear morning the first Women's Commonwealth Games Marathon commenced from the stadium, on a course that went out to the coast for some fresh salt air and wound back again to the stadium. Lisa cleared out early and I sat about 100 metres behind her. My plan was to pass her after 20 miles. *It is always a psychological blow to have someone pass you when you think you have it won*, I gloated to myself as I grabbed my isotonic sports drink — new on the market — which was sure to give me the edge on this warm day.

I should have known better. Those drinks have never sat well with me. Within a half mile I had the stitch so badly that I had to double over to keep moving. The pain intensified and I had to stop. At this stage I thought of quitting. But after a bit of a break and looking around, there was still no-one in sight. I figured that no one ever died from the stitch so I may as well keep going. Why throw away a silver medal?

I resumed running for a mile, crunched over to minimise the stabbing in my right side. Soon the intensity grew again, bringing me to another stop. I dug my fingers in my side, gyrated back and forth, and then walked a while clutching my ribs. After a few minutes it subsided. Lisa was galloping away to gold in the distance. This time I was sure I would have to drop out. But when I turned there were still no other runners close and so very gingerly I resumed running. There were still eight miles to go. But the worst was over and I plugged on to the finish for second place. I had just won a silver medal for my country and, despite two walking intervals, a time for the marathon that would remain the best of my career: two hours, 28 minutes and 17 seconds.

Waiting for the awards ceremony, I sat in a waiting room with Lisa. After all the cursory congratulations were performed I could not help myself.

"So that makes us even," I said.

Lisa looked perturbed. "No," she replied, "that makes it four to three, to me."

As I guessed, she was counting also. We runners cannot help it.

"No, no, I countered, "four all."

Lisa reeled off her list of races where we have both competed, starting with the 1984 Olympics. She finished with this one, "... and that makes four to me and three to you."

I knew then that I had her. "And what about Boston?"

"Boston?"

"Yes, Boston, this year." My run there had been nothing to boast about but now my finish was invaluable.

"But I dropped out of that, it doesn't count."

"Oh, yes it does. If you stand on the start line it counts, that's the way it works."

Lisa was disgruntled but did not refute me. I was satisfied.

When we stood on the podium, the commentators noted how I looked so much happier with my silver than she did with her gold. My guess is that she was still thinking that it was not fair that I had counted Boston. And I was thinking that she had just bought my version of the rules, and that I had just set myself up well for my next encounter with her, in five months' time.

I had two new family 'coaches' for the 1987 Osaka International Ladies' Marathon: my bothers, Gary and Gordon. Unlike my mother and aunt, they eagerly attended the technical meetings and accompanied me on training runs; much more interested in the lead-up to the marathon than in shopping. As we had the same family name, one brother was presumed by some to be my husband and coach, the other his brother and my trainer. We did not bother to find out who was alleged to be what.

Being the reigning Osaka Marathon champion was not enough to earn being hailed as pre-race favourite. Lisa had defeated me in Edinburgh and had run two minutes faster. She was an up-and-coming champion, young and full of potential, while I was tough but, sadly, ageing. I was treated with the utmost respect, but I could feel the tide of expectation turned towards Lisa and against me. I would have to work for this one.

At the press conference the same three standard questions were asked of each of us: What is your condition? What is your goal? And how do you like Japan?

Lisa went first. She said her training indicated that she was in good shape and her goal was to run 2:25. A little jolt went through me. Lisa was fit and ready to declare it. I had learned from Anne Audain at the 1984 Olympics that the press can be used to one's advantage. When it came to my turn, I knew what I had to say, and that I needed to set aside my Kiwi humility and say it with confidence.

"My training indicates that I am in excellent shape," I began, "and my goal is to run 2:24." I said the numbers clearly so there was no mistaking them. I had just committed fraud. Such a time, some four minutes faster than my previous best, was in truth quite a mental stretch for me. I continued, "I know I am in shape to run such a fast time because I ran a personal best time recently at the Commonwealth Games, even though I had to stop and walk due to the stitch … twice." I thought I saw a little jolt go through Lisa.

Afterwards we were taken to a karaoke bar. The TV cameras were stalking the foreign guests, keen to get some news coverage of them enjoying Japanese hospitality. I could not think of anything more embarrassing than singing unaccompanied in public. Whenever I was required to sing in the spotlight only a weak sound was emitted, like water trickling from a leaky tap. I had ceased full-throttle singing at about age six when in hospital my voice took on a timid timbre, a combination of defeat at not being heard and hope that if I was quiet enough I would detect my mother's footsteps returning to get me.

Lisa, along with the other invited runners, refused to take the microphone. Just two days before the big race and they were all too shy. Here was my opportunity to trump them by proving to be a fearless risk-taker. Inside I was trembling as I seized the microphone and did the unthinkable — I sang 'Jingle Bells' on national television, solo. I thought it was an easy song, but I started flat and careered off the musical scale after that. It was so horrible that my hosts loved it. They commented with polite smirks, that "Ms Morrer is much better at running."

Lisa leaned over, "How did you do that? I would never be brave enough."

I shrugged like it was no big deal. Flat or not, I had made my point.

The night before the race, Lisa and I were treated by the race or-ganisers to a special dinner at a Chinese restaurant in the hotel. This quickly became an ordeal for Lisa who fretted about her food 'being of contributing value to her race'. She vetoed dish after dish as she scanned the glossy pictures on the menu for a familiar item. Finally she found something that she could identify — peas. When her meal arrived it was a huge steaming dish of plain old peas, and nothing else. It was a reassuring sign for me. Lisa was micro-managing: focused on the side dishes because she had lost confidence in the main course — herself. As I chowed down fried rice and shrimp in garlic sauce, Lisa solemnly picked at her peas one by one with a fork.

1987 Osaka International Ladies' Marathon — Japan

I shivered as I stepped off the bus. There was snow in the atmos-phere. Along with the other invited women runners I huddled around a kerosene heater in a small concrete room underneath the stadium, waiting until it was time to warm up outside. When we marched out for the short ceremony to open the event, the stands were crowded with spectators despite the chilly weather. These dedicated running fans would cheer us for a lap of the stadium at the start, huddle under their blankets for two and a half hours, watching the race on the big screen as we circled the city, and then stand to enthusiastically cheer us for a final lap around the track to the finish line.

We stripped down to our racing clothes. Lisa and I were both going light: I in my bun-huggers and pink nylon singlet with New Zealand emblazoned across the chest, and a pair of cotton white gloves to keep my fingertips from freezing off, and she in her skimpy nylon one-piece, with two long white sleeves covering her arms. Her hair was tied back in a sophisticated knot at the back; she wore big silver knobs on her ears, her eyelashes thick with mascara. Along with her long white gloves she conveyed an elegance from the waist up fit for a night at the opera.

By fifteen miles the race had developed into a two woman show-down. Much as I loathe leading in the mid-stages of a marathon, Lisa was determined to stick to my tail, drafting in my slipstream while saving herself for the final dash to the finish. This time I was not fazed. While her position was technically the most coveted, leading, being in the winning position, had its own psychological advantage. Besides, in the past few days I had cultivated an attitude of strength, and confidence in any situation. *Look at me, look at how strong I am,* I telepathically transmitted to Lisa behind me, *I'm in front because I'm the winner.* I took to singing it over and over in my head.

For an hour we ran like this, through the corridors of waving Japanese fans, and snow flurries that kissed our red cheeks. With three kilometres to go, Lisa suddenly drew alongside, stripping off her gloves, discarding them to the ground. The gauntlet had been thrown down.

This was my cue. I stole her move, delivering it more decisively and forcefully than she could muster. The commentators called it a 'long hard surge' to the finish line. The race was clearly mine.

By the time we returned to the hotel, as had been the case last time, the evening paper featuring my winning image was already on the news-stands.

There was never much time to relax after the race. The awards were scheduled from seven to eight p.m. Here, this meant *precisely*. The whole affair was rapidly developing into a fashion parade for the runners. Our invitation to the race now included a little prompt: 'Please bring a dress for the awards presentation.'

I had just taken a shower when there was a knock at my door. It was Rita, a Portuguese runner, who had a request of me.

"Do you have any lipstick?"

"Yes of course, borrow what you want."

"Not for me, I don't wear lipstick, it is for Elena. The Russians do not have lipstick, you see."

Yes, I did see. The eastern bloc women always turned up to the race with a coach and a very dour man in a trench-coat who followed them around and made sure they kept to the programme, did their duty, and did not defect. They had neither the resources nor the support to enjoy the shopping mall across the street. I had observed one Russian woman eat exclusively snacks set out in the common room, for the entire week, pocketing her per diem food allowance so that she could purchase a TV which she lugged onto the plane. I remember holding out a bag of cookies and offering her one as we waited in line at the airport. She smiled and took the whole bag, carefully folded the top, and put in it in her pocket.

So now Elena wanted to borrow my lipstick. I felt greedy. I had everything. Plus I had just won the race and would take home all the prizes and a handsome sum of money. She would take home nothing. "Tell her to wait," I told Rita, and I slipped on my sweats and dashed across to the shopping mall. When I returned I had a make-up bag filled with a woman's essential kit: lipsticks, mascara, eye-shadows and blusher. Together with Rita, who spoke some Russian, I presented the gift to Elena. We stood teary-eyed for a few moments in her doorway, then we had to run. The awards were starting in 15 minutes and if we were tardy a Japanese girl would be dispatched to hurry us up. I needed to get dressed and Elena had herself and her team-mates to make over.

At the awards party, the ante for best-dressed had been upped. Lisa could always be relied upon as a strong contender for the sleek black number, and now the eastern bloc had entered the stakes. Running attire was quickly becoming poor taste.

Once again I was presented with gifts: exactly the same set that I had received two years previously, including the Samurai warrior helmet with ornamental box.

The next day the invited runners were taken to Kyoto for sight-seeing and a fancy lunch at a traditional Japanese restaurant. We sat cross-legged around long low tables for a feast of *shabu shabu*. Plates containing all manner of fresh vegetables and meats were neatly waiting until the water boiled in the big central woks. Suddenly there were screams and we turned to see runners shrieking and recoiling and waving their arms. Some had already taken their leave and others were standing on their cushions for lack of chairs. A large prawn had sprung to life and was making his getaway across the table.

It was the East German, Katrin Dorre, who now sprang to her feet with her chopsticks poised, her eyes glinting. With the precision of a sharpshooter she thrust her weapons upon the escapee and raised him triumphantly before plunging him into the boiling stew. The steam hissed off his little body and when she held him up for the second time he was limp and red. I took note. She could be dangerous.

CHAPTER 35

Crackpots and Creampuffs

I have tried to keep an open mind, and it is not the ordinary things of
life that could close it, but the strange things, the extraordinary things,
the things that make one doubt if they be mad or sane.
— *Count Dracula*, by Bram Stoker

1988

Grace wrote to me at my Auckland home. She had seen an article on me in *North and South* magazine and, recognising me as a fellow Sirian, she felt compelled to write and had tracked down my address. I figured she either knew something I didn't or she was a complete crackpot, but her letter was articulate and conveyed a genuine essence. Having been accused as something of a crackpot myself at times, and not wanting to miss what might be my only celestial invitation in this lifetime, I immediately wrote back.

Before long we were pen-pals. I learned that Grace lived on a seven-acre organic farm in the far north with her partner, without running water or electricity to their dwelling. They lived off the fruits and vegetables of their labour. She wrote of her affinity with dolphins and whales, the hidden meanings of words and their sounds and syllables, and of her travels to the stars. She talked of Sirius A and B, their characteristics and the beings that came from them, their connections to the Earth and particularly to ancient Egypt. There were other stars, she said, not yet known around Sirius; Sirius C, soon to be revealed, and even another that she had picked up on, Sirius

D. I loved her way-out letters. I felt closer than ever to discovering answers to the secrets of the universe that I so longed for. When I read a few years later that Sirius C had been discovered I began to wonder whether she was sane and everyone else, hypnotised by their conventional beliefs, were the real crackpots.

I might not have been so excited about climbing to the stars with Grace had I foreseen that shortly thereafter the seesaw of my life would plunge me down into equal depths of darkness.

When I laid eyes on Markov, a lanky, dark, mysterious Romanian, the first image that crossed my mind was of a black magician, a sort of Count Dracula who lived in a dark castle full of secret passageways and demons. I was immediately put off and yet entranced at the same time when we were introduced by my dentist in her waiting room. She knew we were both athletes and might have something in common. *I wonder if I could ever love him?* I mused as I looked long and hard into his golden eyes that gave nothing away. It was a strange thought that did not seem like my own. Already I was hooked.

We parted with no more than a few civilities. Then I started to bump into him around town. On our third chance encounter he asked me on a date which, against my instinct, I felt compelled to accept. He took me to dinner and afterwards we drank wine as we lounged on my living room floor in front of the fire. I was intrigued by him. We talked into the early hours about everything and anything: being a foreigner in Boulder, our disparate upbringings, his escape from the East, running, the communist athletic training camps and their drug regimes, the Olympics, and the arcane. He wanted to hear about my races, the big ones, and especially the Olympics. More than anything he would have loved to be an Olympian, a dream that had passed him by once he joined the business world of the West.

Finally we reached that awkward question of what to do about sleep. Once again I was wondering if I could love him. So when he explained that he would be happy to share my bed but was celibate and had been for ten years, I was relieved if not slightly disappointed. As we climbed the stairs he paused in front of a picture of Mercury.

"That's my favourite guy," he cooed.

"Me too."

Celibate or not, I knew then that we were meant for each other. I put on my pyjamas and piled into bed beside him.

"What's this?" he cried as he reached out for me.

"What's what?"

He tugged at my shirt.

"It's pyjamas."

"Why?"

"To sleep in." I quickly realised that he was naked under the covers.

"But you said you were celibate." I suddenly wondered if I had mistaken his accent and that he had not said celibate but that he had overactive salivary glands and was in fact a salivant who was warning me ahead of time.

"I am celibate. But when I go to bed with you I expect you to be honest enough to get naked with me."

Instantly I felt ashamed. This time because I had my clothes on.

He was fascinating and frustrating. Electrifying and elusive. Charismatic and callous. After my self-imposed fast from passionate relationships, he was an irresistible feast of intensity and I felt as if I was poised on a cliff top, ready to leap into something wonderful and terrifying.

I woke up one morning to the phone ringing.

"Hello."

"Hi, do you want to come to breakfast?" The soft accent was Markov's.

"Sure."

"Meet you at Pour La France at ten."

"Okay." I put the phone down and drifted back to sleep.

The phone rang again. I picked it up sleepily. "Hello."

"Hi, do you want to come to breakfast?" I felt confused. Then I realised that I had dreamed the first episode.

"Sure. Ten, right?"

"Right."

I ran down to Pour la France to arrive at the same time as Markov.

There was a long queue for the popular outside tables and the wait was an hour or so, but that didn't faze him. He saw a couple leaving and leapt over the fence and snagged the table. People yelled at him but he refused to budge and motioned for me to join him. I did, but I was ashamed for my complicity.

My dreams became more vivid, and Markov was often in them. Our nocturnal interactions could best be described as … orange: he wore orange, drank strange orange concoctions from my refrigerator, and spilled orange paint all over my lawn when he left my house.

I dreamt once that I gave him a box of a dozen oranges.

He said, "What's this?"

I said, "Oranges."

He said, "Well I don't like any kind of oranges, just navel ones."

So the next time we met I brought him a box containing a dozen navel oranges. I wanted to see what would happen.

"What's this?" he asked.

"Oranges," I replied.

"Well I don't like any kind of oranges, just navel ones."

"I know," I said, "You already told me."

"Yes, I did."

I hardly noticed how, over the months, I became timid in my self-expression as he became more dominating. Nor did I see the rapid decline in my running fortunes.

I was sidelined for the '88 Osaka Marathon by an injury. Without me to contend with, Lisa ran solo for a world best loop time of 2:23. She was a fabulous time-trialist. This was to have been my qualifying race for the next Olympic Games in Seoul. The selectors agreed that it was folly to make me run another marathon so close to the Olympics and consented to a show of fitness with a 10,000 metre time on the track, I presumed under 33 minutes, since they did not say precisely what it was.

This was no easy task in effort or logistics. Twenty-five laps of the track is a physical and mental grind and such track races are not easy to find, but I tracked one down in Montréal. I was joined by another

Kiwi who was living in Oklahoma: Christine McMiken. She was looking to make a qualifying time for the 10,000 metres and we agreed that we would share the pace.

It was a balmy evening in late June. Christine and I shared the pace for the early stages, after which I took the lead, churning out the laps one after another. With four laps to go, Christine could sense my strength and from behind I heard a simple and desperate plea, "Don't leave me." She was hanging out in my field getting 'pulled along', as we runners say. I stayed steady for another two and a half laps then gave it my all. When I finished I had run a personal best time on the track, of 32:23, with Christine just a few seconds back. We had both qualified for the Olympic team in that event, although I was not interested in running it as an Olympian. We were pleased. This should clinch our selection: her in the 10,000 metres and I in the marathon.

The selectors were not satisfied, however. Perhaps they thought it was a fluke. They wanted us to run another one.

I was angry. I needed to be focusing on the marathon if I had any chance of doing well in Seoul, and chasing track times in other countries was an imposition that detracted from my preparation. But their word was law and so we found another race in Montréal in July, and trudged our way up there again.

It was stinking hot, so hot that the track had water tables set up in the eighth lane for runners to hydrate themselves. It seemed to me absurd: in this sauna there was no way I was going to come close to the time I needed. But I had come all this way and spent hundreds of dollars getting there so I lined up.

Halfway into the race I decided to quit. The truth was that I had decided to quit on the start line but at halfway I enacted that decision. I could not see the sense in frying myself for an effort that would take further precious time to recover from, only to obtain a result that would not serve my purpose. Christine struggled on to the finish, finishing minutes slower than we had previously, confirming for me the wisdom of my decision.

The selectors did not see it my way. In dropping out I had not only insulted my forefathers but the entire nation of New Zealand.

In their eyes I had become a soft American with a remote control, air conditioning and a sense of entitlement: a creampuff in bunhuggers who had lost touch with the rigours of the real world. My actions had shown I was no longer worthy of representing a country founded on hard work. Christine was praised for her effort in sticking it out. It seemed that it was not a fitness trial they were requiring but a test of mettle. Only they had not told me. When the team was announced, neither Christine nor I were on it.

I was dejected. I had thoughts of taking American citizenship and running for the USA from then on, magnificently of course. It was not that I wanted to be an American, I never could be at heart, but the idea of the selectors with egg on their faces was comforting.

In the ensuing weeks it turned out that not everyone in New Zealand saw matters in the same light that the selectors did. I was currently the country's top marathon runner, in fact, that year there were no other contenders for Olympic berths in the women's marathon. "Why was she not selected?" people asked. There were so many letters of support to my brother Gary that they soon evolved into a public petition to urge the selectors to add me to the team. When I heard about it I had mixed feelings. While I was comforted to know that people cared, mentally I had already resigned myself to not going and had adopted the defensive attitude that they could have their stupid Olympics without me.

When the news came that I was added to the team I should have been joyful. I was happy that Christine had also been added, but on my behalf I felt burdened. Now I would have to win a medal to vindicate myself and my supporters. Only weeks away from the Games, my mind had done so much flip-flopping that the sustained focus that I needed to pull it off had been diluted to mere hope. I almost told them to stuff it, but I could not disappoint all those people who had fought so hard to get me there, so I resigned myself to going.

When a reporter called for my comments, I made my excuses. Markov was sitting in the room, eavesdropping on my conversation. We had been dating sporadically for about six months. I found his forcefulness cruel but irresistible.

Afterwards, as we sat in a restaurant, Markov scolded me for not sounding enthusiastic enough towards the press about my selection. He could not understand how I could have reservations about going, and even if I did, it was stupid, he said, to voice them to the media. Then to underscore his point, he picked up my water glass and held it towards me, I thought to offer me a toast, but his hand flew high and he poured it on my head. I choked back the tears. He was laughing, and I thought for a moment that he looked like one of the ghouls from the walnut wardrobe.

CHAPTER 36

Flaming Dove

Serious sport has nothing to do with fair play. It is bound up with hatred, jealousy, boastfulness, disregard for all rules and sadistic pleasure in witnessing violence: in other words it is war minus the shooting.
— George Orwell

1988, SEOUL, KOREA

I shouldn't be here. The thought was lodged in the back of mind when I arrived in Seoul to join my team in the Olympic village. I thought the rest of the New Zealand team was looking at me as an interloper who had not rightfully earned her place with them. I was thankful that I had a room to myself so that I could retreat into my own little world away from my paranoid projections. The sporting bureaucracy did not realize that the medals do not necessarily go to the fastest, strongest and fittest, but to the one with not only high emotional-mental intensity but also the ability to focus it into performance. I was certainly a high-energy generator but after the emotional wrangling of selection I had just gone through, such energies were already misdirected.

What's more I lost Mercury. I was sure I had packed him, but turning my bag inside out he was not to be found. This was not a good sign.

I had been there just a few days when I woke up one morning and found that my identity was missing.

Being without an identity, I discovered, is a very perplexing thing.

I did not know who I was, where I was and even what century I was in. I lay there for a long time searching my mind for something to lock on to that would give me a name. But it was blank. I knew I existed, I was somebody — but I was also nobody. I scanned the interior of the room. Nothing meant anything. I was totally lost. I went to the window and looked outside onto the courtyard and saw the ornamental centerpiece of the famous five ringed insignia, and finally it registered that for today, at least, I was Lorraine Moller at the 1988 Olympics in Seoul.

I had found my identity, but in the aftermath of the Games I wished that I hadn't, for I would have been happier to have been nobody nowhere than an athlete suffering public humiliation.

The opening ceremony was a mixed bag. We were kept waiting for hours for our entrance. In the line-up for our march-in I found myself elbowing with a team secretary for the outside place on the line, the place where your relatives get to spot you because you are facing the cameras. We jostled shoulders but she got the better of me and took the coveted space as we walked outside. I was annoyed. Even she, a paid administrator, felt she had more right than I to be there.

I stood in the center of the field watching the remaining teams enter. I should have had pride overwhelming me and shivers running up and down my spine, but I didn't. I felt no love for mankind, only cynicism. There were so many Arab and African teams coming in with three fat officials and one athlete, and no female representation at all. It only served to annoy me further. I took to yelling at them as they went past, "Where're your women?" My team-mates were giving me dirty looks but that only encouraged my heckling. Then there were the Eastern Europeans marching with their large teams. I rankled to see the diminutive gymnasts in the front rows, rumored to be on hormone therapy to delay puberty and keep them small, and the overstuffed giants in the back, with their acromegalic jaws and hands from too much hGH (human growth hormone). I was so disgusted I hardly noticed the beautiful ceremony, I just remember that when the doves of peace were released, some flew into the Olympic flame and caught on fire.

Now that I look back on it, the race could not have turned out any other way. Mercury had not abandoned me as I thought; he was away busily setting me up for a big lesson.

I dashed to the athlete-assigned porta-potties in the stadium for a nervous pee. There was a long line at one of the boxes while the other had none. "What's wrong with this one?" I knew several of the women, runners from past games, well enough to call them friends. They looked at each other.

"What?" I asked.

"You'll never get in that one. She's been in there for ages," the taller one offered.

"Who?"

"Shhh!" The others didn't want 'her' hearing us. They beckoned me out of hearing range for a tête-à-tête-à-tête and took turns filling me in.

"She's in there with her little kit."

"What for?"

"To pass the drug test."

"How?"

"She's putting someone else's urine in her body."

"Oh, that's sick."

"Yeah, and soooo dirty."

"And cramped, you can hardly fit in those things." My mind boggled at the thought.

"Who cares, fucking cheat, hope she puts her back out and gets an infection." The shorter one's eyes flashed towards the locked door, her voice rising loud enough for all to hear.

I could empathise.

The line filed through and by the time I came out 'she' was still in there. Suddenly the door burst open and she leapt out, bag in hand and raced off to final check-in for her event. I went back to warming up outside and heard a cheer from inside the stadium. Catheter Woman had just won herself a gold medal.

1988 Summer Olympics — Women's Marathon, Seoul, Korea

As soon as the gun went off for the 1988 Seoul Olympic Women's Marathon, I felt light on my feet and fluid in my stride. The first mile of a marathon, when you find your rhythm and feel the spring in your feet and the air moving in and out of your lungs, lets you know if you're going to fly or fight gravity. It seemed this was going to be a good day. But I was mistaken. After the first five kilometres it all went to hell.

Runners have their own water bottles, with their special formulas to give them energy and hydration. After my drink débacle in Edinburgh my bottle contained H2O, pure and simple. Here in Seoul there were close to a hundred runners, so a special drink stop accommodated the same number of bottles, perched alphabetically (by country name) atop three tables, each about as big as an ironing board. These occurred every five kilometres, with other stations containing dixie cups of water and wet sponges evenly interspersed between the personal bottle stops.

Since it was typically warm for a summer Olympic marathon, with temperatures rising into the eighties, I knew it was essential that I drink early on in the race, and not just from the puny cups at the water stops which were good only for a sip and a splash. I needed my bottle to titrate from and absorb while running well under six minutes per mile.

We were bunched up tight. Then we came to the first water station. A runner sprinted ahead, grabbing her bottle then sweeping her arm across the table toppling off as many bottles as she could. I was appalled. I had never seen this tactic before. A runner next to me stopped and crawled under the table to find her bottle. In the flurry of darting legs and reaching arms I missed mine.

At the next water stop I sprinted for my bottle and grabbed it. Gotcha! With one sip I knew it was the wrong one. It was thick and sweet — stitch material. I tossed it to the ground.

By the third stop I was getting anxious and grabbed again. I held the bottle to my face and squeezed. Another runner thumped me on the back. I turned my head as the glucose syrup jarred my taste buds.

She was waving her fist at me. I had her bottle. Chagrined, I handed it over. Slowly but surely I unraveled from there.

My pace slowed to non-competitive and up ahead I saw my Olympic dream disappear with the pack. I was desperately thirsty and the sun bore down on me. I was no longer an Olympic contender; I was an escaped Foreign Legionnaire staggering through the Sahara. Only this was worse; this was televised to the world, my country and my critics, and there was no escape. Soon I would be eaten by vultures.

A wave of tension went through me, starting at my neck and descending down my body. I felt like a sheet wrangled into knots and slipping through the wringer. I wanted to cry but I was too dehydrated and tears would not come. I scanned for places to hide but I was afraid of unwittingly crossing the border into the north and so I staggered on, feeling sorry for myself.

At about 18 miles I came upon an oasis. A volunteer was filling cups from a two-litre bottle at a water station. As I ran past I whisked the bottle from her busy hands and galloped off with it. I took a good guzzle and immediately began to feel better.

It was then I spied a runner walking just in front of me. It was my old rival Carla Buerskens whom I had sprinted off down the Champs d'Elysees four years earlier. I stopped and walked alongside, offering her water.

"What's wrong?" I asked.

"I have a pain in my leg."

"Can you run?"

"I don't know."

So we walked a while.

"Come on Carla," I urged, "Run with me. We can go slowly. You will feel much better if you finish." I was talking as much to myself as I was to her. It was comforting to have someone else in the same boat. We jogged the last few miles to the finish. I could have run faster but I felt bonded to her in my misery and so stayed alongside her to the finish line. I didn't care about squeezing out a few more seconds or sprinting ahead of her. It was first, second, third or nothing at all. And this was nothing, a big zero.

The New Zealand media said it was pathetic that I hadn't even looked like I was trying. When Carla was put ahead of me in the finish results, the New Zealand team put in a protest to have me bumped up a place. I didn't care enough to even find out if it was successful. "See if they can work me up to a medal while they are at it," I sarcastically commented when told of the bid. I was both defeated and embarrassed.

Carla's coach told me a few years later that she had suffered a stress fracture during the marathon and that my urging her to finish had effectively finished her career.

What's more, Anne performed well in the 10,000 metres. In the grand score we kept on each other, she won this time. I begrudgingly admired the way she survived each round, graduating from the heats and semi-finals to the final by the skin of her teeth and, I could see, her sheer grittiness.

It was small consolation to me when Ben Johnson, in the wake of his gold medal record-breaking sprints, got busted for steroid use. His eyeballs were yellow and his hyper-activated muscles threatened to pop out of his skin like over-boiled sausages. They say he had to have breasts surgically removed before the Olympics, a symptom of steroid overuse. The men on steroids change into women, the women into men.

A rumor ran through the village that there were 20 more positives among medal winners and the announcement of them was imminent. It never came. We were all waiting for FloJo to follow Ben Johnson out of the country in shame. I had seen her in Los Angeles four years before and now she had beefed up like a prize bull for a show. For my own curiosity I chased her down in the village, ostensibly to offer my congratulations for her series of gold medals and world records in the sprints. Up close, she had a five o'clock shadow that even heavy make-up couldn't conceal. At least, I rationalised, 'failure' was a preferable label to 'cheat', and definitely preferable to sporting a moustache with red lipstick.

I deliberately did not read the news reports from home of the

Games. I knew they would be depressing. When I arrived back in Boulder my father wrote to me, calling me a quitter. I knew the New Zealand press had trashed me and he was just parroting the common perception. He was ashamed of me. I cancelled my annual trip to New Zealand, preferring to brave the Colorado cold than face my critics, who, I imagined, were the entire country.

Not knowing what else to do, I slung my nose to the ground and carried on for a better day. I was consoled by one thing. Having lost my self for a few hours that first morning in Korea, I now knew that I was something beyond Lorraine Moller competing in the 1988 Seoul Olympics. I was a soul having an experience.

CHAPTER 37

Chop Chop

1989

The day I left Korea for home, a novel and exciting certainty popped into my head. My mate had entered my field and was marching towards me: the man I would marry, settle down and have babies with. I did not know who he was, but I did know that he was no stranger. He was someone I knew already. I wrangled with my mind for more information, but it was staying 'mum' on his identity. Not to be thwarted, I made a list of every single man I could think of during the flight home, and then pared it down until only three names remained. One of these men was 'him'. I was very excited.

In the next few weeks my list was down to two; Markov, the dark, mystical European, and Harlan, the quiet, unassuming American.

Markov only ever asked for a date at a moment's notice and I would sometimes spend the entire weekend waiting anxiously by the phone. I had given up calling him at work. It was futile as he was always 'in a meeting', busy planning a world take-over and I imagined that reports of my trivial calls angered him. When he did call and ask me on a date I was so extremely grateful that I would drop whatever I was doing — even my training runs.

One night I woke up nauseated and crawled to the bathroom and vomited violently into the toilet. What came up was thick and long and slimy. A malevolent black snake lay coiled in the shadows of the bowl. There was more. Insects. I spat them out onto the snake and

270

crawled back to bed, wretched and exhausted. I was still sick to my stomach, knowing such nastiness had been inside of me. Markov was asleep in my bed, still celibating.

In the morning there was no snake blocking my plumbing but it had seemed so real I could not be convinced that it did not happen. I began to wonder, was I once again sleeping with the devil?

I remembered the tarot cards that Jake had given me some 15 years earlier and dug them out of a dusty box. Then I made a fire in a pot in my living room and burned the lot. Perhaps all this devilish stuff was the product of a fertile imagination, and that disposing of the tarot deck was nothing more than alerting Mercury to boot the jerks, past and present, out of my psyche. After that things changed dramatically for me in the romance department.

1989 Osaka International Ladies' Marathon — Japan

As I was packing for Japan, my Mercury medallion fell out of my bag. He had not been lost after all, merely waiting, and was now showing up for his next assignment.

It had been five months since my Olympic débacle in Seoul and so much had changed within me. The Osaka International Ladies' Marathon was willing to bring me back but they were focused on the Olympic Champions and I was brought in as a mere stocking-stuffer for the big presents — four of the top ten at Seoul. Their coup d'état was Rosa Mota, the reigning Olympic Gold Medalist. This was good news for me. She would probably be tired, I was hungry for redemption, and I had Mercury waiting on the course to aid and abet me. Not to mention that I had someone I badly wanted to impress.

I had stopped seeing Markov and started seeing Harlan. In the past two months we had travelled back and forth across the USA to visit each other. At first he seemed too nice, too willing, too relaxed, and I missed the friction I had had with previous boyfriends. But he grew on me. The first time we spent time alone together, Harlan asked me what my worldview was. I was impressed. No-one had asked me that before. Harlan had read all the Seth books so, although he knew nothing about the sporting world, we had plenty to share.

Harlan had never been to a marathon before, apart from the Olympics in Los Angeles five years before, when the race passed by his brother's house while he was visiting and he had stepped out on the street to watch us scamper by. As far as big-time sports was concerned, he was about to be thrown into the deep-end.

When we arrived in Osaka, Harlan was given an ID pass to wear that, unbeknownst to him, said in Japanese 'coach'.

Mizuno made it clear they expected me to win and I knew that my future with them depended on it. They took me to a studio on Friday evening where, dressed in my racing gear, I was asked to thrust myself through a makeshift finish line so that on race day the mock winning shot could be in the evening newspaper with their advertisement.

When I awoke on the day of the race I had a gut feeling that I would win again. When the gun went off my feeling was consolidated. I led because no one else wanted to. This confirmed to me that the top contenders were all tired. Rosa was the only one who concerned me and I was pleased to see her hanging back with the pack, passing by the kilometre mark at a pedestrian pace, something that I had never seen her do before. She always raced as if she was in charge, taking command early and surely, never holding back but setting a mean pace that few others could tolerate. It was obvious to me that today she wanted to coast along and win with the minimum of effort, a strategy that I planned to usurp with one of my own.

I led on and off for the first half, the lead pack dwindling and swelling and dwindling again, as runners wrestled with their limitations and sorted themselves into the positions befitting of their mindsets. By 15 miles I was at the helm of a group of five, poised like a vulture to feed on the carrion of weary heroes. A few miles ago I had paid my respects to Mercury with a silent greeting, and he had urged me to bide my time and be responsive when I needed to. Suddenly Rosa, who had been running steadily at my shoulder, disappeared off the back of the pack. This was all too easy. I increased my pace, and suddenly I was out in front, the pack gone and only the tiny Japanese Kosue Kojima stuck to my rear like a delicate bird on a horse's behind.

As I was contemplating the long haul ahead, which I was now committed to leading, I saw the television truck veer off to my left. I was no longer the focal point. It was Rosa, sprinting past us in a mad dash to regain the lead. I let her go. I knew that the race was mine. Rosa had lost her cool and would pay for this rashness, with interest. Ten metres ahead she settled back into a marathon rhythm. I bore into her back, pulling myself closer with every stride until, once again, I was with her, but this time I was at her side, pushing the pace, and declaring my challenge. We ran this way for a few minutes, sizing each other up: the diminutive Rosa with her low-slung pitter-patter stride and I, the lumbering giant by contrast, trying my best to slink along as inconspicuously as possible. She was in trouble and we both knew it. Her face was scrunched into a grimace, her neck strained and I could smell desperation in the heat emanating from her body. And suddenly she was gone, out of sight. I turned my head briefly to see her clutching her calf. The race was all mine.

Meanwhile, Harlan was sitting in the stadium watching the race on television in the VIP room with all the other coaches when he was tapped on the shoulder. Now that I was clearly winning, the demure little Japanese interpreter kindly requested him to give his expert commentary on the race for television, 'as Miss Morrer-san's coach'. Harlan was cornered. They asked him questions like, "What is her strategy?", "Is she going to win?" And, "How is her form?" To which he replied: "She aims to stay in front but the marathon is a long way": not knowing exactly how far, "Anything can happen." And: "At this stage she looks good to me." The interviewer nodded respectfully at the wisdom of each answer.

At the end of the interview the interpreter pulled out a paper for Harlan to sign. Not knowing what he was getting into he refused. She scurried away and returned a few minutes later with an envelope. When Harlan opened it, it was stuffed full of money. He signed. Now he could add 'professional coach' to his resumé.

I won the race: my third Osaka International Ladies' Marathon victory. The picture of me thrusting across the tape was on the front page (to our way of thinking the back page) of every newspaper delivered to the stands within hours of the race finishing. And there was the congratulatory message from Mizuno with my winning studio shot. They were thrilled. Outside of the Olympics this was the biggest event I could have won for them. The smiling Mizuno brothers, now president and vice-president of the Mizuno Corporation since their father had passed on, wined and dined us that evening. I felt secure that my contract with them would be renewed and that I could ask for a raise.

Now everyone in Japan seemed to know me. Being a head above the Asian crowd with the three-dimensional face of a Westerner, I was easily distinguishable. (One of my Japanese acquaintances did confide to me that to them we all look the same.) Hordes of people followed me whenever I went out on the street, whispering and pointing and tittering to one another, "Rorraine Morrer-san", until one would summon the courage to ask me for an autograph or a photo, which opened the floodgate. Quickly a line would form, growing with every passerby. I would be captive, scrawling my signature on hats and T-shirts, handbags, and across the back of designer leather jackets, until my interpreter would shoo them all away and rustle me on to my next engagement.

A week later back in Boulder I received a letter from the Osaka International Ladies' Marathon Organizing Committee, regretfully informing me that the new race director had had a heart attack and died.

I had sat next to him just the day after the race at the Hand-Dye Centre where the brochure had advertised that 'you can practise dying all by yourself on a handkerchief'. I thought it funny at the time but now it seemed sadly prophetic.

I later heard that he had to answer to the committee for the poor performances of the Olympians to whom they had paid large appearance fees, and that he had hung himself from a cherry tree on his way to the meeting the very next day.

When I arrived home, once again I could not find Mercury. I don't think one can lose him, he does what he wants, but after searching every corner of my house I wondered if he had had enough of me and decided to stay in Osaka. It worried me. I knew that without him I was in for a rough time.

And so it was. A few months later, Harlan and I drove from his home in Pennsylvania to Atlanta, for one of the largest sporting goods trade fairs in the world. Mizuno would be there and Michiyo was keen to see me and discuss my contract. It was a modest one and I thought it fitting that it be doubled. After all, Akito, number two son, had told me, swooshing his hand up in a vertical take-off to illustrate, that each time I had won the Osaka Marathon their shoe sales had soared.

Michiyo started our meeting with a buttery preface about what a nice person I was. I brightened. *Excellent. Nice means promotion. Lots of money.* But, she sighed regretfully, there was Seoul. I nodded … *Yeah, thirty-fourth in the Olympic Marathon is pretty pathetic.* I sagged. *No money at all. Chop, chop.* She continued. But because I had won Osaka again … *Hope. Same money as before* … they were willing to renew my contract but at half the previous amount. I felt a wail go through me, *It's not fair!!* But I swallowed it like a fur ball into my throat.

"No, no," I mustered, shaking my head. She looked at me for a long time. I did not say a word.

"Since you are so popular we can go another twenty-five per cent."

That was the best I was going to get. It was also the worst. A blind-side demotion. Mizuno had become my corporate family, and I had been their Queen of Running, their Number One. Or at least I thought I was. Now they had a new star, to whom they were paying a gazillion dollars – the dubious FloJo. I had outlived my usefulness and was being discarded, reduced in regard to an old horse fit for the meat works and pensioned to a paddock because I was nice. Not because I was a good runner or won big races! Nice, like Miss Goody-Two-Shoes who smiles and bows and signs autographs for hours on end and runs through mock tapes late into the night so they can have the winning shot. Nice enough to astronomically increase their market share in shoe sales. Yes, I had been very nice. I had done everything they asked of me, except win the Olympics. I hated being nice.

I should have told them to stuff it, in a polite Japanese way, of course. Something classy, like, "Due to other commitments I regret that I am unable to avail myself of your kind offer at this time...", and walked off with my dignity. But the surprise had reduced me to an emotional five-year-old. The flashing lights of rejection had me scrambling for acceptance of a lesser kind.

I signed the reduced contract for two years. If I had thought about it in a businesslike manner, I would have seen that I did not need the money. It was peanuts compared to what I made in appearance and prize money from races. I could not see that selling myself short was way too costly. They could have bought the Osaka champion, but they bought the Seoul failure. And in signing, so did I.

No wonder Mercury was shunning me.

CHAPTER 38

Gang-bushed

If Achilles' mother had held him by the hair when she dipped him in the potion of invincibility, I might have won the 1990 Commonwealth Games in Auckland. But she held him by the ankle, leaving a weak spot that eventually caused his death and became the point of vulnerability for all athletes. I was superbly fit but my Achilles tendon hurt like hell. Despite all the treatments physiotherapy could offer, the pain in my foot was getting worse and not better.

The physiotherapist was highly regarded in the sporting field. In her mid-fifties, graying and carrying the mid-torso softness of the older woman, she probed my foot and hooked it to machines with the care of anyone's grandmother. She was excited to play a part in getting me to the podium. My foot had failed to respond to her frequent ultrasound treatments and, running out of options, she had given me a trumpet-blazing, awe-inspiring, heart-rending address about how I needed to rally for the home country and win the gold. "You know you can do it, I know you can do it, and New Zealand knows you can do it, so just get out there and do it!" Her voice rose to a victorious crescendo. I left feeling crushed. She thought it was all in my head and now I too was wondering if it was all mental. I forced myself on another painful run. Mind over matter.

As I limped along the Auckland waterfront I felt close to tears. Rangitoto Island loomed before me, forbidding and mysteriously stark. A large volcanic rock, it is a perfect cone that rises out of the ocean, too barren for habitation but a picturesque backdrop nonetheless. I had run many miles on the waterfront, measuring my speed against the cardiac markers that map out a fitness route for joggers. In just two and a half weeks it would become the marathon course, showcasing the best of scenic Auckland and providing a fast, flat, out and back, out and back, route.

I just had to race; the entire country was depending on me to win. Damn this foot of mine! I would fail, I could see it now: all over New Zealand, sporting fans, that is everyone, staring at their flickering boxes, captivated by the sight of their representative, me, eyes staring down, blanking out the unrelenting focus of the TV camera lens, my stride stuttering to a pathetic limp, my spirit crippled with humiliation. They would be merciless, say I was a head-case and that I couldn't take the pressure of big competition. They would say that I had let them down, that I was a national embarrassment and that I had no business being out there and should go back to America. And when it was all done and the commentators had wrapped it up and smiled into the cameras and said what a disappointment I was, they would continue to discuss it over dinner and declare that I was useless and that they had known it all along. Next morning the newspapers would validate what smart pundits they were, and the public would go to their dreary nine-to-fivers, smug that it was me out there being a loser and not them, and they would puff out their chests, proud to be Kiwis.

I looked off into the distance, and for the first time, Rangitoto Island emerged out of the background and became defined. It didn't look too far away. Suddenly it was shining before me as my salvation. When the pain in my foot becomes unbearable during the race I could veer quietly off the course and into the water. The commentators would be fumbling for words, 'This is a highly unusual manoeuvre,' they would say and the cameras would follow me until I became a black dot in the ocean, swimming towards Rangitoto where I would hide in a lava cave and eat berries, never to be seen or heard of again.

Yes, this would be my fate. 'A baffling disappearance', would footnote my name, 'presumed drowned'. But every now and then someone would maintain they had sighted me and the mystery would grow. The rumour would spread that Rangitoto is a portal to other dimensions, Sirius perhaps, and Grace would confirm that indeed I had been taken home. The idea was becoming quite romantic.

Lorraine, Lorraine! What are you thinking? Listen to yourself. Swim to Rangitoto? You've gone quite stupid. Now face it. You're fried. Give it a break and withdraw. It's the only sensible thing to do. It was Ms Rational and she had no time for such nonsense. I had to admit she was right. But she did not understand the pressure.

I went back to the summer home I kept in Greenlane, the most central suburb of Auckland city, to my cute little Victorian house that sat too close to the motorway. I had had it painted in my favourite combination of colours, green and purple. The sight of it always cheered me no end; it was my haven amidst the madness of the big city. Alone in my room I made a list of pros and cons for running the Commonwealth Games Marathon.

Pros:
1. If I win I will be popular, it will be good for New Zealand and it will please my family and friends.
2. I would avoid the disappointment of abandoning my goal.
3. It is fun to be a part of the team.

For the heck of me I couldn't think of any more reasons to run. So I wrote the cons and thought I would come back to the pros later.

Cons:
1. I could seriously hurt myself by running on an injured foot, possibly finish my career.
2. Chances are I will run poorly and then I will be criticised harshly by the public.
3. I can concentrate on running another race well later on.
4. Competition is relatively poor and the race does not mean much outside of the Commonwealth.
5. I am losing my condition but not resting enough to allow the injury to heal.
6. There is no money for running it.

7. I could possibly do TV commentary instead.
8. I would be looking after myself, particularly paying attention to my emotional well-being.
9. I would be listening to my body.
10. I would be trusting the universe that all is working out fine.

There, I had it covered. Now I was resolved, I would withdraw.

I drove to the Commonwealth Games headquarters. Management had requested a meeting with me. I did not know what exactly they wanted, except to check on my condition, but I knew what I wanted: to officially withdraw. They could replace me with Mary O'Connor, the first alternative, who was itching for the opportunity to run. I did not know that officialdom had failed to register her as a reserve competitor and that the deadline to do so had passed. If I withdrew, that mistake would become apparent.

When I was ushered into the room there were five men present. I knew them all. These were the top-brass blazer-men: doctors and officials dedicated to serving New Zealand sport. Individually I liked each one of them and felt I knew them well enough to have confided my true intentions in the matter. But this was not the friendly chit-chat I had expected — it was an administrative gang-bush.

The doctor took charge and asked me about my heel. I eyed them all suspiciously. They were no longer my esteemed superiors, but a mob of Amway Mafia and I was about to be sold the Golden Opportunity Deal that I could not refuse.

"I can't run. It hurts too much. I don't think I can do it," I started out. My eyes were downcast. This was my pitch, the only one I had. It slipped feebly off my lips and plopped on the floor. *There you have it.* Unfazed, the doctor crouched down and took my foot, probing his fingers into my heel for the sore spot. I was left to the persuasive powers of the medical expert.

"It doesn't hurt to touch," I explained, "only when I move my foot up and down, when I'm running."

He sat back on the wide executive desk, the examination apparently over. "So tell me what's going on?"

"I haven't been able to run for three days," I explained, "and prior to that my foot has been progressively more painful so that my training over the last month has been sporadic."

He nodded sympathetically.

"If I could have you running pain free in three days would you consider racing?"

"I'm not having any injections."

"I'm not talking about injections. I'm talking about oral medication."

"What about the side effects?"

"There are no side effects."

"I took anti-inflammatories once before and they caused my blood count to plummet."

"No, no, these have no side-effects." He shook his head as if I was being ridiculous. "So, if I could have you running pain-free in three days would you consider racing?"

This is where I should have said 'absolutely not' in no uncertain terms and headed for the door. But this was my style only in hindsight. Besides, I had the feeling I was not going to be leaving the room with anything less than a 'yes'.

"Even if I was pain-free I still don't have the confidence that I can go the distance."

"Okay, so what distance would you need to be able to run so that you feel confident that you can run the marathon?"

"Eighteen miles." It was the first number that popped into my head.

"So, if we have you running one mile in three days and add two miles a day …"

"But what about recovery days?"

"Oh yes, of course, well, if we have you running one mile and add two miles every second day … " He quickly saw that he was running out of days so paused to reconfigure. "Let's see, if we added three miles every second day …"

"That's fine except for one thing."

"What's that?"

"I would only be up to sixteen miles on race day," I stated triumphantly.

He could see this wasn't working the way he wanted so he changed tack.

"If I could have you running ten miles pain-free by next weekend would you consider running?"

They were all eyeballing me. This was the head-on hard sell, the clincher, the pitch with the tricky spin.

"I suppose I'll consider it," I muttered feebly.

He jumped up and clapped his hands. "That's all I need!"

I had just been closed, bowled out, and beaten. Satisfied, the others started to file out of the room and I was left to settle up with the good doctor. He wrote me two prescriptions, one for anti-inflammatory pills and the other for the side effects.

As I was heading out the door, the team captain was waiting. "Oh, by the way, don't talk to the press. Let us do it."

I was at my lowest. The System had me by the windpipe. I could barely talk, or take a deep breath, or cry. When I walked into my little house, I scrunched up the prescription and hurled it into the bin, missing by a mile.

As I sat down to commiserate with myself the phone rang. Mercury, working long distance, had sent Hazel to my rescue. Hazel had been on some teams with me and when in New Zealand we usually made contact. She was my age, a local runner and a spirited woman. If she had been in my shoes today she would have told them to shove it, without remorse. It was this spunkiness that I admired and wished that I had today. I poured my heart out to her.

"So pull out of the race," she advised.

"They won't let me."

"It's easy," she said, "just call the media and say you're withdrawing."

"No, I can't, they told me I couldn't talk to the press."

"They may have said you couldn't, but they didn't say I couldn't."

Hazel called the press. The next morning after running some errands, I arrived home to find a television crew camped out in my driveway.

For the next three days it was media pandemonium. Then it all died down, the race was run without me and life went on. Lisa Martin, unfettered by close competition, ran brilliantly to win in a Commonwealth Games record. Mary O'Connor eventually sued Athletics New Zealand for her exclusion from the team and won her case and a settlement. Meantime I busied myself campaigning amongst the New Zealand athletes to support a bill presented by Helen Clark, then the Health Minister of New Zealand, for sport free of tobacco sponsorship. Anne Audain campaigned on behalf of the tobacco companies. The bill was passed.

When I arrived back in Boulder I went to a podiatrist who X-rayed my foot. The bone spur that I had had removed twenty years earlier had grown back and had taken the shape of a drill that was boring into my Achilles tendon with every step. It was so large there seemed no option but surgical removal.

Once more I was under the knife. The surgeon told me I could be running again in six weeks. He did not tell me that meant hobbling for a few hundred yards.

I considered retiring. A new drug, called erythropoietin (EPO) was now easily available on the black market. EPO was developed for kidney dialysis patients who become severely anaemic. It switches on the bone marrow to make more red blood cells — essentially blood doping in a bottle, and was completely undetectable (at the time). It was all so easy it was dangerous. In the last three years 18 Dutch and Belgian cyclists had died from heart failure, suspected to be caused by illegal EPO use, and just lately a spate of Swedish orienteers had suspiciously died from heart failure while running around in the forests, looking at their compasses. This would be a good time to get out and leave them all to their cheating ways. I could be content with a fine career finished by injury — circumstances beyond my control.

Or could I? When Mercury showed up in my jacket pocket, I knew that such an exit would be a whimper and that I was being summoned for another marathon.

Start of 1987 Osaka International Ladies' Marathon. Wearing number '2'.

Courtesy of Osaka International Ladies' Marathon and Sankei Sports

PART FIVE

Medallist

The smile says it all. Barcelona, 1992.

CHAPTER 39

Percolations

1991

1991 Hokkaido Marathon — Sapporo, Japan

Sapporo, with its laid-back ambience, was a pleasant contrast to the high velocity of Osaka, but I was not relishing the idea of racing a marathon there. Being summer it was way too hot for my liking, and over-riding the body's protective mechanisms, to engage in a heat-generating activity such as running, is just plain unpleasant. Also, hot races take so much more of your body's resources and can leave you seriously depleted. I have performed consistently well in the heat in the marathon but such races often take months to fully recover from. But they were paying me well, and, after a year of regaining my fitness, I needed the race, so I was prepared to endure. Besides it was good practice for the heat of Barcelona and if the temperatures did not soar too high I could post a qualifying time. It was over a year since my heel surgery.

I had won the Hokkaido Marathon in 1989 and I was returning this time with Harlan and Dick in tow, hoping to repeat my victory here. I had conscripted Dick to be my coach once again. After years of coaching myself and brief interludes with a few other coaches, I decided that Dick was by far the most dependable and trusted coach I could have. Our relationship had evolved into one of equals and I felt he respected my collaboration in planning my training.

287

As with most Japanese races back then, this was designed to be a two horse race between foreigners. The American, Lisa Weidenbach, was the hired rival: a tall sturdy woman with a likeable, modest nature. She had run and won the Sapporo Half Marathon six weeks before and had remained in Sapporo to train after the race.

I had also run in the half marathon, but my effort had been pathetic and I dropped out at the crunch-point. 'Crunch-point' occurs for most runners somewhere between half and three-quarters of the way along in a race, any race, no matter the distance. At crunch-point you are far enough out from the start for fatigue to be setting in but not close enough to smell the reassurance of the finish line. You get hard-pressed by negative thoughts and find yourself asking, "Why the hell do I do this?" Afterwards I had felt embarrassed and frustrated with myself. The Japanese hate quitters as much as Kiwis. Now that I was back I was determined to make a good showing and redeem myself.

A few nights before the race we joined Lisa and her then-husband, Bill, for dinner. As we walked back to the hotel, Lisa, in her good-natured way, confided to me that her shortcoming in racing was her inability to sprint.

"If anyone is close to me with eight hundred metres to go," she declared, "They'll beat me."

"Really?" I asked, my ears perking up.

"Oh, definitely," Bill confirmed. "This is Lisa's weakness. She can't sprint. Nothing she can do about it."

They had just laid out my race strategy.

I dashed into the hotel restaurant an hour and a half before the race and ordered a three egg cheese omelette and orange juice. I had intended to just order my usual toast with butter and honey so don't know what possessed me to break all my pre-race eating rules, but at the time it seemed quite reasonable. The truth was that I had overslept and I was just plain hungry. I had it in my mind that those winning Kenyans often have a high protein breakfast and that scientifically there was a good case for more protein. Fat too. I was certain I had read somewhere that grease could help in a marathon.

The carbohydrate thing was surely overrated, old science; it was time for me to get with it. I cleaned my plate, chugged a cup of coffee and hurried off to warm-up. The start was only 45 minutes away.

As the race progressed, Dick paced like an expectant father in front of television giving live coverage. "Don't worry," reassured Harlan, "Lorraine told me she was going to win."

"But Harlan," Dick lectured, "You don't understand. It's not that simple."

I stayed with Lisa for 26 miles and then sprinted the last 400 metres. It was a no-brainer.

When I crossed the finish line I had to keep walking. There had been an undigested chain of amino acids in my stomach the entire 26 mile journey and it wanted air. I began to retch. The cute little Japanese girl assigned to follow beside me ran to the sidelines and returned triumphantly seconds later with a plastic bag. I filled it with breakfast, which was now bright yellow and homogenous. As I returned to greet the press and fans and accept awards, she dutifully followed me, carrying the bag containing my stomach contents as if it was a goldfish bowl.

1991 Berlin Marathon — Germany

Even though I had a qualifying time, in that heat it was relatively slow so I decided to go to the Berlin Marathon to run a personal best. I knew I had a much faster time in me if I could just strike the right race. Everyone said that the Berlin race was fast. I had raced there once before on the track in 1985, and led the Olympic Champion until the final stretch of 3,000 metres. Even back then I found the place disconcerting: Hitler's grandiose Olympic Stadium with its stark lines, and that life-sucking wall separating the city in two. Perhaps I should have chosen somewhere to race that made me feel happy.

I missed the start. I didn't even hear the gun go. Everyone just started running and I was still tying my shoes. I leapt up in a panic and rushed after the leaders, jumping medians and weaving my way through the thousands of people as they thronged through the Brandenburg Gates. I was working way too hard way too early, my breathing was laboured and I struggled for oxygen. At 12 miles I simply could not muster more than a jog, so I quit. That surge of adrenaline at the start had taken its toll. The asthma I had held at bay for so many years was making a comeback.

Forget the race, I told myself. Along with my girlfriend, Vicky, I jumped on a train, and we wended our way through Italy and France to Barcelona where I could preview the Olympic course. We checked into a cheap *pensione* and put on our gear for a run.

As soon as I stepped outside to run I knew something was very wrong. I gasped for breath until I was doubled over. This is no good. *How can I win the Olympics here if I can't even breathe the air?*

But there was a job to do, so I put the breathing issue on my 'to-deal-with-later' list and set out to find where the marathon course was. This was not easy. No one at the Olympic office spoke much English and trying to get information over the phone was near impossible. Besides, I gathered from the broken English on the other end of the receiver, the course was not yet set. But what was certain was that the marathon would finish in Montjuïc Stadium, so the next day we headed off to this mini mountain in Barcelona City.

By luck, there I met the Japanese Olympic marathon squad who were also on a marathon reconnaissance mission. The coach showed me his map. I could get a pretty good idea of the course: 26 miles out of town, along the coast, into the city, down La Rambla and heading for the stadium. This part was fairly straightforward and I wasn't much interested in it. It was the last few miles uphill to the finish that were crucial.

I left Vicky and jogged, which was all I could muster with my laboured breathing, over what seemed the best bet for the last four miles of the marathon. As the long hill steepened, the road narrowed into a cobbled walking path that tripped up and down steps and through archways, cafés and what appeared to be little museums.

Yes, I could just see myself in a nimble-footed *pas-de-bourée* up a flight of stairs in first place, barely pausing to hoik a goober on a priceless Dali as I forged my way to gold. My opposition would be struggling in my wake, physically and mentally broken by my superior strength.

Up ahead of me the stadium came into view, the sight of which geared my imagination into overdrive. I could feel my lungs begin to relax. Excitedly I made for the entrance into the arena where next year thousands of cheering fans would hail my arrival as the winner.

My reverie was abruptly interrupted. An official had jumped in my path and was directing me away. It was forbidden to run on the track. So I jogged around the outside on the grass to the finish line and, with a few innovations from the creative imagination, continued with my grand dream. *Olympic Champion! Gold!! I am the winner!* I waved my arms in the air ecstatically, caught up in a moment of total euphoria, totally forgetting that I was a year ahead of myself. *The crowd is going wild.* I blew kisses to the stadium seats. *They love me!*

I snapped back to reality. The official was glaring and heading towards me. While I still had it I quickly rolled this winning image with all the attendant emotions into a golden ball and tossed it into the heavens, leaving it suspended above the stadium to percolate. *You are mine,* I yelled up to it silently. *I will feed you while I am away. Grow strong. I will be back in a year to take you home.*

My job was done. *Adios, until next time!* I waved to the official and blew him a kiss as I ran off.

There was one more place for Vicky and me to visit. While in Europe I wanted to experience that crack in space/time, Glastonbury, England. Supposedly the burial place of both King Arthur and Queen Guinevere, it is revered as one of the world's mystical power points. More than anything I wanted to run up the Glastonbury Tor as if it was Montjuïc and pretend I was winning the Olympics. It was probably overkill, but I was in visualisation overdrive.

Surprisingly, there were no breathing difficulties here. The air was fresh and moist as I headed towards the Tor and began my ascent. Legend has it that the Tor is the lost island of Avalon from ancient times when the surrounding land was submerged in water. Here is the entrance to the underworld and the home of the faerie folk.

As I ran I was strangely excited, my nerves tingling at the enchantment of this hill. The mists were rolling in, so that the air itself became alive, dissolving away the fabric of ordinary reality, and I felt myself lifting. As I wound up the hill, faster and faster I went, gaining speed with every step as if gravity had reversed itself and my feet had sprouted wings. For a few fleet seconds of timelessness I was Mercury himself.

On top of the Tor is the stone ruin of a church. Suddenly it became the finish line of the Olympics in Barcelona and I sprinted in long light strides through the entrance and threw my arms in the air in victory. This place and Montjuïc were one and the same and like a boomerang my wish was now hurtling though other dimensions, gathering the powers of creation to itself, returning to me in the Eternal Now, fulfilled. For a moment I was certain: I could win, I would win, I have won. It was all the same.

Suddenly I noticed I was not alone. A hippie was sitting cross-legged in the center of the structure, wearing a flowered headband and a paisley shirt, joint in hand, staring up at me as if I was his hallucination.

"Coool," he enthused.

CHAPTER 40

Cleared for Take-off

Know the self to be sitting in the chariot, the body to be the chariot,
the intellect the charioteer, and the mind the reins.
—Veda Upanishads (c. 800 BC)

1991 — 1992

Back home in Boulder I found two Greek columns, painted them gold, and constructed an Olympic altar. I wanted to enshrine my dream and daily feed the vision of Gold. I adorned it with winning shots of me, pictures of people who gave me strength, and meaningful knick-knacks such as crystals and rocks and feathers. I bought a statue of Nike the Goddess of Victory and she became the centerpiece. Above her I hung my wish picture. It was a three-dimensional work of art consisting of a shot of me in the victory pose in the doorway of the old church tower on top of Glastonbury Tor, taken by Vicky. I framed it with various tarot cards, such as The Magician and Strength and The Star, archetypes to draw from and embody. At the bottom on each side were my commemorative medals from the Los Angeles and the Seoul Olympics. These would be my basis for success. Forming the apex of a triangle with these two medals, and just above my outstretched hands, I placed a gold medal. It was from Barcelona: chocolate in tin foil. My dream was slowly but surely taking shape.

Harlan moved in with me. He was enthusiastic and amenable to most everything and for a while I was suspicious of such geniality. I kept reminding myself that 'nice is good'.

While I was inspired and emotionally contented, I needed mental house-cleaning. Whenever I thought of the Olympics, memories of Seoul would surface and I would find myself getting rankled. *It's not fair, it's not fair, not fair, fair, fair*, echoed through my head in a whiney tone that jiggered my insides. What exactly was not fair was unclear to me, but I knew enough from my Seth readings to know that a limiting belief was being triggered. I needed help.

Joy Ballas Beeson, a bear-hug of a woman, gave counselling using Psych-K, a form of muscle testing to access one's core beliefs. The arm is used in the same way Miss Whitcombe used the pendulum when I was little. With the lightest of touch from Joy's fingers bearing down on my outstretched arm, my muscle would strengthen and lock for a positive response, and weaken for a negative one. Much as my conscious mind thought it was in control, it soon became evident that many of my body's responses were subconscious and try as I might I could not keep my arm raised if I was not in concurrence with a statement of belief. Joy knew nothing of running but she did understand the human psyche and, what's more, I liked her. She was a comforting mother figure to me and I felt as if I could confide my deepest feelings.

"Joy," I told her, "I want to win the Olympics, but if I don't get this straight, I'm afraid I'll repeat another dismal failure."

We met once a week, sorting through the layers of emotions to capture the sabotaging beliefs beneath. At the beginning I moaned about the pressures that weighed on me, particularly from the New Zealand public, then the sporting bureaucracies and finally from my own family.

Again and again the belief that was triggered was, "The universe doesn't support me." Joy explained that this precept had worked well when I was young, enabling me to develop a greater-than-average sense of self-reliance and to shape and strengthen my willpower. Like many athletes, I believed that I had to put in 110 per cent, and was prepared to do so, driving myself to the limits of my endurance. But this belief had reached the end of its service and was now strangling my progress. One hundred and ten per cent had become counter-productive. My willpower was driving my body into the ground.

Gradually I made progress. With Joy's guidance the mechanisms of my subconscious were becoming conscious, and I felt much more attuned to my body's needs.

As my confidence grew so did my belief that I could tackle anything, not just the pressures surrounding competition but the particular challenges of this next Olympic marathon: heat and hills. Generally I hated them. It was now my task to learn to love them. I sought them out. I wore extra clothes and ran in the heat of the day. I ran up the longest, steepest hills at every opportunity, tuning as best I could into the levity I had felt running up Glastonbury Tor and throwing my arms in the air when I reached the top, as if I had just won the Olympics. As the summer in Boulder wore on the hills started to feel easier, the heat of midsummer bearable. Another summer in New Zealand and I would be ready for Barcelona.

Mizuno dumped me. My contract expired at the end of the calendar year and I had hoped that they would renew it for the coming Olympics. But when my calls were finally returned I was told no. A "no" in Japanese business culture is about as final as you get. Executive decision: *Moller is too old, time to put our advertising dollars into young up-and-coming athletes.* But I attempted one last negotiation. "How about no money, I run just for Olympic bonuses. You pay me only if I win a medal."

Michiyo paused on the end of the phone, "No," she repeated emphatically.

'No' stings. They didn't want me any more.

I marched off to a running store and bought the pair of racing shoes that I liked the most. It was the best therapy I could think of. They were a pair of Brooks and they were light and flexible and pretty. It was the first time in 20 years I had bought my own running shoes. And wearing them, this old has-been would go out and win the Olympics.

Then Anne dumped me. It came to me one morning during my

New Zealand stint while I was reading the morning newspaper. The lead article in the sports section was a dedication to Anne Audain. She had discarded me through one simple act — retirement.

I felt kind of flat; it was like eating chips without salt for the first time. *How can I go to the Olympics without her?* My reaction, visceral and unreasonable, took me by surprise. Already I missed her. Her presence gave me that something extra. I knew that her retirement was timely, that to focus on Anne was limiting, that it was necessary to switch my fuel source from jealousy and anger to the love of excellence: it was time to be the star of my own show. Still, I wanted to call her up and plead with her to race just one more Olympics. But of course I didn't.

These things come in threes. The next one would blindside me the day before my big race.

I arrived back in the USA with a good build-up behind me. Now for my Olympic qualifying time at one of my favourite all-time marathons — the Boston Marathon.

I fizzled in Boston. By ten miles I knew I was a six-horsepower engine running on three. It was a familiar feeling, like losing your upper gears and having to idle along in second. I dropped out somewhere after halfway. Back home, blood tests showed what it had many times before: my ferritin level was at 15, way below the minimum of 25 that I needed to run a marathon. The ferritin test is a measure of iron stores in the body and is considered by sports medicine experts to be the gold standard of iron profiles for distance runners. "No problem," the doctor told me enthusiastically, "we will have you right in six months."

"But I don't have six months!" I exclaimed desperately, "the Olympics are in three!"

I decided to take matters in hand. Time was short but sufficient. I kept reminding myself that I needed to be at my best on one day only — 1 August, the day of the Women's Olympic Marathon. Every day preceding would matter only as preparation and feedback towards that one special day.

I reinstituted my Olympic-commitment routine that I had used before Los Angeles in 1984. The juice extractor was dusted off and put to work. Every morning without fail I began the day with freshly pressed fruit juices. Vegetable juices followed in the afternoon before dinner. I alternated molasses with Vitamin C and green drinks of chlorophyll throughout the day, swallowed iron pills and ate meat while shunning any tea, coffee and sugar — all substances which inhibit iron absorption.

Within three weeks I could feel my strength returning, and my ferritin levels were at 20, hardly the desirable level of 40 to 100 for women but good enough to run a fitness trial in a ten-kilometre race of 32:44. The selectors named me to the team. I did not tell them that the course had been downhill.

My sessions with Joy were progressing. Just a few months away from the Olympics I finally reached the point where I could accept that the universe was in my favour. My perception of the New Zealand public, bureaucrats, sponsors, rivals, past boyfriends and my family had done a 180-degree-turn and the anger towards them was dissipating. Rather than seeing them as a burden on my back, I could picture their interest as a positive force flowing in my direction, pushing me to success and I felt gratitude for their investment in my performance. I was their Olympic athlete delegate, the fortunate representative having this wonderful experience on behalf of those who couldn't. It was nothing less that my moral obligation and spiritual mandate to perform to the very best of my ability.

With that squared away we could get down to dealing with the actual Olympics. I explained to Joy what a pressure-cooker it can be. In Boulder I relied on my home for sanctuary. But the Olympic village can be anything but a soft place to fall and recoup in at the end of the day. I found it hard at times to find 'home' in such a setting, without the comfort of my partner or my familiar things.

"How can I go there," I asked Joy "and maintain this feeling of centeredness when the place is an emotional tornado with so many influences pulling you out of kilter? I don't know if I'm strong enough or experienced enough to hold all these good thoughts."

"Think of something that will keep you centered," she said, knowing that something originating from my own mind would be much more powerful than anything she could come up with.

"I know!" I jumped up and, starting at my feet, pulled a giant imaginary pink bubble up and over my head, sealing it at the top.

"This is my magic bubble," I explained to her, assuming that she could see it as well as I did. "This pink membrane will allow only what is helpful to penetrate; anything else will just whiz on past, leaving me unfazed."

From then on the pink bubble stayed intact, and I began to see everything through a soft haze of rose.

"Now what about the race? Where do we need to focus?" I was back with Joy a week later and she was finally zeroing in on the Olympic marathon.

"Crunch-time. It can occur at any point but most often just after halfway. If I can hang in there through crunch-time then I have a good chance."

"What happens at crunch-time?"

"Everyone else starts looking good and the better they look the tireder I feel."

"So how can you give yourself more positive feedback?"

I thought about it for a few moments then it became obvious. "I run to the front of the pack. Everyone feels good at the front, initially at least. You instantly feel like you are winning! I don't have to stay there for long; I wouldn't want to lead the whole thing, just long enough to feel positive again. Then instead of me looking at them all the time, they can look at me and see how good I look!"

"Mentally see yourself doing this and note how it feels." Joy pushed on my arm while I held the picture of me running in front. It held strong.

"Okay, now how do you win a race?" Joy knew little about competition.

I took a deep breath. I needed to comb through my mind to capture the crucial element of winning for me. It was an elusive thing I had not yet defined for myself.

"It's like a doorway opens at just the right moment, and you need to move through it or it closes again. You never know ahead of time when it's going to open, though in a marathon it's probably not going to be before eighteen miles. When it does though, it's like a rush of fresh air hits you and you just want to break out of where you are and surge into it."

"What does the doorway look like?"

I closed my eyes to see it.

"Just a door, it looks like any door in any house, dark wood with a gold handle but it's open and it's in the middle of the street leading into a different version of reality. One thing I do notice though is that Mercury is standing beside it!"

"Excellent! Hold that image in your mind so that when the time comes in your Olympic race you can recognise your Doorway of Opportunity."

The world's greatest coach, Arthur Lydiard, was staying at the home of my friends Priscilla and Dave Welch. I was invited to join them for dinner. The Olympics in Barcelona were just a month away.

Arthur asked me how my training was progressing. I told him that my coach had me on a programme of running about 90 miles a week, no track work but lots of long runs that just kept getting faster. "Good, good," he muttered, then paused as he carefully conveyed mashed potatoes on the back of his fork and sipped on his lager. He was mulling my situation over in his head while he chewed, and I sat poised for the verdict which I knew was about to be delivered.

He put down his fork and paused as he looked me straight in the eye in true Arthur style: unblinking, absolute, omniscient. "Just remember that ninety per cent of runners perform below what they are capable of in the Olympics. You're smart and experienced. You have trained the right way for years. You can win."

I don't know where Arthur got his statistic from, and I wonder if he just made it up on the spot, but I held that number in my head. Ninety per cent. That left ten per cent. There were 60 entrants. That would mean that I would be competing against just six people!

Suddenly my task seemed so simple. I could feel myself lifting. The God of Running had just spoken to me. A hope in my heart had now become a distinct probability. Not for a moment did I consider that I would be in that 90 per cent. Sitting in front of Arthur that evening, I was knighted by his words as a ten per cent person. Being a ten per center himself, Arthur most surely intended that.

When Arthur returned to New Zealand he made a bold move and announced to the papers that I was ready to win a medal.

As usual he was right.

CHAPTER 41

Broadsided

JULY 1992, SPAIN

When I arrived at the Olympic Village in Barcelona I was once again greeted warmly by the athletics team captain, Graeme McCabe. Shades of Los Angeles. This time he had carried bottles of the Putaruru spring water on which I was raised, surely the purest water in the world, to put in my water bottles for the race. The gesture was touching and a good omen. Already the universe was supporting me.

I was taken to the New Zealand headquarters and left to 'check in'. The Chef de Mission, Ralph Roberts, whom I had not previously met, enthusiastically received me. I felt at home, wanted, accepted into the Kiwi fold — not at all like the outcast that I had felt in Seoul.

"I have a good feeling about you," Ralph waxed. In response, my own good feelings about myself upgraded themselves to first class. I liked this guy.

Just then one of the administrative assistants walked into the room. Ralph gestured for her to join our conversation and landed his hand affectionately on my shoulder as he drew her in,

"I was just telling Anne that I had a good a feeling about her."

She smiled at me. "Hello, Anne. I wish you the best of luck." I forced a smile back and excused myself. It was an understandable mistake but I was momentarily staggered.

By the time I leave here, I vowed to myself, they will all be saying, "*Anne who?*"

301

Anne's lingering presence was to be but a flicker. It was Ron's presence, on the eve of my big day, which roared into my life.

I was sitting in the athletes' dining hall, when Janis Klecker, a Minnesotan runner and fellow competitor in the marathon, tapped me on the shoulder.

"Did you hear about Ron?"

"No."

"He had a heart attack."

"Is he okay?"

"No. He's dead."

I did not know how to respond and left the dining room in a hurry. My pink bubble had been penetrated and my head was spinning. Emotions flooded me in quick succession: the cold wall of denial, the heaviness of remorse, the stickiness of guilt, and the ache of sadness. Following on their heels was hot indignation beating its well-worn path to my central nervous system and I could feel the warm, sharpening rush surge through my body. With it came memories of Ron and his immaculate timing to create everlasting moments in my life's album: Ron in Rio on the stage, biting on my medal; Ron on our honeymoon telling me I made him sick; Ron in Auckland picking a fist fight while I am on stage; Ron in London setting up my demise, and then rubbing my nose in it. On the heels of these pictures the pressing question, *Of all days why did he have to die now?*, came along with the answer that lodged in my mind and refused to budge: *The bastard did it on purpose just to sabotage the most important race of my life!* And then I cried, a few tears of shock, a few more of self-pity, and then some big ones of outrage.

I did not cry for long. Too many questions were whizzing through my brain that needed answering. *What do I do with this? Does it change anything? Can I still win?* I had only a few hours before I would be going to bed, so it was imperative that I get this straight, quick. I could see only two choices: run well despite Ron, or run well in tribute to Ron. Somehow finding motivation for winning the Olympics out of spite didn't quite work. It seemed too petty, too little for something so big, and I was sure, in the eyes of the Olympic gods, unworthy of

Gold. I knew what I must do: honour Ron by using all that he taught me about marathons to run well. And to do this I must forgive.

When night fell I headed to the Barcelona pier with a little boat I had made from a cardboard box, decorated with flowers and holding one lone candle rummaged from team headquarters which I lit, and then cast out on the sea. As I watched it float away, my eyes filled with tears. I knew that this was an era of my life that was leaving; not only was I saying good-bye to Ron but to the dependent girl-woman who had given herself away in return for his stewardship and then blamed him for the hollowness it had carved inside her. I felt a weight lift from me.

As I sat staring into the inky sea I sifted through my memories of Ron, asking for the grace to thank him for them: both the happy times and the angry, painful times. I could not dwell on them, for the painful memories kept shoving the happy ones out of the way. While intellectually I could frame that time of my life in a positive context and give thanks to Ron, emotionally I could not find it in me to fully forgive. My marathon was tomorrow and I was not willing to give up my anger completely. I needed it in order to race. I was not yet comfortable with using love and there was too much at stake. Complete forgiveness would take some help. That would not come until much later, and from a most unexpected source. I recalled my mother's advice when Ron had left me in Wellington and now, ten years later, her words would serve me as soundly as they had back then: "Forget Ron. Go run your race."

I sealed up my pink bubble, shutting Ron out. I had a job to do.

CHAPTER 42

Into the Fire

*If you aspire to the highest place, it is no disgrace to stop
at the second, or even the third place.* — Cicero

1 AUGUST 1992, BARCELONA

1992 Summer Olympics — Women's Marathon, Barcelona, Spain

As I watched my competitors warming up the following afternoon at the start line of the Olympic marathon in the outskirts of
Barcelona, I could see that Arthur was right. Ninety per cent of these
women were already in the throes of selecting their demise from
the unwritten running manual, *101 Ways to Run Below Your Best*. The
heat was already proving today's popular choice, next would be the
hill where many would quit, followed by the distance, the smog, the
pressure, the side stitch, tummy ache, shoes that blister, muscles that
hurt, not enough water, too much water, not enough sleep, indigest-
ible breakfast, last week's cold, etc., etc., etc. I had used them all at one
time or other in the last twenty years. Now, inside my bubble there
was room for none of them. Even the asthma that had bothered me
so badly over the past year had become a non-issue, although I carried an inhaler in my pre-race kit as a precaution. My ferritin levels
had topped out at 28, as high as they had ever been. I felt fit. This was
time for business. I was here to collect on the energy investment I had
made a year before: to meet my future waiting just 26 miles away in
the stadium: to win.

Bang! We were underway — a caravan of 60 women vying for

glory at the top of the hill where the Olympic stadium stood, 26 merciless miles away.

We ambled along, cagily saving ourselves for the battle. For the first time in the Olympic Women's Marathon there were no heroics at the outset with some frisky whippersnapper from nowhere racing ahead of the pack thinking she could steal the race. We knew the fiery dragons of Barcelona would eat such foolishness for an appetiser. I ran at the side of the front pack, biding my time and keeping out of trouble. The first ten miles were my warm-up.

Occasionally, when doubts began to surface in my mind, I ran to the front of the pack for a few yards. It made me feel as if I was winning. Just a few steps and I had enough of a shot of confidence to settle back into the pack for another few miles.

At precisely half way, several runners fled from the front of the pack for their winning bids. They were following their coaches' instructions: "Stay in the pack until half way, then take the lead and win!" I could bet they would not finish well, for they still had fat in their cheeks and had not yet learned to feel the race for themselves. But I knew I needed to be within covering distance, for it would take only one unknown prodigy to hang on to that lead and take my place on the podium. Along with the other sets of mature legs defined by sinuous pistons and pulleys working under translucent skin, I gave chase.

Over the next few miles, runners burst ahead like Icarus taking flight, and one by one they fell back to earth with melted wings and were swallowed up by the ensuing flurry of feet. These bids swiftly reconfigured us from a running sisterhood to a frantic string of chased, chasers, and stragglers.

Soon tall, terraced apartments buildings with wrought iron balconies enclosed the streets that were thick with cheering onlookers. We were approaching downtown. I was expecting to see the honeycombed towers of Gaudi's Sagrada Familia cathedral at around 14 miles. I had deliberately selected this landmark as a mental milestone, but we were almost at 15 miles and I must have missed it. It did not occur to me that I had raised my eyes from the ground only long enough to sight my next turn and plot a straight line to it. I wondered how I could have overlooked such a glaring structure but I would not commit the sacrilege of turning my head away from my goal. "Don't look back!" the peppery old coaches back home would bark to lanky, barefooted lads and lasses on grass tracks. Such pragmatism had made an indelible impression on me. I rarely looked back and never cast my thoughts back either. My concentration was purposefully locked in forward gear.

I first became aware of my surroundings on the long stretch of Las Ramblas. I had walked this famous avenue many times and I was comforted to recognise where I was in relation to the finish. I was a chaser and I could sense the aura of the Japanese runner hitchhiking on my pursuit as I picked off runners in front of me: first two other young Japanese in dark sunglasses, striding together, next the reigning bronze medallist, East German, Katrin Dorre, and then the seasoned Russian, Madina Biktagarova. There was no response from any of them and they let our carriage pass them by as they began their death march to the finish. Soon there was just one runner in front of us.

My attention was taken by a familiar voice from the sidelines, yelling "Go Lorraine!" I looked up to see Harlan. I was heartened. From the first time we met, the sight of him had always lifted me. I could tell he was excited and I looked straight at him and flashed my hand in acknowledgement. I did not want to use my precious energy in words so I wanted my eyes to convey that I had this under control and not to worry about me. I had just passed the 16-mile mark and I felt fantastic.

The crossroads. The point of reckoning. The defining moment. Unwittingly I had just passed into Mercury's territory and was about to be tested. I should have known that the minute I thought I had it in the bag was the same minute I would fall prey to my own hubris. I should have recognised that my foe was not out there but in my own self. But I didn't. I was not aware that the title of Olympic Champion required my fortified walls be razed and my fears emptied out, that I needed to die to my past insufficiencies right then and be filled anew, with a heart open and courageous enough to bear such an awesome responsibility.

This was the cue for my Rational Mind to step in. She looked snappy in her pressed and pleated power suit, selected just for this special occasion. While I had been busy with my imagination the past weeks, erecting magical pink bubbles and lighting incense to invoke Greek Gods at my Olympic altar, she had busied herself with a postgraduate course in 'Judicious Personal Energy Management for Status Quo Maintenance' at Harvard Business School. She had been dispatched urgently by her boss, The Ego, to rein me in. Unlike the directness of the dragon's fire, her breath was cold and her agenda insidious, cultivated specifically to dampen the fever of unbridled dreaming.

Lorraine, what do you think you are doing? she asked with a little sigh in her voice.

I'm chasing down that Russian up ahead so I can win the Olympics.

Oh, really? She raised her eyebrow. *Just remember, it is very hot, and you are not a good heat runner.*

You know, I haven't given the temperature a thought. I really don't feel hot.

Yes, but there are still ten miles to go. The heat can grab you just like that. She snapped her fingers. *Ten miles at the end of a hot marathon can seem like twenty. This is no time to be rash. Slow down.*

But if I slow down I may not catch the leader.

And risk blowing up? Come on, Lorraine. The course goes uphill. You know you are not a good uphill runner. Chances are the Russian will come back to you.

But I feel so good.

Hey, you know not to trust your feelings. They always get you into a hell of a lot of trouble. Slow down, there's a smart girl. The race doesn't start till 20 miles. You know that.

But this is the Olympics, I won't get another chance.

You're absolutely right. And look, you have third in the bag. Third is more than you can hope for. Hold onto it. Everyone is watching. We don't want you making a fool of yourself. Now slow down before you blow it.

So I slowed down. The young Japanese runner, Yuko Arimori moved past me in pursuit of the white-vested runner up ahead, gaining ten,

20 then 50 yards on me. I watched her swaying form chip into the lead of the upright Russian, then catch her. As the two of them merged strides, my heart sank. Her onslaught had been met with renewed vigor from her rival and I knew they would now gain strength from each other. The race for first was 70 metres ahead of me and they were slowly but surely drawing away. I dug in and could feel that I was far from spent. We ran equidistant for a long time, slowly climbing the base of Montjuïc, but I knew that on this ever-steepening uphill that I would not catch them. Soon the curves around the mountain took them out of view. Our energetic bond had now been severed. I was on my own. The road was newly paved, re-cut for the smooth passage of this grand event. Up, up, up it wended to the Olympic stadium, a magical kingdom in the sky beckoning me on in the twilight. I was still strong but now the snap in my ankles was deadened by the weight of knowing I had blown my chance for gold.

Third! Wow, that's great for you. Best you're ever going to do. Sure beats fifth, Ms Rational Smarty-pants chirped as I head for the tunnel into the stadium. *Now look good, everybody is watching.*

I straightened my back and lifted my arms. As I stepped into the arena, a roar rose to greet me. I scanned the stadium stands. Eighty thousand people were standing on their feet, heralding my entrance. My body jolted with the realisation that such rampant jubilation was directed towards me. I had not expected that a third place would surpass a hundredfold the exhilaration of all my other wins put together. The cheering swirled around the stadium and filled me up so that I felt I might burst with goodness. This was the collective sound of enthusiastic appreciation: the sound of humanity welcoming me as theirs. Who would have ever thought that I, Lorraine Mary Moller, from little old Putaruru in New Zealand, would be here at the centre of the universe? For the first time ever, I felt ecstatically alive. I held it in, trying to immortalise this feeling. *This,* I said to myself, *is the finest moment of my life.*

When I crossed the finish line, the gold medalist, Valentina Yegorova was already jogging around the stadium on her victory lap. I hesitated.

Can I do a victory lap? After all, I didn't win. Then I spied Yuko Arimori, the silver medallist, on the other side of the track, jogging around, waving her arms to the crowd, smiling excitedly. *If she can do it so can I*, and I set off around the track again, my legs surprisingly fresh with a new surge of adrenalin.

At the end of my lap, amid the throng of reporters and agents pushing their business cards into my face, I was ushered into the catacombs under the stadium to the drug testing room. Here I was required to urinate in a jar, no easy task after running 26 miles in 90-degree temperatures. There was no leaving until I was done and so I drank water and more water until I felt my stomach would explode. An hour later I summoned my 'escort' that I was ready. She was an older woman whose brusque manner reminded me in type of Miss Hedgerow, Matron, and Miss Baxter. Her job was to ensure that the urine did in fact come from my body. With my shirt pulled up to show that I had no suspicious tubes carrying someone else's urine concealed on my body, I emptied my bladder under her watchful eye. In spite of my embarrassment, I couldn't help giggling to myself as I handed her the cup to carry. When I was little, pissing in company meant that I was unhealthy, deficient, flawed. Now my pee had become a rare and precious fluid that verified my new status: Olympic Medallist.

About midnight when I was finally done with testing and press conferences, the team manager summoned a car to take me back to the village. I desperately wanted to see Harlan and share my joy but he had become trapped in the crowds and had been unable to make it to the stadium. I would not see him until the following afternoon.

That night as I lay on my bed I was ecstatically happy. I had never known such elation. It seemed to burst from me and I had the urge to jump up and do something, anything, like hug and kiss myself and bounce on the mattress, while shouting "I did it! I did it!!" But my roommates were sleeping and so I lay with a big silly grin on my face and my eyes wide open, staring at the ceiling until the sun rose. Life would never be the same again. Inside I felt invincible, as if I had flown to the heavens with Mercury and unlocked the secrets of the universe. I was Superwoman, convinced there was nothing I couldn't do if I put my mind to it.

But while I was filled with a rock-solid confidence, disappointment was strumming a melancholy note in the background. I knew how to do it but I still had not done it. And now that chance for gold was gone forever.

CHAPTER 43

All that Matters

It's wrong to keep on raging, heart inflamed forever.
— Achilles, from *The Odyssey* by Homer

1992 — 1993

When the Games finished I wanted to be with my own people. I had visions of stepping off the plane in my homeland as a hero: riding down Queen Street in the ticker tape parade, going on talk shows and television, being stopped in the street by every second person and signing autographs. New Zealand would welcome me home with open arms and I would retire there and live my life happily ever after as a famous person beloved by all.

There was just one small hitch. With no sponsorship for the past year, I was cash broke and did not have the funds to buy a ticket home. So I asked the New Zealand Olympic Committee if they could trade my ticket back to the USA, so that I could travel back to New Zealand with the team. They had chartered their own plane, issued all the tickets, and since they had been singing my praises for the past week, I thought surely they easily and happily would pull some strings. But I was met with a terse and final 'no'. My ticket originated in the USA and I had to return to the USA, they said. This request was clearly outside the bureaucratic box and could not be accommodated. I was crestfallen. Like the little girl who had just wanted her mother, once again I had hoped for too much. I had done well, but bronze was not quite good enough for a ticket home.

I returned to Boulder. There was no hero's welcome. I hinted to my girlfriend to organise a party for me. I thought it would seem crass to organise one in my own honour. But even asking left me feeling a tad like a beggar. She happily obliged but the gathering of my friends, while touching, was not the grand display of adoration that I was hoping for.

When I read in the paper that they were calling on Olympic Medallists for a parade through the streets of Denver, I rang hopefully and left a message with the organisers. They never called back. It was obvious: I was an outsider, a foreigner, and although I had called this place home for the past ten years I did not really belong.

Meantime there was a big welcoming party in New Zealand for all the Olympic Medallists but me. I could not bear to hear about it. Here or there, this piece of metal on a ribbon was a Joker's invitation. It had not bought me a golden carriage to the ball, merely a pumpkin without a fairy godmother. Time to face up to it. I did not really belong anywhere.

Dissatisfaction gnawed away at me like a dripping tap in the bathroom. In the ensuing weeks I ran and re-ran the race in my mind, analysing every step until I came to the unyielding conclusion: I could have won. When I pulled back at the 16-mile mark I gave away my chance for gold or silver and settled for the bronze. At that crucial moment I betrayed myself. I had failed, not to win, but to risk it all. I was fearful of winning 'The Big One'. I knew it and they knew it. Of course I wasn't invited to the party.

The pink bubble had burst. When I brought my bronze medal out to show, I could not resist the urge to apologise for it not being gold.

Osaka Marathon wanted me back in January. When it came to running, I was tired and apathetic in a defeated way and I knew it. The Olympics and the ensuing weeks had used me up. I didn't really care to go, so I asked for a suitcase of money to see how high they would go. It soon became apparent that I had previously been negotiating too low. They offered me three times what they had before. Of course

I accepted. I needed the money. I justified it as back payment for my previous wins.

When the race came around I found myself in a line-up of weary Olympians. Even Mercury could not rouse my fire. I was stalked by younger, ambitious runners and ended up in my old safe finishing place — fifth. I didn't care.

I followed suit with the London Marathon a few months later. Princess Diana arrived at the start to talk to a few selected runners. She was as tall and willowy as a mannequin in a shop window at Milne and Choice's. She asked me where I was from. I told her. She gazed off into the stratosphere for a few moments, then pulled herself back as her mind scrolled her checklist of appropriate questions for runners. I waited politely until she had downloaded one. "How many miles a week do you run?" I told her about 80. She nodded and went back to question access mode. I wondered what would have happened if I had said 800. Would she have noticed? I wanted to ask her if she was happy, to tell her that she should have stayed in bed and enjoyed a good sleep-in instead of standing here at six-thirty a.m. trying to remember the right questions to ask runners.

I finished in fifth place. Another soulless run collecting dough. After London I decided to take a long-needed break from running.

I returned to Osaka three months later, this time to give a talk at a university about my training. They could not believe that someone as old as me could win a medal without some special secret, which now, they were certain, I was about to reveal. I was asked to photocopy my training diary of the last three weeks before my Olympic run, to give as handouts to the audience, which I did.

As I explained my training I suddenly noticed that the entire roomful of Japanese coaches, athletes and exercise physiology students appeared puzzled as they flipped through the pages. Then my interpreter politely called my attention. "There seems to be some pages missing. Do you know where they are?"

I quickly flicked through the pages. "They are all there."

She relayed this to my audience. A discussion ensued. Again she interjected. "Excuse me, but this is so little? Are you sure there is not a page missing? Perhaps the other side did not print?"

"No," I assured her. "That is all." And I continued with my talk which included how to construct a wish picture and a big pink bubble, my two biggest training secrets. They were still not satisfied.

I tried to explain that the only secret was that there was no secret and that I trained according to what worked for me. I could see that in their scheme of things my training volume was too small and could not produce the results I had from this old body. I realised then the folly of trying to look at my training outside the framework of my journey. I wanted to explain that the lure of transformation kept me going, and that I was not done until I was done, but I didn't. I am sure that they left feeling that I had withheld the big secret, and perhaps I did, but I had no choice. The only secret is that you have to figure it out for yourself.

Ron had been dead for about a year. I had thought of him now and then: mostly with the regret that we had never made our amends with one another. This night in Osaka I was jetlagged and lay down for one of those delicious sleeps where a horizontal stretch-out is a luxury.

I awoke gradually. I found myself sitting on the loveseat with Ron in his little house on Fifty-sixth Avenue South in Minneapolis. He had his arm around me, Snarf was sitting at his feet and we were reminiscing over a photo album full of snapshots of our good times together.

We flicked though the pages, dusting off each memory like a relic rediscovered in an attic: Snarf with his head hanging out the window of the rusted Toyota; Ron in his black, woollen captain's hat from Edinburgh; me in my first pair of New Balance shoes dressed for snow running with a pointy hat and fat gloves; Ron holding a coat over my head as I dash through the pelting rain in my wedding dress; and so they went on. In the last ten years I hadn't been able to remember all those good times, and now they were laid out in front of us, page after page. Some we laughed at until the tears ran down our cheeks, others we smiled over and snuggled closer, and with each one our circle of warmth grew until we were bathed in a soft haze of nostalgia.

But the best was to come. Ron turned the page. I was taken aback. Here I was in Barcelona, my arms outstretched to the heavens on the victory dais. In the background crowd Ron's face was visible, his eyes beaming with the quiet pride of Apollo's gaze.

This was unsettling.

"You were there?"

He nodded. It didn't make sense. "Is this okay?" I asked.

"What do you mean okay?"

"Sitting here like this, you know, considering all that went down, you know, me and Clint, us fighting, leaving mad, never talking."

Ron looked puzzled.

"Remember, you get married to the lady you met at the post office and then you die of a heart attack, right before my race. I'm now with Harlan. What I mean is, considering all that, is it okay for us to be sitting here like this?"

"Oh, all that." For a few moments he seemed to be accessing distant memory banks, and finally clicking, he waved his hand in dismissal. "Lorrainey-Babes, from my perspective now, none of that stuff matters. All that matters is this." Ron pulled me closer to him and squeezed my hand affectionately.

Once again he turned the page, then pointed to the last photo. In it Ron and I are sitting on the couch with Snarf at Ron's feet. Ron has his arm around me, and we are both looking at a photo album. This was a snapshot taken 20 years ago when we were contented to be with one another: a moment of tenderness and rightness. The memory of that moment erupted through the overlays of resentment and bitterness with the gentle power of a spring columbine breaking through the morning snow: we were experiencing that very same moment in the photograph right now! I was here and there at the same time, as clearly as I have been anywhere. I looked into Ron's eyes, suddenly suffused with the awareness that time had just crossed itself like a snaking river. We had come full circle.

When I awoke again, my whole being was immersed in a soft white luminescence. I was buoyant as I had never felt before, and filled with an immense gratitude for the gift of Ron. He was right. The gritty details didn't matter — it had all been necessary grist for the mill, fodder for ruminating, and now the dam of resentment had finally broken and past hurts were released back to the ocean.

I understood what forgiveness was: to give it all up until all that remained was all that mattered — the love that was shared.

I was now free to move on.

CHAPTER 44

Three Weddings and a Funeral

1992 — 1993

Harlan asked me to marry him. Not a strong proposal, it appeared as a slip of the pen: a 'by the way, let's get married when you get back' thrown in at the end of his letter to me while I was in New Zealand for my annual summer sojourn. When I arrived back in Boulder he acted as if he couldn't remember writing it. I figured that he was teeter-tottering between the comfort of his old single life and the lure of a new one with me as his wife and that all he needed was some gentle coaxing to cross the threshold of legal entanglement. Using my womanly wiles, I proceeded so carefully and skillfully to pre-empt the decision to my advantage, that by the end of the year he was married to me not once, but three times.

Handfasting in the Celtic tradition, Evan explained, takes place on August the first. At this time a couple commits for a year and a day. After that time they are free to quit or to renew the vow. August the first I enthusiastically noted was the day I had won my Olympic medal. I had been doing a weekly class with Evan Hodkins on Wicca and Celtic Christianity and reporting back to Harlan after each class. Evan is a bard of old and, like Andy and Joy, is one of those agents of Mercury who opens doors to the heart and gently nudges you through to a greater truth than the one you are presently comfortable in.

"Let's do it," I urged Harlan. "I'll arrange it. Nothing official and it is not forever." I was presenting it as a sort of marriage by lease-agreement, rather than a cash-up-front irrevocable deal. He went for it.

My friend across the street is a real Wiccan priestess who goes by the name of Morwyn. She knew a guy who was a civil servant by day and a pagan minister by night who was willing to perform the ceremony. I called my best friends, Colleen and Vicki, and asked them to come. We all headed up into the mountains to Morwyn's secret site, which she claims is a vortex of potent energies, and the exchange of vows took place. In the eyes of the Goddess, Harlan and I were now fasted by hand, for a year and a day, at least.

We headed for Japan to the city of Sapporo for the Hokkaido Marathon a few weeks later. Harlan was getting pretty comfortable with the idea of calling me his wife and had more or less agreed that we could get married in the eyes of the greater community when we returned.

When it came to the marathon I was still running tired, but like Osaka and London they were willing to pay well for an Olympic medallist. I finished third. At the post-race press conference I mentioned that we were to be married. This caused considerable interest and shortly afterwards I was approached by the race director to see if Harlan and I would like to get married in the morning.

It just so happened that the hotel we were staying in was a 'wedding hotel' with chapel attached. Conveyer-belt weddings were their specialty, where packages starting at about US$30,000 would process two single people through the wedding factory, from which they would emerge several hours later, married. The race director was prepared to foot the bill for it, or, more likely, he sold the rights to television networks.

I was told to report to the lobby at eight a.m. Monday. Two ladies in kimonos led me away to the bridal preparatory chambers. From a rack of coloured chiffon and silk and starched petticoats I was asked to select a dress. Not bound here by western sensibilities, I chose a black one with gold brocade. I was then ushered into the dressing room where four excited women descended upon me, stripped me down to my underwear and went to work: one on my hair, two on my make-up and one running around to the orders of the other three.

They clucked and tutted and tsked as my freckled skin was buried under layers of white powder. Soon I was transformed into a porcelain round-eyed doll, my dress sewn onto my body to a perfect fit, and flowers, jewellery and shoes to complete the transformation from sporty girl to decorous bride.

Meantime Harlan had run into town to find a cheap ring that would do in a pinch, and on his return to the lobby was whisked away for similar treatment in the groom's room. We both emerged precisely on time at the chapel for the practice run-through.

Stand, bow, turn, hold bride's arm, walk slowly, stand here, turn, bow … and so our directions were given and we dashed through a quick rehearsal. Both of us were relying on the other to remember.

We were then introduced to the Presbyterian minister, a sweet, humble Japanese man. Any objections? we were asked. Harlan and I shook our heads. We were just going with the flow. "I am sorry I have very broken Engrish," the minister informed us.

We entered the chapel for the second time to 'The Wedding March', with automatic cameras recording every precious moment for posterity. The pews were filled with race officials, some bellboys and maids from the hotel, and even several chefs who had been gathered from the kitchen and were still wearing their tall hats. The few non-Asians amongst the audience stood out — a smattering of Russian and South African runners from yesterday's race.

The organ started with 'What a Friend We have in Jesus' which the minister's lone broken-Engrish voice carried for three verses and choruses since few of the audience could read the English programme, Harlan did not know the words, and I had done my dash singing for Japan on national television.

The ceremony then began. To Harlan and me it sounded something like this:

"Radies and Gentremen, We are gathered here today to join this man and this ermine in ho-ry matrimony."

I dared not look at Harlan in case I got the giggles.

"Har-ran Smiff," he said weighing each syllable and eyeing Harlan as if making sure he did indeed have the right Caucasian, "do you take this ermine, Rorraine Morrer, to be your rawfull redded rife, to ruv and perfect as long as you both shall riv?"

"I do."

(The Japanese language does not have a separate sound for 'r's and 'l's but rather one sound that is blended. To us Westerners their pronunciation of 'l' sounds like 'r'. My name was always somewhat of a mouthful here.)

The minister turned to me: "Ro-rraine Morrer." He made an emphatic pause to convey the heaviness of the promises to come. "Do you promise to take this man Har-ran Smiff to be your rawful redded husband, to ruv and obey and to cheap yourself only for him as long as you both shall riv?"

"I do."

"I now pronounce you husband and rife."

When we exited the church as a married couple the Japanese media greeted us with flashbulbs and television cameras. We were showered with rice and then asked to ring the hanging bell, a custom that signifies the ringing in of our new life as a couple — for an extended period so that all three national networks could get their footage, but I took it to signify that we would have a very, very long marriage together.

We were escorted into a reception where a banquet table holding a magnificent six-tiered cake awaited us. The whole affair turned out to be a press conference and we were politely handed a microphone and questions were fielded. The first question was directed to Harlan.

"Mr Smith, how do you feel?"

"Married," he replied. This was dutifully interpreted and everyone wrote it down.

"How long have you been Mrs Smith's coach?"

Harlan could not be bothered explaining that he wasn't. "About five years."

What with my mother and aunt, my two brothers, Dick and now Harlan, not to mention that I claimed to be self-coached, these reporters must be so confused, I thought. I quietly kicked Harlan under the table.

A few more questions and they announced it was time to cut the cake. I was so impressed and very touched by the sheer enormity of it. *For us? Really they shouldn't have gone to so much trouble, and at such short notice.* The thought just about brought tears to my eyes. We were then instructed to move the knife in and out, not up and down. When we got up close we realized why. The cake was a fake; a big prop made of cardboard and plaster sitting atop a barrow that had been wheeled in for the photos and would be wheeled out again for the next wedding.

After the reception one of the African runners sidled up to Harlan. "How much" he asked "did you have to pay her father for her?"

"Nothing" Harlan replied.

He was shocked. "I had to pay three cows and six pigs for my wife!" He walked away shaking his head at the bargain Harlan had scored. Skinny and old, but still a bargain.

When we returned to Boulder we got married once AGAIN, this time with friends and family present. The owner of the bridal store in Sapporo had been so happy with the publicity our wedding had generated for her business that she had given me a bridal gown, this time an elaborate white wedding dress which I wore for this one last occasion. I think I can safely say that Harlan and I were now well and truly hitched.

I searched but I could not find Mercury. Harlan and I turned the house inside out but to no avail; he was well and truly gone. I thought of flying out to LA and buying a new one, but it did not seem right.

Time had come to flee from the snowy winter in Boulder for the warmer climes of New Zealand. Harlan planned to follow shortly after. The night before my flight I was prancing around in my summer outfits, figuring out which ones to wow them with back home, when I noticed that most of my clothes were much tighter than usual. Surely I couldn't be — but the two pink link lines on the stick the next morning confirmed that indeed I was pregnant. How perfect! Now Mercury's disappearance made sense. My time had come to retire from running and raise children.

On New Year's Day of 1994, I miscarried. I had been in New

Zealand just five days when I was razed to the ground. The super-being that I had supposed myself to be had just been annihilated by a handful of cells that I had failed to nurture. I wept. My belly wept. Once again I was a sad little girl, alone and empty. *How could I have been so stupid for thinking that I could have it all,* I berated myself.

By the time Harlan arrived a few weeks later it all made sense to me. Fate had interceded so that I could fulfill my destiny. The baby was not to be. Instead I was to run another Olympics, this time for the gold medal. Without it I would remain incomplete and would be doomed to living my life out knowing that my mission here on earth was a failure.

Back in Boulder a few months later I walked into my bathroom. I called Harlan urgently. Did you put this here? He shook his head in astonishment. Mercury was dangling on a towel holder next to the washbasin.

CHAPTER 45

Last Call

1994

In June I turned forty. According to running lore, I was technically over the hill and now I was precariously facing downhill. Any moment, I was told, I would lose my footing and make a quick slide to retirement. I spurned the notion. Age had less to do with it than attitude. Ron had often said that "age is a structure by which society tricks you into giving up the things you love doing." I was not giving anything up. As far as I was concerned, my athletic potential had not yet been realised, especially now that I was fast discovering that there was a boundless reservoir of psychic/spiritual energy to be tapped. I was born to run and in doing so to stretch the limits, not just for myself, but for all of humankind. *If they all thought I was rather old to win a bronze medal at 37*, I chuckled, *wait until I win a gold medal at 41!*

These lofty ideals gave me the motivation to push through my 20-mile runs, for as inspired as I was, my breathing on some days was laboured and my recovery not what it used to be. But I managed my training, so that decent performances were still forthcoming and as a masters runner I maintained an unbeaten record. But as an open runner the same performances were, by my own standards, middling and I knew it. I was just hoping that when the time came I would 'come right'.

As the pressure mounted to make my qualifying time, I fell apart. I was bone tired and training was dragging me down rather than enhancing my fitness. When I ran the Cal International Marathon in Sacramneto at the end of the year I was hoping to run under the 2:35 time I needed to make the team. Once I would have run through such a time as a training run but now I was not so cocky. I was hoping that destiny would provide me with perfect conditions and some spring in my legs. I was fast losing faith in my own ability to perform.

A health practitioner friend offered to inject a live cell adrenal extract into my arm muscles to boost my flagging adrenal function.

"This is the good stuff imported from Germany," he told me. "They say it is the fountain of youth. I've been trying it on myself and can personally vouch for its potency."

I rejected the idea outright at first. Just the idea of needles is discomforting, and injecting foreign tissue from bovine embryo organs seemed Frankenstein-ian. It reminded me of a story I had read in the newspaper ten years earlier about athletes who had been injecting themselves with black market human growth hormone before the synthetic stuff became available. The only source was from cadavers, which were hard to come by and exorbitantly expensive. Officials had become concerned because monkey growth hormone was being pedalled instead and unsuspecting athletes had begun exhibiting ape-like characteristics.

But adrenal extract was not illegal, and I was not looking for the winning edge; I just wanted to get to the launching pad of good health. Over the weeks Ms Rational worked on me. As usual she was concerned with failing. Faith in Mercury was fine, she argued, but the physical indicators were that I would fall short. *Get real*, she urged. So on the verge of desperation I let him inject one dose, half in each arm.

Both my deltoids went into spasm. My arms ached day and night. (I would have taken it up with him shortly afterwards but after all his focus on youth potions, he committed suicide. It made me wonder what was in the stuff.) On the plane to Sacramento I went to the bathroom and could barely move my arms enough to pull my pants up. So I sat on the toilet and bawled for ten minutes before I made a concerted effort to get myself dressed for landing. "If I can't pull my pants up, how can I run a marathon?" I wailed to myself.

I couldn't. I knew from the start of the race I was done for. The first five miles should breeze by, but five minutes into it I was already hitting the wall. I felt like a puppet dragging myself against a dead puppeteer. It hurt to swing my arms. It hurt to hold them. It hurt to feel the shock of each footfall in my shoulders. At five miles I knew it was over. At ten I dropped out. I considered this just punishment for going against my better judgment.

I remained undeterred. This was a small hiccup on my road. My arms would recover. I was still certain that if I was not to have a baby then I was meant for another Olympics. Otherwise the past two years would be pointless, and I could not imagine the universe being set up in such a mean way. I would come right after some solid training in New Zealand and then I would run the Los Angeles Marathon and qualify for the Olympics — where I would win. This reasoning made perfect sense.

After a few weeks in New Zealand I began to come around, running consistently and feeling more like my old self. My arms relaxed and rejoined the group effort of my body, the spring returned to my step and running became joyful again.

One day I was out running around the Auckland Domain, a popular running spot near the city center. I had a favourite four-kilometre loop around the border of the park and enjoyed the variety in terrain as I loped along lost in my thoughts. I loved the feeling of power generated by my own body moving freely through the atmosphere, at my own pace, on my own terms, with my own thoughts. The sense of flying was with me today, and now and then blue orbs flashed in the trees like little imps playing hide and go seek. Magic was in the air. I smiled inwardly — *It's so good to be alive!*

She caught my eye, her forlorn little face framed with dark hair. I had run past the high-rise building to my right hundreds of times. I knew it was a hospital but today, for the first time, it demanded my attention so urgently that I did something I rarely do during runs — I stopped. My eyes were drawn to the third floor where I noticed a child at the window, distant behind glass, but I could see the V-neck of white regulation pyjamas beneath her red dressing gown. I waved and she waved back. I thought of myself at that age and how I would stare out the window. *Hang in there, kiddo, it is worth living for,* I found myself transmitting to her, *you won't believe how good it gets. How good? How about Gold at the Olympics!*

I ran on. I had a feeling of being connected to all things, and an overwhelming sense of inner strength. Nothing in life could ever break me. I was, from that moment on, most assuredly, eternally, safe.

When I next saw my mother a week later, the image of the pale little girl staring at me through the window still haunted me.

"Mum," I asked "Where was the hospital that I was in when I was little?"

"Auckland Hospital," she replied, "next to the Auckland Domain, where you run."

Dick had begun coaching a young woman called Nyla Carroll who was hugely talented, having recently broken Anne Audain's New Zealand record for the 5,000 metres. Nyla consistently ran big mileages and Dick thought that if I trained with her for a few weeks I would temper her tendency to overdo it and get in some solid training myself.

But that is not quite how it worked.

We ran morning and evening from her house in New Plymouth, Nyla often starting ahead of me to get in some extra miles. I would meet her some 30 minutes later after her prolonged warm-up. I probably needed it more than her: my body took some 20 minutes of cranking before the oil circulated into my feet, but I tagged along as best I could, drawing her into conversation so she would have to stay with me until I was ready to chomp into the meat of the work-out with her. We ran hard, neither relenting for the other, she drawing from the replenishing well of youthful exuberance, and I, from the calculated appropriation of dwindling resources. By the end of my stay I had logged my biggest week's mileage ever of 130, and was well into a second week of 120. I thought I was safe because Nyla had, by my calculations, run over 150. What's more, I ate what Nyla ate, simple fare deficient in calories for such high expenditure, and after a week I was looking like a greyhound on an Atkins diet, my ribs sticking out like washboards and my cheeks sunken.

When I called in to home in Putaruru, Dad took one look at me and said I was peak-ed. He liked to make that distinction, the difference between being peaked and peak-ed. Peaked was just right, peak-ed was overdone. He said I needed to stay with him and get a few decent feeds and some leisurely forest runs to bring me around. He was right. But I was on a tight schedule.

The Los Angeles Marathon came and went. I struggled for ten miles and then dropped out. My gas gauge was on empty. For all my training, I was as far away from qualifying for the Olympics as I had ever been.

My last chance was the Boston Marathon in six weeks' time. In a last-ditch attempt to pull myself together I ran mostly in the pool and took days off from running when the air was so polluted that I could not breathe. My lymph glands were swollen, a sure sign of overwork and chronic stress, and I was suffering from a persistent sore throat. What's more, my foot was out of place and all the adjusting, padding and taping did not help it. It took me 20 minutes of running before I could put my full weight on it.

The night before the Boston Marathon I knew that if I dropped out of this one it was all over, not just for this round, but for my whole career. I could not finish on this note, broken down and pathetic. My story could not end with a whimper. Mercury had something magical in mind for me, I was sure of it.

The next morning as I warmed up around Hopkinton for the noon start of the Boston Marathon, I knew only one thing: that I was destined for another Olympic Games and this was a mere formality. My willpower was at its peak and it would drag my half-dead body to the end on schedule.

My foot hurt like hell. A Japanese team coach stopped me. "Morrer, are you injured?" His brow rose with concern. "No," I replied, "Just warming up. I will be okay." He shook his head, and I went on with my limp to the start line, knowing that my foot just needed an extra long warm-up and would probably come right by the end of the race.

From the very start of the Boston Marathon I felt as if I had a stone in my shoe. Every step gave a sharp stab to the pad of my foot. A bone was out of place and I hoped that the pounding would push it back in. There was no way I was pulling out. *Can I run one more step?* I continually checked with myself. And that is how I ran the 1996 Boston Marathon, one painful 'yes' after another, for 26.2 miles.*

I finished eighth overall, first master, and made my Olympic qualifying time. When I saw Harlan back at our room in the Copley Plaza, he did not know the result and scanned my face for clues. "Two thirty-two!" I blurted. Tears of relief spilled onto his face and we stood together and cried like actors in a B-grade movie. This was the hardest race I had ever run in my life. The bottom of my foot was bruised black and blue and it hurt to put my weight on it.

That evening I called Dick. I could hear the surprise and relief in his voice.

"Now you need to get down to training."

"I can't," I told him. "I have to go to Greece."

"What for?"

"Don't ask. I just have to. I'll train when I get back."

Greece, the birthplace of the Olympians, was calling to me.

---

* At the 1908 Olympic Games in London, the marathon distance was changed to 26.2 miles to cover the ground from Windsor Castle to White City Stadium, with the 2.2 miles added on so the race could finish in front of the royal family's viewing box.

CHAPTER 46

Meeting Zeus

... inquire of Zeus of the flashing thunderbolt, if he has any message to give you concerning men whose spirits are seeking to attain great excellence ...
— excerpt from the 'Eighth Olympic Ode',
by Pindar (c. 522-420 BC)

APRIL — MAY 1996

Just a few weeks later I landed in Athens and headed north to Delphi: the magical world of gods and goddesses, oracles and athletics. 'Know thyself', the inscription over the entrance to the Temple of Apollo says in its Greek translation.

I climbed up the hill of this sacred site to the highest point in the complex where the athletic stadium stood, still intact with hundreds of years of history embedded in the earth of the track and the large stones that formed the audience seating. I drew in a deep shuddering breath. Nostalgia flooded my being. The struggle, the triumph, the roar of the crowd, hung in the air like eternal ripened apples just waiting to be picked and eaten. I lay down on the grass at the northern end of the track and fell into a deep, restful state.

"Thesalus?" a voice called.

"Yes," I heard myself responding.

"It's time."

"I'll be there in a minute."

I needed a few more minutes of silence to focus my intent. The stadium was filled with spectators and in a few moments I would be racing for top honours in these, the Delphic Games. This competition was what I was here for, the pinnacle of my existence, and now it was essential that I call upon all powers to be with me. It sounded first like a whisper emanating from a crack in the earth, but the words of the Oracle were clear. They seemed to be carried on the wind and on my breath all at once, inside and outside, then and now, to me, Thesalus, and every other warrior that ever existed and ever will. My heart quickened. This was what I had been seeking.

"You *can* win but I cannot say that you *will* win. That is up to you." The voice was etheric and haunting. "Your destiny is not to win, your destiny is in the bid to win. That is all you need to know." The voice faded with the vapors.

I understood. Attachment to the outcome of winning or losing was a mortal invention, whereas performing for performance's sake was the realm of the gods. Now was the time to surrender to the greater powers, not to transcend the flesh but to fully incorporate the spirit into every cell of my being. This was my destiny as an athlete. I was ready to do battle. I opened my eyes.

I was no longer Thesalus, and the stadium was empty and anti-quated as it had been when I first walked in.

That night I dreamed I was trying to enter the Delphi site. The ticket attendant offered me a cut rate if I pretended to be someone else. "But," I was adamant, "I am me," and I insisted on paying full price — the cost of authenticity.

Mount Olympus is the home of the original Olympians and so I headed north to the mountain. While I had discoursed with Mercury since 1984, I knew that this time it was impera-tive that I go without intermediary to the source, directly to the CEO of the Olympian Corporation, to the almighty Zeus. According to Greek mythology, Zeus rules the heavens and lives on the top of Mount Olympus. I figured the only way I was going to meet him was to go to his hang-out on the peak of this mountain.

When the road up the mountain ran out, I left the car and on foot with my little backpack I headed along a narrow hiking trail. Despite the struggles I had had with my sore foot and stiff legs from the Boston Marathon, today I felt fresh and nimble-footed. I was excited. Magic was in the air and I sucked it in.

As I climbed, the trail turned to snow and I found myself trudging deeper and deeper through the crunchy cover until I was in a wide open space above tree line. When I came to a standstill I was not at the very top, which would have been impossible at this time of year, but it seemed that the expanse of white I was standing on was Zeus's beard and that this would be the perfect place for a meeting. I stood on a rock and faced the mountain. The silence was immense and I could feel the gaze of the mighty God bearing down on me. Suddenly I felt like an insignificant gnat on the face of the Almighty. *Who am I to talk to Zeus?* My heart was trembling. I knew what I must do to have audience with the awesome King of Olympians. So I stood down, stripped naked, and climbed back on the rock. Mustering all my courage and holding my arms high, I beseeched Zeus.

"Oh Zeus, Great and Glorious Father of the Olympians, I, a mere mortal, with the greatest of humility, come to seek your audience. I have journeyed far to deliver this, my plea and my wish. I ask for your assistance in my bid to win the Gold in the Women's Marathon in Atlanta on July 28th 1996. For this I pledge to you my service and promise in every way to make myself worthy of being an Olympian. I will conduct myself with truth, honour and valor and with love in my heart not just in competition but as a way of life. Please grant my plea. I give you this gift as a symbol of my wish and of my sincerity. I remain your most humble servant always, Lorraine Mary Moller."

I held up a gold medal made from wood and paint. It had my winning photo upon it and the back was inscribed with the place, time and date of the Olympic Marathon. Using a stick and my fingers to scoop a hole in the cold, wet earth under my rock pedestal, I buried my token under a pile of stones. Then, I bowed to the mountain. My job was done.

I put on my clothes and proceeded down the trail. I had gone but a short way when it occurred to me that I could well have been just a crackpot waving her arms on top of a boulder in her birthday suit, and that Zeus was no more than a flicker of my imagination. The thought stopped me in my tracks and I turned back to face the spot where I had been. *Please, Great Father, I have to know if you have heard me. Give me a sign! Give me a sign!*

From above I heard a deep rumble that echoed through the clear blue sky. *Baooooomm!* It sounded like a jet plane cracking the sound barrier. I jumped. Goosebumps danced all over my body. *What was that?* I gasped. And on cue it happened again, this time unmistakably — a second great roll of thunder, louder than the first. *Baaaooooooomm!* "Thank you, thank you, thank you!" I cried out, clapping and dancing as tears of appreciation welled up in my eyes. Zeus had answered me and now I knew that magic was real. I flew down the mountain, my adrenalin pumping and my mind racing, pausing only to gather every piece of rubbish I came across, the least I could do as a servant to Zeus and for my ignorant fellow mortals.

The next morning as I was sitting in a village cafe having breakfast, a little elderly woman entered and made a beeline for my table. She looked as if she belonged in a fairy tale for she was wearing a long peasant skirt, encircled by an apron, a black cotton scarf covering her head, and on her arm was a basket containing jars of clear, golden honey. I knew this was no ordinary honey, this was nectar from the gods, Olympic gold. Mercury had sent her to deliver this to me. I bought a jar and put it in my bag. Then I thought better of it and turned to buy a second jar, but she had vanished from sight.

I had already collected water from the sacred spring at Delphi and now I had one more magical elixir to collect, olive oil from Zeus's grove in Olympia. I had read that the ancient Olympians anointed themselves with this before competition and so I decided, with that in my hands, the ingredients for making Gold would be complete.

The word Olympic is derived from the ancient village of Olympia where the Games were held every four years. The site of the ancient Olympics is fairly well preserved. The athletes who competed there lived in the Olympic compound where they were trained both academically and physically. There was no brains/brawn split in the psyche as there is in our modern Western world. Back then the athlete was seen as an all-round universal prototype for man: conversant in the arts, sciences and philosophies while physically gifted and honed to perform. This striving for mental, physical and spiritual perfection was the key to excellence in competition. And while the Gold medal and the adulation of the Greek world was the earthly reward, the bestowal of immortality by the gods themselves was the ultimate attainment.

Lining either side of the entrance to the stadium were life-sized statues known as Zanes. These were erected to the cheats of the games, paid for by levies from the offenders' hometowns, and a chilling reminder to the competitors on the way to the arena that one could be remembered for posterity for either fame or shame, depending on how they chose to play to the game. How I wished that tradition had been resurrected with the modern Olympics.

When I checked into a modest hotel on the border of the town, I found myself in conversation with the manager. She was American and had married a Greek man who had been an Olympian himself. She was excited to hear that I was bound for the Olympics in Atlanta for my fourth time.

I asked "Where can I find olive oil from Zeus's grove?"

"Zeus's grove?"

"Yes, the ancient Olympians used to smear themselves with it before competition. I want to do the same."

"I don't know. But I will find out."

That evening when I returned from my day at the Olympic compound, she proudly presented a glass bottle full of the precious lubricant, processed from the revered trees of Zeus found next to the stadium.

I carried my precious water, honey and oil in my hand luggage on my flight back to the USA. When the plane stopped in Houston for customs clearance I was last in line. Customs always made me nervous. My insides felt jittery and my palms began sweating as I approached the counter. But this time my edginess was usurped by my mission: to protect my godly elixirs.

I clutched my wares in my hands as the rest of my luggage went through the X-ray machine.

"Just put your items though the machine, ma'am." the official in the uniform instructed.

"No thank you," I replied, "I would prefer you to hand-check them."

"Just put them through the machine ma'am."

"No, please hand-check them. I don't want them X-rayed. It's food."

"X-rays are harmless. Just put it through."

"X-rays are not harmless, the effects are cumulative. I have been over-exposed to X-rays and I'm going to eat this food."

"Listen lady, put it through. Everybody has to put it through."

"But you can see right through each one of these containers and the liquid too." I held up the bottle of honey to the light, "What more can you see in an X-ray that you can't see by looking?"

He looked at me and huffed. I knew I was dangerously close to the edge. He threw up his hands. "Look, we can't spend time checking everyone's luggage by hand. Just put them through."

I scanned to the right. I scanned to the left. I turned to look behind me. My movements were deliberately exaggerated to emphasize my point. Everyone else had cleared and I stood alone, the last person, the crazy lady with the food who was not budging. There were three other customs agents leaning on their podiums chatting amongst themselves.

"So it's an issue of time, is it?"

He glared at me. I held his gaze, searching to see if I had gone too far. At the very moment my hand was about to place my goodies on the X-ray belt, he waved me on through.

CHAPTER 47

Rock Bottom

Truth, like gold, is to be obtained, not by its growth,
but by washing away from it all that is not gold.
— Leo Tolstoy

JUNE — JULY 1996

When I returned to Boulder I threw myself into training with renewed vigour. If my mind had not been playing tricks, then the Gold was most assuredly mine. I had Zeus on my side; he had spoken to me and I knew I could not fail.

Without that confidence I would have given up, for my body was falling apart. I felt like an old car that had too many miles on it. My foot hurt, my digestion was poor, my muscles stiff and asthma plagued my runs. I sought relief in alternative healing with chiropractors, massage therapists, movement specialists and counsellors. They kept me from total dissolution. My daily routine was back to where it had been in 1984, only a little more frantic as I ran from one appointment to another, hoping that by the end of the day, my treatments had rejuvenated me enough to complete my work-out. My immediate goal was just to run consistently and yet I was anything but consistent. Some days I ran with the old spark. And then I would crash. On my training runs I resembled a person cheating in a walking race.

Frequently I dreamt I was running on my knees, my lower limbs literally worn off from overwork. In waking life my hormone levels were those of a 70-year-old; I was in chronic adrenal exhaustion, my blood nutrients depleted.

Harlan could see I was struggling but knew better than to attempt to dissuade me from my course. He remained 'on call' to massage my legs, and ease my stress in any way he could.

"The key word is 'delight'." My spiritual mentor, Evan, delighted in the word 'delight'. He was like that, a gourmet wordsmith. He enjoyed the smell of words, the way the syllables rolled around in his mouth, the subtle flavours of their meanings. I often imagined that he had a secret vault full of onomatopoeic words that he liked to roll around in.

"I can hear how delighted you are. Think of the word de-light and its implications," he instructed.

I thought, *Dis woman here runs in de light of de silvery moon*. From then on the song, 'By the Light of the Silv'ry Moon' ran like a continuous-play record in my mind, taking every opportunity to strike up whenever there was a pause between my thoughts.

The problem, I confessed to Evan, was that I needed to train hard but it hurt to run, just one thing after another. Lately I doubted that Zeus had spoken to me, I wondered if it had just been an airplane overhead. I felt like Sisyphus repeatedly pushing a boulder up a hill. How did you stop pushing without having the boulder come back and crush you?

Evan never failed to find an answer that would send me out of the room uplifted and brimming with hope.

"Lorraine," his eyes glinted kindly, "Your task is to find a way to integrate the magic of the trip into your daily training. It is time to shed the old and the heavy and to run in delight."

Of the sil-ver-y moon …

"As for the plane … let's reframe the experience on the mountain. What if Mercury had sent planes over Olympus to fool you into thinking Zeus had made a thunderbolt?"

I hadn't thought of that one. But why would Zeus be any less real than Mercury? As I considered the idea, I became more resolute that there were no planes (after all, in the vast blue sky I did not see any) and that they were Ms Rational's concoction for something that was outside of her limited understanding. Evan's point was taken.

He continued. "Don't be like Sisyphus any more, pushing the rock up a hill. That takes too much of your energy. What if you took your twenty-eight years of training and said, 'I've got it all, done it all. No more pushing. Now I let it happen and run with delight.'

"Do not think of winning the gold, Lorraine. Be the gold."

For a week I ran my schedule as best I could, letting my body dictate the parameters of my training. Intellectually I understood that Evan was right; I had done all the training I needed. Pushing at this stage was counterproductive.

But completely detaching from the rigours of training and not doing was in reality more difficult than doing. I had 28 years of a highly habituated athlete's mindset still driving me. Pushing in one form or another was a knee-jerk reaction to being awake. Quite simply, I was addicted. While I pulled back on the land-running, I punished myself pool-running, pumping my legs like a drowning rat for hours on end in hot water, telling myself that I was conditioning for the heat of Atlanta. Because these work-outs were not measurable in miles, I fooled myself that they did not really count.

One day I went out for a run, on land, as I had done thousands of times before. I stretched my legs out, but they would not go. I felt like a puppet with strings missing. I was at a standstill. My watch said 30 seconds. I had intended to run for two hours. I cried tears of frustration. "Fuck it," I muttered and walked home. When I got in the door, I thought to myself, *I didn't try hard enough. I must be able to run!* So I tried again, out the back door just in case the neighbours were watching. This time, I was armed with willpower. I ran for three minutes before I seized up and walked home.

I was at my lowest: tired, depressed and overwhelmed. My defences were down and I should have known that at such a time Mercury was busy flitting back and forth, arranging the rest of my day. I was about to be sprung — big-time.

That afternoon I was at the supermarket when I met a runner that I had not seen for a few years. Cindy was something of a running prodigy but had never fulfilled her potential because of anorexia. I had talked to her a few times previously but did not know her well. Now when I saw her I was shocked. She was thin and pale, her round eyes sunken into her bony head, her life force dulled. I asked her if she was running.

"No," she replied through a clenched mouth that moved like a ventriloquist's. "My health is too poor to run and I'm so obsessive-compulsive that it's better to leave it be for now."

"Are you getting help?"

"No. I'm trying a few things on my own."

I didn't want to ask what and swing into a crevice so deep I was stuck down there with her. She seemed so helpless, so pathetic, so trapped, that I just felt like crying.

Then the impulse to hug her suddenly overcame me and I pulled Cindy's bony body to mine. Her torso was rigid with the rigor mortis of the half-dead and I let her go just as quickly. She found my ambush disconcerting, but just for a moment she held my gaze and a flicker of a smile grazed her mouth before she turned her head back down to the sorry-me position. As I paid for my groceries I felt tears welling up in my eyes once again. She had shaken me and I felt guilty for leaving her there.

As I walked in our home, Harlan was on his way out to a meeting. I had not seen him all day. Now as he dashed out the door, I felt the tears returning. I needed him and he was leaving me. For the longest time I walked around the house, emotionally distraught and not knowing what to do with myself. Finally I got out for a run and went to the track to do a few strides.

When I arrived home Harlan was there, cheery and chatty as usual. His levity annoyed me. I ate my dinner in silence, ignoring his attempts to engage me. Finally he left and went downstairs to be alone with his own more enjoyable company. That annoyed me even more. I sat up until late and finally went to bed after midnight. Harlan was asleep. Now I was angry. When I got in, he snuggled over to me but

I rebuffed him and read my book, so he rolled over and went back to sleep. When I could no longer see the words on the page I turned off the light and closed my eyes. I was tired but my anger would not release me to sleep's care. Instead, thoughts of the ways that Harlan failed to love me circulated through my brain like dirty laundry in a clothes dryer and so it went on and on until I was sure that he truly did not love me. Harlan had always been fully supportive and helpful of me and my running career in every way possible, but in my state I was blind to that truth. I worked myself into a knot and now, suitably convinced that I had been emotionally trampled, I began to sob. On this cue Harlan woke up and asked me what was the matter.

I was momentarily caught. I could not just launch into my accusations without seeming unreasonable, so I cried for a little longer, before I blurted it out. "I can't do it! The Olympics is so close and the task is overwhelming. I'm running out of time. I can't do it!" The outburst was a little disingenuous, for it did not express the truth of the moment. But it was a relatively safe segue to a discourse that was now out of my control. From this point on, Mercury was meddling full-time.

Harlan and I danced through familiar territory, he attempting to be helpful while remaining blameless, I rebuffing his positivism with "yes, but, yes, but" in ever-tightening circles that would take me close enough to fire an arrow that would strike and hurt. As I circled I talked fast, in whiney, self-pitying torrents, stumbling around in a stream of consciousness and half-formed ideas, throwing bits out at him, sorting and searching until I could find something solid and sharp.

"I saw Cindy at the store today. She looked so bad, it really upset me."

As the words tumbled out of my mouth, I knew instantly what I was really crying about. Then it all came flooding out and very soon I was sobbing deeply with hurts from long, long ago, open and defenceless. I was not crying about the forthcoming Olympics or Cindy or anything that Harlan had done — when Harlan walked out that evening I had become an abandoned two-year-old.

"I am so scared that you will leave me. I feel that I need you so much that if you did leave me, it would be like you had died and I would want to die too, just like I felt when my parents left me at the hospital all alone, when my mother walked away without looking back. I wanted her so much. I would pray at night to die first because I couldn't bear the thought of losing her." I wept uncontrollably and Harlan held me, rocking me gently, and crying with me.

After a long while I was all cried out and ready to talk once again. Our bed had become a warm snuggly haven. The darkness had softened and dispersed the pain.

"I'm sorry," I whispered. "I know I have been angry, aloof, blaming, but I never knew how sad and insecure I was underneath it all. There's been this little kid sitting on my doorstep all this time who was just so scared that her terrible secret would be revealed."

"What secret is that?"

"That she is ugly."

"You're not, you know."

I took a long pause.

"I know that, but she doesn't."

"It's time to take her in and let her know."

"I know. I know. Until I do I can't go forward. I know that now. You know, I saw me in Cindy, the one who thinks she is so unloved that she will sabotage, manipulate — even give her life to find love. She's the one who will strive and strive and strive to be good enough but knows she never is. That's me."

"And look where it got you."

"Yeah. Right here."

I squeezed his hand.

As I lay there, the little girl standing at the window of the hospital came into focus, looking wistfully out, searching for a future. I remembered running by that day and seeing her. *Come with me,* I heard myself calling to her. *You are so loved and so beautiful. Come into my heart and be with me forever. You will never be left behind again. I'm taking you to the Olympics. We are going to get Gold together.*

The next day I ran a great work-out. Two two-mile back-to-back runs, in 10:21 and 10:03, on my slightly downhill course at Eldorado Springs. I was back to my old self. *Whoa-ho-ho-ho — Olympics — here we come!*

CHAPTER 48

Gold

It is better to conquer yourself than to win a thousand battles.
Then the victory is yours. It cannot be taken from you,
not by angels or by demons, heaven or hell.
— Prince Gautama Siddhartha (563-483 BC)

AUGUST 1996

Most of the Olympic Games in Atlanta went on without me and I did not mind. I just wanted to turn up and collect my gold medal without all the brouhaha that goes on beforehand. These were certainly my last Games and I was already in the throes of distancing myself, as one does when about to break up with a long-term lover.

When I met with the team doctors they were concerned about my asthma. My lung capacity was functioning at about 60 per cent of what it should be. I was given a new medication, non-steroidal, but it would not be fully effective until after about three weeks, they said. I had eight days.

I did not know how I was going to win. I only knew that I would. I was unflinchingly thunderbolt confident. Zeus had it all arranged. I wondered if it would come about through some freak accident, like a flash-flood that wiped out the other runners but left me standing, or something of a more cosmic nature, like a time warp that would suddenly transport me into the lead at a critical point, or, as I really hoped, I would be granted the Wings of Mercury and would run without my feet touching the ground. All I had to do was get out of my own way and let Zeus work his magic through me. These were my thoughts, as I smeared the mighty god's olive oil over my legs, took a swig of Delphi water, and spooned Mercury's honey into my mouth. As I lined up for the start I was ready to claim my gold.

1996 Summer Olympics — Women's Marathon, Atlanta, USA
Uta Pippig launches out from the gun ridiculously fast. Her body expresses an effort that she can sustain for an hour or so, but not for a marathon. As she hammers away up the long Georgia hill, I wave her goodbye. I am content to sit back and move up through the field later for my surprise come-from-behind victory.

As the miles click off, the hills became arduous, the heat sapping, the distance interminable. I stay somewhere in mid-field. Later I can admit that I know I need to be up closer to the front but I am running as hard as I can just to stay where I am.

As I approach the halfway mark the course loops back upon itself and one by one — a parade of sinewy runners — who have already made the turn and are on their home journey — pass me by. My morale sags. I can now gauge how far ahead of me they are, and it is not good.

I snap my attention away from the leaders and for the first time look to the sidelines, at the spectators enthusiastically cheering the runners on. They are applauding even me, in my mediocre position. Up till now they have been faceless blurs, their voices muffled out by my own thoughts but now I feel strangely uplifted and my body tingles. Something odd is happening. Time seems to telescope into slow motion wherever I look, yet zoom by wherever I am not looking. I know this feeling. I have stepped out of linear time and entered Mercury's realm where the ordinary becomes extraordinary.

I scan the faces in the crowd and they begin to look familiar. For a flicker of a moment I think I see doctors and nurses from the hospital in Auckland, teachers from my school, runners from my club in Putaruru, past coaches, old friends, boyfriends, rivals and acquaintances. It seems like my entire hometown is there, and a Boulder contingent, and even some familiar Japanese faces, all cheering for me. I see John Davies, Dick, Arthur, Ali, Kathrine, Andy, Joy and Grace. Trevor and

Clint, even Anne is there spurring me on. And yes, so is Ron, his smile shining kindly towards me.

I think of my mother's unrelenting faith in my ability and my father's enthusiastic stewardship and their faces, too, flash from the sidelines, along with my brothers and sisters, proudly beaming. Mr Drummond stands behind them. He has tears in his eyes.

It seems that all the players of my past are lining my path now to be with me and I am flooded with appreciation for them all. I know that I am weary and that my imagination is playing tricks with me, that the characters I see are not out there, but in me, and that they have been with me all along. I hear Evan's words reverberating clearly through the din of the crowd, "Do not think of winning the Gold, Lorraine; be the Gold."

I turn my attention back to the race passing by me.

Fatuma Roba from Ethiopia, a relative newcomer, is striding out the front, her lithe ebony limbs skimming the road. She is running as a symphony of brain and body, spirit and matter, a sight so awesome that for a moment I forget what I am doing in order to behold her. I can see fire in her eyes burning for the gold. I recognise that fire. It was there the first day I ran one lap of the track, my first ten-kilometre race, my first marathon. It is the flame of intensity and freedom; the uninhibited expression of physicality; a runner's gift of gratitude to creation. That fire within me is now a glow. I know that she will win. It is fitting, and I feel happy for her.

In focused pursuit for the silver are three runners: Valentina Yegorova, the reigning gold medallist, her arms pumping like pistons driving a reliable communist vehicle, Yuko Arimori, her eyes transfixed in a steely gaze that sees only the finish line 13 miles away, and clinging to her shoulder is the gritty prawn-stalker from the Osaka marathon, Katrin Dorre, her shock-white legs locked in rhythm with the churning pair in front. While Roba is my distant past, these women are my recent past. Brow-crinkling, will-over-fatigue, snot-snorting, tactical experts.

A wave of luminosity washes over me. As I witness each runner's personal odyssey and see the struggle, the hope, the need to prove that they are faster and therefore better than the next person, I also see their passion, their courage and their magnificence. They are out there, Olympians all, willingly processing themselves through this great human factory of triumphs and tragedies. Suddenly I understand the prophecy from Delphi and know why I am here. The finishing result for me will be inconsequential. My moment is now.

Here I am at Mercury's crossroads once more, but this time the signpost has not been turned. He has become my ally, my trusted friend, and he no longer has need for guile with me. My path is unmistakably obvious and I have no cause for resistance. There are only 13 more miles to run, not just to the finish of this race, not just to the finish of the 28 year run, but to completion. When I cross the line, my marriage to racing will end, and we will part ways, to always remain good friends. Never again will who I am be measured by a race result. It is over. Lorraine the Runner is fading into a memory.

This is oddly satisfying, like reading the last few pages of an engrossing novel. I know I will never have the world stand for the national anthem on my behalf, nor have an Olympic gold medal hung around my neck.

But I do have a bronze medal. Before this I have hardly recognised it, now suddenly that third-rate prize seems pretty darn wonderful. Right now I am amidst the world's best, who are running their hearts and guts out to claim one of these, rarest-of-rare, and I already have one. It belongs to me.

No, I correct myself, it belongs to us: Lost Little Girl and Running Woman. Yes, the girl with the big nose, the ugly one who pissed on everything, the one so flawed that even her parents would leave her to be tortured by strangers, it is her I have been running for all this time. After 28 years and enough miles to circumnavigate the globe several times, we have joined forces and the struggle is over. The little girl is finally home.

When I cross the finish line, I announce that I have just run my last Olympics. The quest is over. The Runner's line has finally become a circle.

True to his word, Zeus has given me Gold.

CHAPTER 49

Death

1996 — 1999

When I ran the Olympic Marathon in Atlanta I did not know that I was already pregnant. At the Falmouth Road Race two weeks later I strongly suspected I was. My breasts were tender, and such cyclic fluctuations rarely occurred while I was Olympic-lean. The asthma drugs had kicked in, just as the doctors said they would, and I raced like my young self, holding my own in a star-studded field of new champions, mostly Kenyans, 20 years my junior. I won the masters division in a record time. It was amazing what a difference air made. I was glad to once again feel the smooth power of my body moving as an integrated unit from breath to stride. This was the last competitive race I would ever run.

That afternoon I took a pregnancy test. The two pink lines confirmed what I had hoped. I tossed the asthma drugs into the bin, and walked into my new life. Little did I know the old warrior I had become would hold on tenaciously, and that it would take another full Olympiad to ease her into retirement so I could transition into motherhood.

I remember clearly the day of my next miscarriage. It was the middle of October and I was 11 weeks pregnant. It came like the devil comes, when things are so good they can no longer be trusted. It came slyly and unannounced, interrupting another day of crisp, cloudless skies,

345

trees that reached out and waved their warm autumn hands, and strangers who smiled and said, "Good morning", as they passed by on the street. They could read the rose in my cheeks and the fullness of my lips and knew I was special. They sensed the way I walked in my husband's space of protection and pride, even when I was alone. I was woman: the bearer of new life.

I remember how the day turned dull the afternoon they told me the baby had died inside, and the way the grey sky seemed to bear down, and how the leaves lay decaying in clumps in the gutter.

I remember the numbness as Harlan and I lay down to sleep that night, and the wail that rose from my belly, waking me from my half-sleep. It was loud and long and primal. When my mouth closed, the spirit that sought life in my body had returned to the ethers and my womb had become a casket. I felt Harlan's arm encircle my chest, his head nestle onto my shoulder, his breath cooling my tears.

Doctors blamed the running. My friends blamed the running. Strangers blamed the running. Soon I blamed the running. Surely all those years of jiggling my insides had done something contra-indicative to my child-bearing ability. Perhaps I should have taken notice of my high-school headmistress. I stopped running. I gained 20 pounds. People nodded in approval. We all knew that fat women grew babies with chubby cheeks, and that skinny girls couldn't even get pregnant. I did not feel like me. I kept thinking I was being followed, but when I swung around there was no-one there. It was my adipose renovation, a foreigner who would help me bear a baby. I stopped weighing myself and bought bigger clothes.

I got the late-night phone call in Boulder that told me Dad had died. Exactly a year had passed since I had lost our baby.

As I boarded a plane for Auckland the next day, I suspected I was pregnant again. It was confirmed for me a few days later. My father's body lay in the next room.

Death of a loved one is like a whirlpool. It seizes everything in you that is dying and sucks it into its black vortex. My baby went with Dad; I could not hold onto it. I pleaded and prayed but its life slipped through my fingertips to the other side.

I mourned my father for almost a year. I had fallen into a dark hole where my heart turned grey and my blood cold and vaporous. The fire that had fueled my life for so long had been extinguished and I had not found a new light to guide me back into full-throttle living. I could see nothing to rebel against, no cause to fight for, no grudges to uphold. The thought of running depressed me. Instead I thought about dying.

Gradually I came back to life as winter passed and the snows thawed. Somewhere buried underneath my gloom were treasures gleaned from my running days, sustaining me: *I am eternally safe, the universe supports me, I can do anything I will to do, magic is real.*

The problem, the doctor said, was me. My eggs were too old. Unless I used donor eggs from a younger woman, statistically, my chances of having a baby were very slim.

When I walked out of the clinic there was one thing I knew: that my chances of having a baby far exceeded the odds of winning an Olympic medal. When I had another miscarriage a year later, I did not even bother to cry. It was merely another bump on the road to my next dream.

Old eggs. The phrase was thrown out as a well-established fact. But nobody could tell me what old eggs were exactly. For sure I got the picture: I was worn-out, withering, a woman past her use-by date. My pile of eggs was dwindling and those left had become dried up, rubbery, cross-linked, irradiated, toxic duds. They were no longer fit for human consummation. I should just shrivel into cronehood and spend the rest of my days making bland spells that didn't bother any-one, and leave the love-making and procreating to the youthful.

Then one night I had a dream. I was Lorraine on the Plain in Spain and a feisty black bull was charging me. I ran for cover into an old barn and closed the doors. Shafts of sunlight beamed though the cracks in the walls, enlivening the warm red glow that permeated the interior. It was safe and dry inside and I felt comforted. As I scanned the rustic wooden structure, I noticed that there were rows upon rows of cartons of eggs stacked floor-to-ceiling around the walls. There must have been tens of thousands of extra-large, organic, free-range, fertile, white eggs — the sort I would be willing to pay extra for in the health food store. Outside I could hear the bull snorting.

I was heartened. My instinct was right. 'Old eggs' was a counter-reproductive belief. It was time for me to take charge. There was a little soul circling the periphery of my universe, looking for a landing clearance. My job was to clear the fog.

When we move in a certain direction, the universe moves with us. Mercury is always on hand to deliver our thoughts to The Creative Force who arranges our circumstances accordingly: 'She's going forward with the baby thing! Send her help!'

CHAPTER 50

Making Magic

2000

D r Michael Catalano looked up my name in a phone book and
called me. He had read an article about me in the newspaper
and wanted to meet. We met at a coffee shop. He had a Robert de
Niro look and a soft New York accent and wanted to talk about ideas,
sports, and the power of the mind. I told him about remote viewing
— a top-secret programme developed by the US military during
the Cold War to teach their soldiers how to psychically spy on their
enemies. Remote viewing was made public when it was declassified
in the early nineties, and its methods are used as a fast-track means
of developing one's powers of extra-sensory perception. I had been
practising remote viewing for the past year and had been a teaching assistant to my teacher, Dr Hein. Michael and I agreed to meet
weekly and trade sessions. He would take me through his creative
visualisation programme and I would teach him to accurately per-
ceive through his non-ordinary senses. I thought he was getting the
better end of the deal but I was pleasantly mistaken.

In my first session he directed me to do some basic creative
exercises to stretch the visualising mind muscle. Largely because of
the influence of television, many people rely on an outside source to
create pictures for them — pictures that are someone else's version
of reality — rather than using their own imaginations. Exercised
regularly by my years as a runner, my mind was already fluent in self-

imaging. Now that I was relaxed and inner-focused, Michael asked me to come up with an issue in my life that I would like to address. Not knowing him well, I was unwilling to divulge my personal affairs to him.

"I can't seem to keep my house tidy." It was innocuous enough to delve into with a stranger. He was unfazed.

"Okay, now I would like you to come up with a statement of intent and affirmation for how you would like your house to be."

The words instantly popped into my head. "I make the room for new and wonderful things to come into my life."

"Remember that," Michael instructed. "We will work on it in our next session in two weeks' time. Meantime, be aware of what comes up for you around this issue."

Ming told me my kidney chi was 3.6 on a scale of one to ten. "You must not try to get pregnant," she warned, "We must first build your chi to at least seven so you can hold the baby." She shook her head when I told her my history as a marathon runner and that I was travelling regularly to exotic lands such as Japan, Mongolia and Cambodia for charity races. "Running is very bad, you must not run. The same energy you use for running is the energy you need for baby. And no travel. Same thing." After an acupuncture treatment, she sent me home with some disgusting herbs to boil and drink three times a day. They looked like the sweepings from the bottom of an aviary and they stank so badly I almost puked when I walked into the room where they steeped. But I drank them religiously with the same stoicism with which I had eaten sulfur when I was a kid.

Ming was an acupuncturist and herbalist from mainland China and by hearsay had remarkable success with those seeking fertility.

Every two weeks I returned for a treatment and replenishment of aviary sweepings. My chi energy was restoring steadily. I marvelled at how Ming could calculate it to one-tenth of a decimal point just by holding my wrist. I did not tell her that I sneaked in the occasional jog.

"Can you remember your affirmation?"

I was back for my next session with Michael.

"Of course. I make the womb, I mean the room for new and wonderful ..."

"Stop right there. What did you say?"

By October my chi was at 6.8. I was almost there but I needed to take a trip down to New Zealand for a few weeks. Ming chastised me. "Travel is very bad. Do not get pregnant. You will have to start all over."

When I retuned to Ming my kidney chi had dropped to 5.6. She tut-tutted and chastised me about travel, then poked my meridians as I lay on her table. Every ten minutes she returned to zing them with a few twirls of the needles. This time the herbal concoction she sent me home with appeared to include seashells, entire bonsai tree branches and miniature fossilized creatures. After a few sessions I was fast approaching the magical mark of seven.

There were five versions of me, all residing under the one umbrella of Lorraine. One by one I introduced them to Michael: Lorraine the Little Girl who needs to belong, Lorraine the Runner, Lorraine the Fiery Career Woman with work to do, Lorraine the Mother, and Lorraine the Wise Old Woman who knows magic. Under Michael's guidance they were all gathered here today for a round-table discussion so that these various aspects of self could come to a group consensus about having a baby. Each one got to have her say.

The Little Girl was pretty happy. Since the last Olympics she had found her sense of security in the heart of the group. Lorraine the Fiery Career Woman was the pragmatist. Her life's work was to get things done. She was the one with a temper but, she emphasised, such fire is needed to burn away the obsolete and break through barriers. She was excited about the baby project and had been largely responsible for getting the group to this meeting. Lorraine the Mother was soft and empathetic, not wanting to appear pushy but hopeful of a full-time job. The Wise Old Woman sat quietly in the background, observing. She was the tour guide for the journey and oversaw the spiritual welfare of the group. Everyone deferred to her ultimately. Finally, Lorraine the Runner piped up. She had tears in her voice.

"Hey, everyone, I've worked my butt off for years. Haven't I done well? Really, I need the rest of you to tell me how well I've done. It's all been for you, you know that, don't you?" They all nodded. They knew it. "Hey, I'm really, really tired, I can't do any more. Is it okay if I give up running? Can I stop now?"

A little discussion ensued. There was no problem; they just didn't know that she needed acknowledgement and an official announcement of retirement.

The Wise Old Woman finally spoke. "You have done a magnificent job. All these years you ran your heart out, and we deeply appreciate how well you did on behalf of all of us." She looked around the table and everyone nodded in agreement. "We hereby, in acknowledgement of your fine contribution to this soul, give you full pension to live out the rest of your days as you please. I say this with the deepest gratitude from all of us."

Lorraine the Mother stood up. "If you don't mind, now that Lorraine the Runner has officially retired, I would like to take the workload for a while."

Everyone clapped. The meeting was adjourned.

Two weeks later my chi was at 7.5. I was ripened. I did not tell Ming that I had snuck off to Japan and Cambodia between sessions. I had put my wish for a baby out there into the heavens from the centre of the universe at Angkor Wat Temple, and a few days later to the giant Buddha in Nara, Japan. Somehow I felt that I had got through to the Source of Creation and I returned with that same spiritual determination that had come over me when I knew I was going to win a big race.

It was the end of the year. Y2K was approaching. The planets were lining up in extraordinary configurations and people were buying batteries and duct tape as they anticipated a global computer system breakdown, and with it the destruction of the world.

The energy generated from such universal excitement was eagerly harnessed for baby-making. I invited Harlan to join me on the full moon in the backyard where I lit a little fire in a pot and prayed to any and every fertility deity who would listen. Then we went inside and made love.

The next time Ming gave me herbs they stank so badly I had to put them in the trunk of the car where I forgot them. When I approached the car a few days later and threw up on the sidewalk from a pungent whiff emanating from it, I knew for sure I was pregnant.

My womb was a pizza oven, warm and dry, glowing with enough heat to make perfectly baked pizza. I kept the door closed — hermetically sealed for this special one. I had no ultrasounds, no amniocenteses, and no tests. No-one was invading the womb and trespassing on this new and wonderful thing that was coming into my life. I could trust that this time a baby was growing happily in the belly of Lorraine the Mother.

When I went into the fourth month of pregnancy I knew that we would make the finish line. As my belly expanded so did my contentment.

"Congratulations! It's a girl. Girls are the best!!" the doctor's enthusiastic voice rang out. A chubby, wet baby was hoisted up by her shoulder, her marinated skull formed into a cone shape. A shiny face turned and alert black eyes surveyed the surroundings. Experts would say she was too young for any cognizance but I knew better; she had just arrived and she was truly amazed.

With my 'Golden Girl', Jasmine, 2000. *Annie Krause*

Dreamer

There was a world … or was it all a dream?
— Helen of Troy, from *The Iliad* by Homer

AUGUST 2004

The Athens Olympics had just begun. Life had been full the past four years, with raising our daughter and doing Zeus's work: coaching runners and travelling to foreign countries for charity work. But it was none of these things I dreamt about this one night. Rather, my dream was a familiar one from my days as an athlete.

I am preparing for the Olympics. The women's marathon is due to start in one hour. But I am totally unprepared and cannot find my running clothes. I rifle through drawers of sports apparel that I have not worn for years, in order to find my silver-ferned shirt and shorts. I am panic-stricken. The clock is ticking down the minutes and I know I will be hard-pressed to make the start line on time. My mother appears. "Can I help?" she asks. I anxiously instruct her to start searching. "I need my Olympic gear – now!"

Together we pull things out of boxes and search under stacks of items until I am totally exasperated. The race is sure to go on without me. I don't even know if I can run a marathon. I am really out of shape. Come to think of it, I have been retired for years. I laugh out loud.

"Stop, stop!" I yell to my frantic mother. "Stop looking. You can relax. This is a dream. It's not real."

"Well, what do we do now?" she asks.

"Anything we like," I reply. "Since it's a dream, the possibilities are endless. What would you like to do?"

It was at this point that I woke up. And then I woke up again: it is all a dream in which we are the both the dreamer and the dreamed.

And the possibilities are endless.

Running at Mount Santias, near Boulder, Colorado, 1993. *John Kelly*

CAREER HIGHLIGHTS

1973 5th, 800 m, Pan Pacific Conference Games — Toronto, Canada
NZ record 4 X 400 m relay, team member — Victoria Games, Canada

1974 5th, 800 m (2:03.6), Commonwealth Games — Christchurch, NZ

1975 5th, World Cross-country Championships — Rabat, Morocco

1979 1st, Syttende Mai, 20 miles (in World Best: 1:58:28) — Madison Wis, USA
1st, Grandma's Marathon, debut (2:37:36.5) — Duluth Minn, USA

1980 1st, Syttende Mai, 20 miles (in World Best: 1:55:36) — Madison Wis, USA
1st, Grandma's Marathon (2:38:35) — Duluth Minn, USA
1st, Avon Women's World Championship Marathon (2:35:11) — London, England
1st, Nike OTC Marathon (2:31:42) — Eugene Oreg, USA
1st, Maratona Atlantica Boavista (2:39:10) — Rio de Janeiro, Brazil

1981 1st, 3,000 m Pan Pacific Conference Games — Christchurch, NZ
1st, Grandma's Marathon (2:29:34) — Duluth Minn, USA
1st, Maratona Atlantica Boavista (2:35:56) — Rio de Janeiro, Brazil
1st, Nike OTC Marathon (2:31:15) — Eugene Oreg, USA

1982 2nd, London Marathon (2:36:15) — London, England
1st, Avon Women's World Championship Marathon, San Francisco Calif, USA
Bronze medal, Commonwealth Games 1,500 m (4:12.6) — Brisbane, Australia
Bronze medal, Commonwealth Games 3,000 m (8:55.7) — Brisbane, Australia

1983 Finalist, 3,000 m World T&F Championships (8:51.7) — Helsinki, Finland

1984 1st, Boston Marathon (2:29:28) — Boston Mass, USA
1st, Chicago Distance Classic, 20 k (1:08:12) — Chicago Ill, USA
1st, Beverly Hills Buick, 10 k (32:12) — Los Angeles Calif, USA
5th, Olympic Games Inaugural Women's Marathon (2:28:28) — Los Angeles Calif, USA
1st, Avon Women's World Championship Marathon (2:32:44) — Paris, France

1985 NZ record 1,500 m track, Van Damme Meet (4:10.3) — Brussels, Belgium

1986 1st, Osaka International Ladies' Marathon (2:30:24) — Osaka Japan
1st, Steamboat Classic, 4 miles (in World Best: 20:23) — Peoria Ill, USA
1st, Cascade Run-Off, 15 k (49:08) — Portland Oreg, USA
Silver Medal, Commonwealth Games Marathon (2:28:17) — Edinburgh, Scotland
1st, Falmouth Road Race — Falmouth Mass, USA

1987 1st, Osaka International Ladies' Marathon (2:30:40) — Osaka, Japan
1st, Steamboat Classic, 4 miles (in World Best: 20:16) — Peoria Ill, USA
2nd, Cascade Run-Off, 15 k (49:30) — Portland Oreg, USA
Finalist, 10,000 m, World T&F Championships — Rome, Italy

1988 1st, Boston Milk Run, 10 k (32:06) — Boston Mass, USA

1989 1st, Osaka International Ladies' Marathon (2:30:20) — Osaka, Japan
1st, Hokkaido International Marathon — Sapporo, Japan
1st, Revco-Cleveland, 10 k (32:58) — Cleveland Ohio, USA

1991 1st, Hokkaido International Marathon — Sapporo, Japan

1992 Bronze medal, Olympic Games Marathon (2:33:54) — Barcelona, Spain

1993 World best, 10 miles track (54:29) — Auckland, NZ
5th, Osaka International Ladies' Marathon — Osaka, Japan
5th, London Marathon — London, England
3rd, Hokkaido International Marathon — Sapporo, Japan

1996 Undefeated as a masters runner
1st, Master, Boston Marathon (2:32:02) — Boston Mass, USA

Winner, 1986 Osaka International Ladies' Marathon.
Courtesy of Osaka International Ladies' Marathon and Sankei Sports

ACKNOWLEDGEMENTS

I discovered that producing a book is a marathon effort that takes a team, and a neophyte such as I could not have done it without the help, support and encouragement of many. My utmost appreciation goes out to everyone who has given their expertise and critical praise to make this a better book than one I could have produced on my own.

My writing coach, Max Regan, a brilliant teacher and, more importantly, a thoroughly decent human being, drew out the finest in me with true Mercurial playfulness. I am forever grateful for the confidence he instilled in me as a writer.

I started with a good feeling about my publisher Longacre Press and over the past months that feeling has only grown. The professionalism, kindness and good humour of Barbara Larson, Annette Riley and Penelope Todd in particular, has made publishing a pleasure.

Very special thanks to Leslie Daniels, who started me off on this book odyssey with a simple question, "Have you written anything?" eight years ago. Her guidance has been invaluable.

My childhood running hero, Peter Snell, and his wife, Miki, have generously given their time and valuable input and I am deeply honoured.

Many accomplished writers willingly shared their knowledge, experience and networks, and cheered me on: Michael Sandrock, Janis Hallowell, Eugene Bingham, Robyn Langwell, Warwick Rodger, Christina Negron, Bobby MacGee, Anna Chi, Greg Lautenschlager, Kathrine Switzer, Roger Robinson, Rich Benyo and Joe Henderson.

My running friend David Mastbaum generously gave his professional expertise.

Many readers gave me valuable criticism through first drafts: Chris Pilone, Nina Rillstone, Jessica Ruthe, Lynn de Hart, Dr Andrew Ness, my mum Maisie Moller, Evan Hodkins, Keith Livingstone, Steve Torrente, and my biggest supporter and valued confidante, Gary Moller — their input has been invaluable. The same goes for my many listeners: the Wings of Mercury Running Team, my friends — Colleen Cannon, Allison Roe, Heather and Jeff Matthews, Sharon Wilson, Jan Hayhow, Dick Quax, Rod Dixon, Nobby Hashizume, Paul Hamblyn, Mary Lou Firth Irving and Marjorie Perine — many thanks to them all for indulging me and especially for laughing in all the right places.

Special tribute to all those life-graduates who graced the pages of this book: my dad Gordon Moller, Mr and Mrs Drummond, Nancy Reid, Ron Daws, Euan Robertson, Fred Lebow, John Davies, Jack Foster, Arthur Lydiard, and David Welch. With love to my dear friend, Annie Krause, who did not stay long enough to hear the finish, but she and I both know that the story never ends.

Although some of my early childhood experiences were harrowing, my life with my five brothers and sisters, Vivienne, Gary, Gordon, Bruce and Delwyn, along with my mother, Maisie, and father, Gordon, was filled with the vibrancy of full-on living. My family has always been there for me supporting all my endeavors and I am very grateful to be have been born into such a remarkable and loving group.

Finally, my rock, Harlan, and my precious golden girl, Jasmine, have made many concessions while I was lost to computer world. None of this could have happened without their love lifting me every moment. I am surely the luckiest woman ever.